NO FEAR

D0724029

The Canterbury Tales
The Scarlet Letter

SHAKESPEARE

As You Like It
The Comedy of Errors
Hamlet
Henry IV, Parts One and Two
Henry V
Julius Caesar
King Lear
Macbeth
The Merchant of Venice
A Midsummer Night's Dream
Much Ado About Nothing
Othello
Richard III
Romeo and Juliet
Sonnets
The Taming of the Shrew
The Tempest
Twelfth Night

NO FEAR

THE
CANTERBURY
TALES

Cover Illustration by Michael Wertz
Book layout by Christina Renzi

SPARKNOTES is a registered trademark of SparkNotes LLC.

Spark Publishing
A Division of Barnes & Noble
120 Fifth Avenue
New York, NY 10011
www.sparknotes.com

ISBN: 978-1-4114-2697-9

Library of Congress Cataloging-in-Publication Data

Chaucer, Geoffrey, d. 1400.
    Canterbury tales / Geoffrey Chaucer. SparkNotes contributers: Josh Cracraft, Hilary Teplitz, and John Crowther.
        p. cm. — (No fear literature)
        ISBN 978-1-4114-2696-2 (pbk.)
        1. Christian pilgrims and pilgrimages—Poetry, 2. Storytelling—Poetry. 3. Middle Ages—Poetry. 4. England—Poetry. I. Title.
        PR1870.A1C6 2009
        821'.1.—dc22
                                                2009005178

Please submit changes or report errors to www.sparknotes.com/errors.

Printed and bound in the United States

10 9 8 7 6 5 4 3 2 1

FEAR NOT.

Have you ever tried to read *The Canterbury Tales* but realized that you have to look up the definitions of half the words on the page? You want to enjoy Chaucer's poetry, but decoding it one word at a time is beyond slow. *No Fear: The Canterbury Tales* will fix that problem. When you can't decipher the original, look across to the right-hand page and you'll know what each word means and how they fit together. Soon you'll be reading Chaucer's own verse fearlessly—and actually enjoying it.

No Fear: The Canterbury Tales puts Chaucer's language side by side with a facing-page modern English translation—the kind of English people actually speak today. When Chaucer's English makes your head spin, our translation will help you sort out what's happening, who's saying what, and why.

Contents

Characters

The Pilgrims

THE NARRATOR—A character called Geoffrey Chaucer. We should be wary of accepting his words and opinions as Chaucer's own. In the General Prologue, the narrator presents himself as a gregarious and naïve character. Later on, the Host accuses him of being silent and sullen. The narrator writes down his impressions of the pilgrims from memory. What he chooses to remember about the characters tells us as much about the narrator's own prejudices as it does about the characters themselves.

THE KNIGHT—The first pilgrim Chaucer describes in the General Prologue and the teller of the first tale. The Knight represents the ideal of a medieval Christian man-at-arms. He has participated in no less than 15 of the great crusades of his era. Brave, experienced, and prudent, the narrator greatly admires him.

THE WIFE OF BATH—A seamstress by occupation and an "expert on marriage." The Wife of Bath has been married five times and had many other affairs in her youth, making her well practiced in the art of love. She presents herself as someone who loves marriage and sex, but, from what we see of her, she also takes pleasure in rich attire, talking, and arguing. She is deaf in one ear and has a gap between her front teeth, which was considered attractive in Chaucer's time. She has traveled on pilgrimages to Jerusalem three times and elsewhere in Europe as well. Bath is an English town on the Avon River, not the name of this woman's husband.

THE PARDONER—A charlatan, who "officially" forgives people's sins for a price. Pardoners granted papal indulgences—reprieves from penance in exchange for charitable donations to the Church. Many pardoners, including this one, collected profits for themselves. Chaucer's Pardoner excels in fraud, carrying a bag full of fake relics. For example, he claims to have the veil of the Virgin Mary. The Pardoner has long, greasy, yellow hair and is beardless. These characteristics were associated with shiftiness and gender ambiguity in Chaucer's time. The Pardoner also has a gift for singing and preaching whenever he finds himself inside a church.

THE MILLER—Stout and brawny, with a wart on his nose and a big mouth, both literally and figuratively. He threatens the Host's notion of propriety when he drunkenly insists on telling the second tale. Indeed, the Miller seems to enjoy overturning all conventions: He ruins the Host's carefully planned storytelling order, he rips doors off hinges, and he tells a tale that is somewhat blasphemous, ridiculing religious and scholarly clerks, carpenters, and women.

THE PRIORESS—A nun who heads a convent. Described as modest and quiet, this Prioress aspires to have exquisite taste. Her table manners are dainty, she knows French (though not the French of the court), she dresses well, and she is charitable and compassionate.

THE MONK—A monk given to corporeal pleasures. Most monks of the Middle Ages lived in monasteries according to the Rule of Saint Benedict, which demanded that they devote their lives to "work and prayer." This Monk cares little for the Rule; his devotion is to hunting and eating. He is large, loud, and well clad in hunting boots and furs.

THE FRIAR—An example of the unscrupulous friars of Chaucer's time. Roaming priests with no ties to a monastery, friars were great objects of criticism in Chaucer's time. Always ready to befriend young women or rich men who might need his services, the friar actively administers the sacraments in his town, especially those of marriage and confession. However, Chaucer's worldly Friar has taken to accepting bribes.

THE SUMMONER—An official who brings persons accused of violating Church law to ecclesiastical court. This Summoner is a lecherous man whose face is scarred by leprosy. He gets drunk frequently, is irritable, and is not particularly qualified for his position. He spouts the few words of Latin he knows in an attempt to sound educated.

THE HOST—The leader of the group. The Host is large, loud, and merry, though he possesses a quick temper. He mediates and facilitates the flow of the pilgrims' tales. His title of "host" may be a pun, suggesting both an innkeeper and the Eucharist, or Holy Host.

THE PARSON—The only devout churchman in the company. The Parson lives in poverty but is rich in holy thoughts and deeds. The pastor of a sizable town, he preaches the Gospel and makes sure to practice what he preaches. He's everything that the Monk, Friar, and Pardoner aren't.

THE SQUIRE—The Knight's son and apprentice. The Squire is curly-haired, youthfully handsome, and loves dancing and courting.

THE CLERK—A poor student of philosophy. Having spent his money on books and learning rather than on fine clothes, the clerk is threadbare and wan. He speaks little, but when he does, his words are wise and full of moral virtue.

THE MAN OF LAW—A successful lawyer commissioned by the king. He upholds justice in matters large and small and knows every statute of England's law by heart.

THE MANCIPLE—A clever fellow. A manciple was in charge of getting provisions for a college or court. Despite his lack of education, the Manciple is smarter than the 30 lawyers he feeds.

THE MERCHANT—A trader in furs and cloth, mostly from Flanders. The merchant is part of a powerful and wealthy class in Chaucer's society.

THE SHIPMAN—A well-traveled and well-tanned veteran sailor. The Shipman has seen every bay and river in England, as well as exotic ports in Spain and Carthage. He is a bit of a rascal, known for stealing wine while the ship's captain sleeps.

THE PHYSICIAN—A talented doctor with expertise in diagnosing the causes and finding cures for most maladies. Though the Physician keeps himself in perfect physical health, the narrator calls into question the Physician's spiritual health: He rarely consults the Bible and has an unhealthy love of financial gain.

THE FRANKLIN—A man of leisure. The word *franklin* means "free man." In Chaucer's society, a franklin was neither a vassal serving a lord nor a member of the nobility. This particular franklin is a connoisseur of food and wine—so much so that his table remains laid and ready for food all day.

THE REEVE—A shrewd steward of a manor. This reeve's lord never loses so much as a ram to the other employees, and the vassals under his command are kept in line. However, he steals from his master.

THE PLOWMAN—The Parson's brother and an equally good-hearted man. A member of the peasant class, he pays his tithes to the Church and leads a good Christian life.

THE GUILDSMEN—A hatmaker, carpenter, weaver, clothing dyer, and a tapestry maker. The Guildsmen appear as a unit. English guilds were a combination of labor unions and social fraternities: Craftsmen of similar occupations joined together to increase their bargaining power and live communally. All five Guildsmen are clad in the livery of their brotherhood.

THE COOK—The Guildsmen's cook. The Narrator gives little detail about him, but he does mention a crusty sore on the Cook's leg.

THE YEOMAN—The servant who accompanies the Knight and the Squire. The Narrator mentions that the Yoeman's dress and weapons suggest he may be a forester.

THE SECOND NUN—Not described in the General Prologue. She tells a saint's life for her tale.

THE NUN'S PRIEST—Also not described in the General Prologue. His story of Chanticleer, however, is well crafted and suggests that he is a witty, self-effacing preacher.

NO FEAR

Characters in the Knight's Tale

THESEUS—A great conqueror and the duke of Athens in the Knight's Tale. The most powerful ruler in the story, he is often called upon to make the final judgment, but he listens to others' pleas for help.

PALAMON—One of the two imprisoned Theban soldier heroes in the Knight's Tale. Brave, strong, and sworn to everlasting friendship with his cousin Arcite, Palamon falls in love with the fair maiden Emily, which brings him into conflict with Arcite. Though he loses the tournament against Arcite, he gets Emily in the end.

ARCITE—The sworn brother to Palamon. Arcite, imprisoned with Palamon in the tower in the Knight's Tale, falls equally head-over-heels in love with Emily. Arcite gets released from the tower early and wins Emily's hand in a tournament, but he then dies when a divinely fated earthquake causes his horse to throw him.

EMILY—The sister to Hippolyta, Theseus's domesticated Amazon queen in the Knight's Tale. Fair-haired and glowing, we first see Emily as Palamon does, through a window. Though she is the object of both Palamon's and Arcite's desire, she would rather spend her life unmarried and childless. Nevertheless, when Arcite wins the tournament, she readily pledges herself to him.

AEGEUS—Theseus's father. Egeus gives Theseus the advice that helps him convince Palamon and Emily to end their mourning of Arcite and get married.

NICHOLAS—A poor astronomy student in the Miller's Tale. Nicholas boards with an elderly carpenter, John, and the carpenter's too-young wife, Alison. Nicholas dupes John and sleeps with Alison right under John's nose, but Absalom, the foppish parish clerk, gets Nicholas in the end.

ALISON—The sexy young woman married to the carpenter in the Miller's Tale. She is bright and sweet like a small bird. She also dresses in a tantalizing style: her clothes are embroidered inside and outside, and she laces her boots high. She willingly goes to bed with Nicholas, but she has only harsh words and obscenities for Absalom.

ABSALOM—The local parish clerk in the Miller's Tale. Absalom is a little bit foolish and more than a little bit vain. He wears red stockings underneath his floor-length church gown, and his leather shoes are decorated like the fanciful stained-glass windows in a cathedral. He curls his hair, uses breath fresheners, and fancies Alison.

JOHN—The dim-witted carpenter to whom Alison is married and with whom Nicholas boards. John is jealous and possessive of his wife. He constantly berates Nicholas for looking into God's "pryvetee" ("private parts"), but when Nicholas offers John the chance to share his knowledge, John quickly accepts. He gullibly believes Nicholas's pronouncement that a second flood is coming, which allows Nicholas to sleep with John's wife.

Characters in the Wife of Bath's Tale

THE FIRST THREE HUSBANDS— "Good" husbands, according to the Wife of Bath, because they were rich and old. She could order them around, use sex to get what she wanted, and trick them into believing lies.

THE FOURTH HUSBAND—A reveler who had a mistress. The Wife of Bath says comparatively little about him. She loved him and had fun singing and dancing with him, but she tried her best to make him jealous. She fell in love with her fifth husband, Jankyn, while she was still married to her fourth.

JANKYN—The Wife of Bath's fifth husband. Jankyn was a twenty-year-old former student, with whom the Wife was madly in love. His stories of wicked wives frustrated her so much that one night she ripped a page out of his book, only to receive a deafening smack on her ear in return.

THE KNIGHT—Arthur's young knight who rapes a maiden, and, to avoid the punishment of death, is sent by the queen on a quest to learn about submission to women. Once he does so, and shows that he has learned his lesson by letting his old ugly wife make a decision, she rewards him by becoming beautiful and submissive.

Characters in the Pardoner's Tale

THE THREE RIOTERS—The three protagonists of the Pardoner's Tale. All three indulge in and represent the vices against which the Pardoner has railed in his Prologue: Gluttony, Drunkenness, Gambling, and Swearing. These traits define the three and eventually lead to their downfall. The Rioters at first appear like personified vices, but it is their belief that a personified concept—in this case, Death—is a real person that becomes the root cause of their undoing.

THE OLD MAN—A very old man whom the Three Rioters encounter. The old man's body is completely covered except for his face. Before the old man tells the Rioters where they can find Death, one of the Rioters rashly demands to know why the old man is still alive. The old man answers that he is doomed to walk the earth for eternity. He has been interpreted as Death itself; as Cain, punished for fratricide by walking the earth forever; and as the Wandering Jew, a man doomed to roam the world, through the ages, without rest because he refused to let Jesus rest at his house when Jesus proceeded to his crucifixion.

Characters in the Tale of Sir Thopas

SIR THOPAS—A frivolous young knight who sets off in search of an elf-queen. Driven by adolescent sexual urges and dreams of an elf-queen, Thopas seeks out a magical land where he might find such a queen. When he finally finds a faerie country, a huge man named Sir Elephant thwarts his quest. Sir Thopas returns the next day to battle for the elf-queen, but before the listeners hear the outcome, the Host interrupts the meandering story.

SIR ELEPHANT—Sir Thopas's foe. Sir Elephant refuses Sir Thopas access to the elf-queen, the object of Thopas's dreams. He dismisses Thopas as a "pissant."

Characters in the Nun's Priest's Tale

CHANTICLEER—The heroic rooster of the Nun's Priest's Tale. Chanticleer has seven hen-wives and is the most handsome cock in the barnyard. One day, he has a prophetic dream of a fox that will carry him away. Chanticleer is also a bit vain about his clear and accurate crowing voice, and he unwittingly allows a fox to flatter him out of his liberty.

PERTELOTE—Chanticleer's favorite wife in the Nun's Priest's Tale. She is his equal in looks, manners, and talent. When Chanticleer dreams of the fox, he awakens Pertelote in the middle of the night, begging for an interpretation, but she will have none of it, calling him foolish. When the fox takes Chanticleer away, she mourns him in classical Greek fashion, burning herself and wailing.

THE FOX—An orange fox, interpreted by some as an allegorical figure for the devil. The Fox catches Chanticleer the rooster through flattery. Eventually, Chanticleer outwits the Fox by encouraging him to boast of his deceit to his pursuers. When the fox opens his mouth, Chanticleer escapes.

NO FEAR

THE CANTERBURY TALES

General Prologue

HERE BIGINNETH THE BOOK OF THE TALES OF CAUNTERBURY.

Whan that Aprille with his shoures sote
The droghte of Marche hath perced to the rote,
And bathed every veyne in swich licour,
Of which vertu engendred is the flour;
Whan Zephirus eek with his swete breeth
Inspired hath in every holt and heeth
The tendre croppes, and the yonge sonne
Hath in the Ram his halfe cours y-ronne,
And smale fowles maken melodye,
10   That slepen al the night with open yë,
(So priketh hem nature in hir corages):
Than longen folk to goon on pilgrimages
(And palmers for to seken straunge strondes)
To ferne halwes, couthe in sondry londes;
And specially, from every shires ende
Of Engelond, to Caunterbury they wende,
The holy blisful martir for to seke,
That hem hath holpen, whan that they were seke.

Bifel that, in that seson on a day,
20   In Southwerk at the Tabard as I lay
Redy to wenden on my pilgrimage
To Caunterbury with ful devout corage,
At night was come in-to that hostelrye
Wel nyne and twenty in a companye,
Of sondry folk, by aventure y-falle
In felawshipe, and pilgrims were they alle,
That toward Caunterbury wolden ryde;
The chambres and the stables weren wyde,
And wel we weren esed atte beste.
30   And shortly, whan the sonne was to reste,
So hadde I spoken with hem everichon,
That I was of hir felawshipe anon,

General Prologue

THE CANTERBURY TALES STARTS HERE.

1-18 People want to go on religious pilgrimages to spiritual places in the springtime, when the April rains have soaked deep into the dry ground to water the flowers' roots; and when Zephyrus, the god of the west wind, has helped new flowers to grow everywhere; and when you can see the constellation Aries in the sky; and when the birds sing all the time. Some people go to other countries, but many people in England choose to go to the city of Canterbury in southeastern England to visit the remains of Thomas Becket, the Christian martyr who had the power of healing people.

20-32 One spring, when I was making my own humble pilgrimage to Canterbury, I stayed at the Tabard Inn in the city of Southwark. While I was there, a group of twenty-nine people who were also making the same pilgrimage arrived at the hotel. None of them had really known each other before, but they had met along the way. It was a pretty diverse group of people from different walks of life. The hotel was spacious and had plenty of room for all of us. I started talking with these people and pretty soon fit right into their group. We made plans to get up early and continue on the journey to Canterbury together.

And made forward erly for to ryse,
To take our wey, ther as I yow devyse.

But natheles, whyl I have tyme and space,
Er that I ferther in this tale pace,
Me thinketh it acordaunt to resoun,
To telle yow al the condicioun
Of ech of hem, so as it semed me,
40   And whiche they weren, and of what degree;
And eek in what array that they were inne:
And at a knight than wol I first biginne.

A KNIGHT ther was, and that a worthy man,
That fro the tyme that he first bigan
To ryden out, he loved chivalrye,
Trouthe and honour, fredom and curteisye.
Ful worthy was he in his lordes werre,
And therto hadde he riden (no man ferre)
As wel in Cristendom as hethenesse,
50   And ever honoured for his worthinesse.

At Alisaundre he was, whan it was wonne;
Ful ofte tyme he hadde the bord bigonne
Aboven alle naciouns in Pruce.
In Lettow hadde he reysed and in Ruce,
No Cristen man so ofte of his degree.
In Gernade at the sege eek hadde he be
Of Algezir, and riden in Belmarye.
At Lyeys was he, and at Satalye,
Whan they were wonne; and in the Grete See
60   At many a noble aryve hadde he be.
At mortal batailles hadde he been fiftene,
And foughten for our feith at Tramissene
In listes thryes, and ay slayn his foo.
This ilke worthy knight had been also
Somtyme with the lord of Palatye,
Ageyn another hethen in Turkye:
And evermore he hadde a sovereyn prys.

NO FEAR

33-42 But before I begin my story, I should probably tell you all about the twenty-nine people in this group—who they were, what they did for a living, and what they were all wearing. I'll start by telling you about the knight.

43-50 There was an honorable KNIGHT, who had devoted his life to chivalry, truth, and justice. He had fought for his king in many wars throughout Europe and the Middle East and had won many awards for his bravery.

51-78 This knight had been there and done it all. He had helped conquer the city of Alexandria in Egypt in 1365 and had dined with royalty in Prussia on many occasions. He'd fought in Lithuania and Russia more times than any other Christian knight. He'd been at the siege of Algeciras in Grenada, Spain, and had conquered enemies in North Africa and Eastern Europe. He'd been all over the Mediterranean Sea. He'd been in fifteen battles—three of them against the heathens of Algeria—and he'd never lost once. This knight had even fought with the pagan king of Istanbul in Turkey against another non-Christian. Despite his huge success and his noble lineage, he was practical, self-disciplined, and humble. Never had he said anything bad about another person. He truly was the most perfect knight in every way possible. Now, to tell you about his clothes. He rode fine quality horses, but he didn't wear flashy clothes. He wore a simple cotton shirt that had stains all over it from the chain mail he'd worn in the war he'd won just before starting out on the pilgrimage to Canterbury.

And though that he were worthy, he was wys,
And of his port as meke as is a mayde.
70   He never yet no vileinye ne sayde
In al his lyf, unto no maner wight.
He was a verray parfit gentil knight.
But for to tellen yow of his array,
His hors were gode, but he was nat gay.
Of fustian he wered a gipoun
Al bismotered with his habergeoun;
For he was late y-come from his viage,
And wente for to doon his pilgrimage.

With him ther was his sone, a yong SQUYER,
80   A lovyere, and a lusty bacheler,
With lokkes crulle, as they were leyd in presse.
Of twenty yeer of age he was, I gesse.
Of his stature he was of evene lengthe,
And wonderly deliver, and greet of strengthe.
And he had been somtyme in chivachye,
In Flaundres, in Artoys, and Picardye,
And born him wel, as of so litel space,
In hope to stonden in his lady grace.
Embrouded was he, as it were a mede
90   Al ful of fresshe floures, whyte and rede.
Singinge he was, or floytinge, al the day;
He was as fresh as is the month of May.
Short was his goune, with sleves longe and wyde.
Wel coude he sitte on hors, and faire ryde.
He coude songes make and wel endyte,
Iuste and eek daunce, and wel purtreye and wryte,
So hote he lovede, that by nightertale
He sleep namore than dooth a nightingale.
Curteys he was, lowly, and servisable,
100   And carf biforn his fader at the table.

A YEMAN hadde he, and servaunts namo
At that tyme, for him liste ryde so;
And he was clad in cote and hood of grene;

79-100   The knight's son was also with us, a young SQUIRE boy who was his father's assistant. He was a gentle, happy boy who was well on his way to becoming a knight himself. He was about twenty years old, of average height, and had very curly hair. He was also very strong and physically fit. He'd served in the army in some wars in Holland and France and had won honors there too, which he hoped would impress the girl he loved. In fact, he was so madly in love with this girl that he couldn't even sleep at night. He wore a very colorful long shirt that had wide sleeves, and it looked like a field full of red and white flowers. You could tell he was young and carefree because he sang and played the flute all day. He'd write poetry and songs, draw, dance, and joust. All in all, he was a nice young man—humble, polite, and always willing to help out his dad.

101-117   A YEOMAN, or servant, accompanied the knight and his son, ◄――――― and since he was the only servant with them, he got to ride **Yeoman:** A servant in one of his master's horses. This servant wore a green hooded a noble household.

A sheef of pecok-arwes brighte and kene
Under his belt he bar ful thriftily;
(Wel coude he dresse his takel yemanly:
His arwes drouped noght with fetheres lowe),
And in his hand he bar a mighty bowe.
A not-heed hadde he, with a broun visage.
110 Of wode-craft wel coude he al the usage.
Upon his arm he bar a gay bracer,
And by his syde a swerd and a bokeler,
And on that other syde a gay daggere,
Harneised wel, and sharp as point of spere;
A Cristofre on his brest of silver shene.
An horn he bar, the bawdrik was of grene;
A forster was he, soothly, as I gesse.

Ther was also a Nonne, a PRIORESSE,
That of hir smyling was ful simple and coy;
120 Hir gretteste ooth was but by sëynt Loy;
And she was cleped madame Eglentyne.
Ful wel she song the service divyne,
Entuned in hir nose ful semely;
And Frensh she spak ful faire and fetisly,
After the scole of Stratford atte Bowe,
For Frensh of Paris was to hir unknowe.
At mete wel y-taught was she with-alle;
She leet no morsel from hir lippes falle,
Ne wette hir fingres in hir sauce depe.
130 Wel coude she carie a morsel, and wel kepe,
That no drope ne fille upon hir brest.
In curteisye was set ful muche hir lest.
Hir over lippe wyped she so clene,
That in hir coppe was no ferthing sene
Of grece, whan she dronken hadde hir draughte.
Ful semely after hir mete she raughte,
And sikerly she was of greet disport,
And ful plesaunt, and amiable of port,
And peyned hir to countrefete chere
140 Of court, and been estatlich of manere,

jacket and carried a bow and a bundle of arrows made with bright peacock feathers. The quality of the peacock feathers alone told you that he was a pretty meticulous guy who always paid attention to the little details. He was also an excellent woodworker. He had tan skin, short hair, and wore a wrist guard and a sharp, shiny dagger. He also wore a silver Saint Christopher's medal around his neck and a hunting horn with a green strap over his shoulder. He also carried a sword and a shield. I guess he was a forester who spent a lot of time in the woods.

118-164   There was also a PRIORESS, a nun named Madame Englantine, who ran a convent. She had a sweet and modest smile and was very friendly and easy to get along with. She sang hymns kind of through her nose, which actually sounded pretty good. She spoke French fluently—though still with an English accent. She prided herself on her proper manners and etiquette. For example, she always served herself small portions and took small bites of food so that none would fall out of her mouth or get her fingers too messy. And before taking a drink, she would dab her lip with a napkin so that food didn't get all over her cup. She went to great lengths to appear well mannered and worthy of being a prioress. She was one of those people who felt so strongly for others that she would burst into tears if she saw a mouse caught in a trap. In fact, the only time she'd swear would be to say "By Saint Loy!" She had a few small dogs with her and would feed them only the finest food—roasted meat, milk, fine bread. She'd cry if one of those dogs died or was abused by someone else. She really did wear her heart on her sleeve. She had a fine nose, bright eyes, a small red mouth, and a broad forehead. In fact, her forehead was almost as wide as the span of my hand, since she was a good-sized woman. She wore a pretty cloak and a well-pressed cloth around her neck. Around her arm she wore a rosary made of coral and green beads, and on this string of beads hung a golden brooch with the letter A and the inscription *Amor vincit onmnia*—love con-

And to ben holden digne of reverence.
But, for to speken of hir conscience,
She was so charitable and so pitous,
She wolde wepe, if that she sawe a mous
Caught in a trappe, if it were deed or bledde.
Of smale houndes had she, that she fedde
With rosted flesh, or milk and wastel-breed.
But sore weep she if oon of hem were deed,
Or if men smoot it with a yerde smerte:
150 And al was conscience and tendre herte.
Ful semely hir wimpel pinched was;
Hir nose tretys; hir eyen greye as glas;
Hir mouth ful smal, and ther-to softe and reed;
But sikerly she hadde a fair forheed;
It was almost a spanne brood, I trowe;
For, hardily, she was nat undergrowe.
Ful fetis was hir cloke, as I was war.
Of smal coral aboute hir arm she bar
A peire of bedes, gauded al with grene;
160 And ther-on heng a broche of gold ful shene,
On which ther was first write a crowned A,
And after, *Amor vincit omnia*.
Another NONNE with hir hadde she
That was hir chapeleyne, and PREESTES three.

A MONK ther was, a fair for the maistrye
An out-rydere, that lovede venerye;
A manly man, to been an abbot able.
Ful many a deyntee hors hadde he in stable:
And, whan he rood, men mighte his brydel here
170 Ginglen in a whistling wind as clere,
And eek as loude as dooth the chapel-belle,
Ther as this lord was keper of the celle.
The reule of seint Maure or of seint Beneit,
By-cause that it was old and som-del streit,
This ilke monk leet olde thinges pace,
And held after the newe world the space.
He yaf nat of that text a pulled hen,

quers all. She was accompanied by three priests and another nun, who was her assistant.

165-269 There was also a MONK, a splendid chap, who inspected his monastery's lands. He was a man's man who loved to hunt and who might one day become the head of his monastery. He kept many elegant horses, and when he rode them you could hear their bridle bells jingle as clearly as the bells of his monastery. He liked all things modern and new and didn't care for old things, especially St. Benedict's rule that monks should live simply and devote themselves to prayer and work. He didn't give a damn for the notion that says monks can't be hunters or anything but churchmen. I myself agreed with him. Why should he drive himself crazy reading books and working inside all the time? How is that going to accomplish anything useful? To hell with St. Augustine's stupid rules. Instead, the monk was a horseman, and he kept fast greyhounds. He loved to go hunting,

That seith, that hunters been nat holy men;
Ne that a monk, whan he is cloisterlees,
180   Is lykned til a fish that is waterlees;
This is to seyn, a monk out of his cloistre.
But thilke text held he nat worth an oistre;
And I seyde, his opinioun was good.
What sholde he studie, and make him-selven wood,
Upon a book in cloistre alwey to poure,
Or swinken with his handes, and laboure,
As Austin bit? How shal the world be served?
Lat Austin have his swink to him reserved.
Therfore he was a pricasour aright;
190   Grehoundes he hadde, as swifte as fowel in flight;
Of priking and of hunting for the hare
Was al his lust, for no cost wolde he spare.
I seigh his sleves purfiled at the hond
With grys, and that the fyneste of a lond;
And, for to festne his hood under his chin,
He hadde of gold y-wroght a curious pin:
A love-knotte in the gretter ende ther was.
His heed was balled, that shoon as any glas,
And eek his face, as he had been anoint.
200   He was a lord ful fat and in good point;
His eyen stepe, and rollinge in his heed,
That stemed as a forneys of a leed;
His botes souple, his hors in greet estat.
Now certeinly he was a fair prelat;
He was nat pale as a for-pyned goost.
A fat swan loved he best of any roost.
His palfrey was as broun as is a berye.

A FRERE ther was, a wantown and a merye,
A limitour, a ful solempne man.
210   In alle the ordres foure is noon that can
So muche of daliaunce and fair langage.
He hadde maad ful many a mariage
Of yonge wommen, at his owne cost.
Unto his ordre he was a noble post.

and his favorite catch was a fine fat swan. He spared no expense pursuing this hobby. It was therefore no surprise to see that the finest fur lined the cuffs of his sleeves or that he used a fancy golden pin to fasten his hood. In fact, it appeared to be a love knot, a symbol of enduring love. He had a shiny bald head and his face seemed to glisten. His eyes rolled about in his head and seemed to burn like fire. His brown horse was well groomed, his boots were well worn, and his skin looked healthy, not pale like a ghost's. Indeed, he was a fine-looking churchman.

208–269 There was also a FRIAR named Hubert, who lived happily ◄──────
and excessively. He was a beggar, but a sweet talking one. Of **Friar:** A roaming
all the friars in the world, he was the most playful. He was the priest with no tie
best beggar in town and was so smooth that he could even to a particular
get the poorest little old ladies to give him money. As a result, monastery.
he made more money than he actually needed, which meant that he could play like a puppy all day long. He was good at resolving legal

Ful wel biloved and famulier was he
With frankeleyns over-al in his contree,
And eek with worthy wommen of the toun:
For he had power of confessioun,
As seyde him-self, more than a curat,
220   For of his ordre he was licentiat.
Ful swetely herde he confessioun,
And plesaunt was his absolucioun;
He was an esy man to yeve penaunce
Ther as he wiste to han a good pitaunce;
For unto a povre ordre for to yive
Is signe that a man is wel y-shrive.
For if he yaf, he dorste make avaunt,
He wiste that a man was repentaunt.
For many a man so hard is of his herte,
230   He may nat wepe al-thogh him sore smerte.
Therfore, in stede of weping and preyeres,
Men moot yeve silver to the povre freres.
His tipet was ay farsed ful of knyves
And pinnes, for to yeven faire wyves.
And certeinly he hadde a mery note;
Wel coude he singe and pleyen on a rote.
Of yeddinges he bar utterly the prys.
His nekke whyt was as the flour-de-lys;
Ther-to he strong was as a champioun.
240   He knew the tavernes wel in every toun,
And everich hostiler and tappestere
Bet than a lazar or a beggestere;
For unto swich a worthy man as he
Acorded nat, as by his facultee,
To have with seke lazars aqueyntaunce.
It is nat honest, it may nat avaunce
For to delen with no swich poraille,
But al with riche and sellers of vitaille.
And over-al, ther as profit sholde aryse,
250   Curteys he was, and lowly of servyse.
Ther nas no man no-wher so vertuous.
He was the beste beggere in his hous;

disputes too, and did so wearing thick, bell-shaped robes that were so splendid he looked like the pope instead of a poor friar. He even pretended to have a lisp to make himself sound more dignified. He had married off many young ladies—much to his own dismay. Oh, he was one of the Church's finest all right! All the guys in town—and the women too—thought he was just great because, as he himself put it, there was no one who could hear confessions better than he could. All you had to do was slip him some change and he'd swear up and down that you were the most penitent person that ever lived, no matter what you'd done or how sorry you really were. And since bribes are easier than actual remorse, this guy had a lot of nice stuff, including a fair amount of jewelry in his robes that he'd use to woo the ladies. He could also play the fiddle and sing the sweetest songs with a twinkle in his eye. He knew all the bars in town and every bartender and barmaid too. He knew them much better, in fact, than he knew any of the lepers or beggarwomen or other poor people whom he was supposed to be helping. It wouldn't have been fitting for him, the powerful man that he was, to be seen with such people. Besides, there's no money to be made hanging out with the likes of them. Instead, he'd spend all his time with the wealthy, flattering them so that they would give him money. Nope, no one was more virtuous!

For thogh a widwe hadde noght a sho,
So plesaunt was his "*In principio*,"
Yet wolde he have a ferthing, er he wente.
His purchas was wel bettre than his rente.
And rage he coude, as it were right a whelpe.
In love-dayes ther coude he muchel helpe.
For there he was nat lyk a cloisterer,
260 With a thredbar cope, as is a povre scoler,
But he was lyk a maister or a pope.
Of double worsted was his semi-cope,
That rounded as a belle out of the presse.
Somwhat he lipsed, for his wantownesse,
To make his English swete upon his tonge;
And in his harping, whan that he had songe,
His eyen twinkled in his heed aright,
As doon the sterres in the frosty night.
This worthy limitour was cleped Huberd.

270 A MARCHANT was ther with a forked berd,
In mottelee, and hye on horse he sat,
Upon his heed a Flaundrish bever hat;
His botes clasped faire and fetisly.
His resons he spak ful solempnely,
Souninge alway thencrees of his winning.
He wolde the see were kept for any thing
Bitwixe Middelburgh and Orewelle.
Wel coude he in eschaunge sheeldes selle.
This worthy man ful wel his wit bisette;
280 Ther wiste no wight that he was in dette,
So estatly was he of his governaunce,
With his bargaynes, and with his chevisaunce.
For sothe he was a worthy man with-alle,
But sooth to seyn, I noot how men him calle.

A CLERK ther was of Oxenford also,
That unto logik hadde longe y-go.
As lene was his hors as is a rake,
And he nas nat right fat, I undertake;

270-284   There was also a MERCHANT who had a forked beard and wore clothes that looked like a jester's. This businessman wore a beaver hat from Holland and had expensive-looking boots. He spoke very seriously, making sure that everyone knew how wealthy and successful he was. He was particularly obsessed with making sure that the navy maintained order in the North Sea between England and Holland. He played the markets well and sold a lot of Dutch money in currency exchanges. This guy was pretty smart all right: He carried himself so well that no one suspected he was really heavily in debt. Whatever. He was actually a good guy, and it's too bad I never learned his name.

285-308   There was a CLERK from Oxford who studied philosophy. His horse was a lean as a rake, and so was he for that matter. He looked hollow and serious. He wore a threadbare cloak because he didn't make any money. He didn't have a

Clerk: This clerk is a poor student of philosophy.

But loked holwe, and ther-to soberly.
290　Ful thredbar was his overest courtepy;
For he had geten him yet no benefyce,
Ne was so worldly for to have offyce.
For him was lever have at his beddes heed
Twenty bokes, clad in blak or reed,
Of Aristotle and his philosophye,
Than robes riche, or fithele, or gay sautrye.
But al be that he was a philosophre,
Yet hadde he but litel gold in cofre;
But al that he mighte of his freendes hente,
300　On bokes and on lerninge he it spente,
And bisily gan for the soules preye
Of hem that yaf him wher-with to scoleye.
Of studie took he most cure and most hede.
Noght o word spak he more than was nede,
And that was seyd in forme and reverence,
And short and quik, and ful of hy sentence.
Souninge in moral vertu was his speche,
And gladly wolde he lerne, and gladly teche.

A SERGEANT OF THE LAWE, war and wys,
310　That often hadde been at the parvys,
Ther was also, ful riche of excellence.
Discreet he was, and of greet reverence:
He semed swich, his wordes weren so wyse.
Iustyce he was ful often in assyse,
By patente, and by pleyn commissioun;
For his science, and for his heigh renoun
Of fees and robes hadde he many oon.
So greet a purchasour was no-wher noon.
Al was fee simple to him in effect,
320　His purchasing mighte nat been infect.
No-wher so bisy a man as he ther nas,
And yet he semed bisier than he was.
In termes hadde he caas and domes alle,
That from the tyme of king William were falle.
Therto he coude endyte, and make a thing,

job because he didn't want one. He'd rather own twenty philosophy books than have nice clothes or nice things. He used all the money his friends gave him to buy books, and he prayed for the souls of his friends for helping him to pursue his passion. Not surprisingly, he spent most of his time reading. He was polite, but he spoke only when it was necessary and important to do so. His speeches were short and quick but very insightful and often about morality. He was both eager to learn and eager to teach.

309-330   There was a SERGEANT OF LAW too, who was both wise ◄────────────
and slightly suspicious of everything. He spent a lot of his   **Seargant of Law:** A
time consulting with his clients outside St. Paul's Cathedral   lawyer commis-
sioned by the king.
in London. He was very wise and well respected and chose
his words carefully when he spoke. He had served as the judge in
a criminal court before, and his vast knowledge and wisdom had
made him famous. He'd earned a lot of money as a judge and had
become a great and powerful landowner. He had memorized all of
the laws, court cases, and decisions in England over the last 300
years and could therefore write the most perfect legal document. He
was an incredibly busy person but always made himself look busier
than he really was. He traveled in a simple multicolored coat that
was tied together with a silk belt and some small pins. And that's all
I really have to say about his clothing.

Ther coude no wight pinche at his wryting;
And every statut coude he pleyn by rote.
He rood but hoomly in a medlee cote
Girt with a ceint of silk, with barres smale;
330 Of his array telle I no lenger tale.

A FRANKELEYN was in his companye;
Whyt was his berd, as is the dayesye.
Of his complexioun he was sangwyn.
Wel loved he by the morwe a sop in wyn.
To liven in delyt was ever his wone,
For he was Epicurus owne sone,
That heeld opinioun, that pleyn delyt
Was verraily felicitee parfyt.
An housholdere, and that a greet, was he;
340 Seint Iulian he was in his contree.
His breed, his ale, was alwey after oon;
A bettre envyned man was no-wher noon.
With-oute bake mete was never his hous,
Of fish and flesh, and that so plentevous,
It snewed in his hous of mete and drinke,
Of alle deyntees that men coude thinke.
After the sondry sesons of the yeer,
So chaunged he his mete and his soper.
Ful many a fat partrich hadde he in mewe,
350 And many a breem and many a luce in stewe.
Wo was his cook, but-if his sauce were
Poynaunt and sharp, and redy al his gere.
His table dormant in his halle alway
Stood redy covered al the longe day.
At sessiouns ther was he lord and sire;
Ful ofte tyme he was knight of the shire.
An anlas and a gipser al of silk
Heng at his girdel, whyt as morne milk.
A shirreve hadde he been, and a countour;
360 Was no-wher such a worthy vavasour.

331-360 The judge traveled with a FRANKLIN. He had a fleshy red
face and a snow-white beard. He loved to eat a piece of bread
soaked in wine for breakfast every morning. He was an epi-
curean and believed that the pleasures of the world bring
true happiness. He owned a large house and frequently enter-
tained guests who came from miles around. He always had the best
bread and beer, and there was so much meat and fish that it must
have rained wine and hailed food at his house. He also liked to mix
up his diet according to the seasons. His chicken coops were actu-
ally filled with partridges and his stewes filled with fish. I pity the
chef who served him bland food! His dining room table was always
loaded with food no matter what time of day it was. He wore a dag-
ger and a white purse. He was a powerful member of Parliament and
a former sheriff. Nowhere was there a more worthy landowner.

Franklin: A free and independent man who also owned some land

An HABERDASSHER and a CARPENTER,
A WEBBE, a DYERE, and a TAPICER,
Were with us eek, clothed in o liveree,
Of a solempne and greet fraternitee.
Ful fresh and newe hir gere apyked was;
Hir knyves were y-chaped noght with bras,
But al with silver, wroght ful clene and weel,
Hir girdles and hir pouches every-deel.
Wel semed ech of hem a fair burgeys,
370   To sitten in a yeldhalle on a deys.
Everich, for the wisdom that he can,
Was shaply for to been an alderman.
For catel hadde they y-nogh and rente,
And eek hir wyves wolde it wel assente;
And elles certein were they to blame.
It is ful fair to been y-clept "*ma dame*,"
And goon to vigilyës al bifore,
And have a mantel royalliche y-bore.

A COOK they hadde with hem for the nones,
380   To boille the chiknes with the mary-bones,
And poudre-marchant tart, and galingale.
Wel coude he knowe a draughte of London ale.
He coude roste, and sethe, and broille, and frye,
Maken mortreux, and wel bake a pye.
But greet harm was it, as it thoughte me,
That on his shine a mormal hadde he;
For blankmanger, that made he with the beste.

A SHIPMAN was ther, woning fer by weste:
For aught I woot, he was of Dertemouthe.
390   He rood upon a rouncy, as he couthe,
In a gowne of falding to the knee.
A daggere hanging on a laas hadde he
Aboute his nekke under his arm adoun.
The hote somer had maad his hewe al broun;
And, certeinly, he was a good felawe.
Ful many a draughte of wyn had he y-drawe

NO FEAR

361-378　There was also a HABERDASHER—a hatmaker—a CARPENTER, a WEAVER, a clothing DYER, and a TAPESTRY MAKER. These men all belonged to the same workingmen's union, called a guild. Because they belonged to the same guild, they all wore the same clothing too, which seemed to have been made just recently. They wore expensive accessories, including purses, belts, and even fancy knives with handles made of pure silver. Each of them seemed like he could have been a powerful leader of their guild or even a town council. They were certainly all wise enough and wealthy enough to do so. Their wives would no doubt have pushed them to take such positions of power because they too would benefit from being married to men of such prestige.

379-387　The guildsmen brought a COOK with them to make them tasty dishes on their journey—spicy chickens and tarts and whatnot. The cook certainly knew a good beer when he saw one and could roast, broil, fry, and stew with the best of them. His chicken stew was particularly good. Too bad he had a nasty sore on his leg.

388-410　There was also a SHIPMAN, who came from the West, maybe as far away as the city of Dartmouth. He wore a cheap shirt that came down to his knees, and he rode an old, shabby horse. He also wore a dagger tied to a strap that hung across his chest. He had just recently brought over a wine merchant from Bordeaux on his ship—the Magdalen—and had gotten tan and more than a little drunk during the voyage. He was a good guy, but didn't let his conscience bother him. When he won battles at sea he would release his captives. He was an excellent navigator too and knew how to read the stars bet-

From Burdeux-ward, whyl that the chapman sleep.
Of nyce conscience took he no keep.
If that he faught, and hadde the hyer hond,
400   By water he sente hem hoom to every lond.
But of his craft to rekene wel his tydes,
His stremes and his daungers him bisydes,
His herberwe and his mone, his lodemenage,
Ther nas noon swich from Hulle to Cartage.
Hardy he was, and wys to undertake;
With many a tempest hadde his berd been shake.
He knew wel alle the havenes, as they were,
From Gootlond to the cape of Finistere,
And every cryke in Britayne and in Spayne;
410   His barge y-cleped was the Maudelayne.

With us ther was a DOCTOUR OF PHISYK,
In al this world ne was ther noon him lyk
To speke of phisik and of surgerye;
For he was grounded in astronomye.
He kepte his pacient a ful greet del
In houres, by his magik naturel.
Wel coude he fortunen the ascendent
Of his images for his pacient.
He knew the cause of everich maladye,
420   Were it of hoot or cold, or moiste, or drye,
And where engendred, and of what humour;
He was a verrey parfit practisour.
The cause y-knowe, and of his harm the rote,
Anon he yaf the seke man his bote.
Ful redy hadde he his apothecaries,
To sende him drogges and his letuaries,
For ech of hem made other for to winne;
Hir frendschipe nas nat newe to biginne.
Wel knew he the olde Esculapius,
430   And Deiscorides, and eek Rufus,
Old Ypocras, Haly, and Galien;
Serapion, Razis, and Avicen;
Averrois, Damascien, and Constantyn;

ter than any other man. He could sail in any waters and knew all the safe spots from Tunisia and Spain to Sweden. He was hardy and had weathered many storms. He was both wise and practical in everything he did.

411-444   There was also a medical DOCTOR with us, the best doctor in the whole world. This doctor knew astrology and the workings of the natural world and would only treat his patients when it was astrologically safe to do so. He knew the movement of the planets and had studied all the great theories of disease and medicine. He knew the cause of every disease and where it came from. He was really a great doctor. Once he'd figured out which disease his patient had, he immediately gave him the cure. He and the pharmacists had quite the racket going and were quick to prescribe drugs so that they'd both profit. He ate simple food that was nutritious and easy to digest—nothing more—and he mostly read the Bible. He wore bright red and blue clothes made of the finest woven silk, but he saved the rest of his money because he really loved gold more than anything else.

Bernard, and Gatesden, and Gilbertyn.
Of his diete mesurable was he,
For it was of no superfluitee,
But of greet norissing and digestible.
His studie was but litel on the Bible.
In sangwin and in pers he clad was al,
440 Lyned with taffata and with sendal;
And yet he was but esy of dispence;
He kepte that he wan in pestilence.
For gold in phisik is a cordial,
Therfore he lovede gold in special.

A good WYF was ther of bisyde
But she was som-del deef, and that was scathe.
Of clooth-making she hadde swiche an haunt,
She passed hem of Ypres and of Gaunt.
In al the parisshe wyf ne was ther noon
450 That to the offring bifore hir sholde goon;
And if ther dide, certeyn, so wrooth was she,
That she was out of alle charitee.
Hir coverchiefs ful fyne were of ground;
I dorste swere they weyeden ten pound
That on a Sonday were upon hir heed.
Hir hosen weren of fyn scarlet reed,
Ful streite y-teyd, and shoos ful moiste and newe.
Bold was hir face, and fair, and reed of hewe.
She was a worthy womman al hir lyve,
460 Housbondes at chirche-dore she hadde fyve,
Withouten other companye in youthe;
But therof nedeth nat to speke as nouthe.
And thryes hadde she been at Ierusalem;
She hadde passed many a straunge streem;
At Rome she hadde been, and at Boloigne,
In Galice at seint Iame, and at Coloigne.
She coude muche of wandring by the weye.
Gat-tothed was she, soothly for to seye.
Upon an amblere esily she sat,
470 Y-wimpled wel, and on hir heed an hat

NO FEAR

445-476 There was a WIFE from the city of BATH, England. She had a striking, noble face that had a reddish tint to it, though, sorry to say, she had a gap in her front teeth and was a little bit deaf. She wore a hat that was as wide as a shield, sharp spurs, and a pleated cloak over her legs to keep the mud off her dress. She also wore tightly laced red stockings and comfortable new shoes, and her kerchiefs were made of high-quality fabric. In fact, the ones she wore on her head every Sunday were so nice they must have weighed ten pounds. She was so good at weaving cloth that she was even better than the famous weavers from the cities of Ypres and Ghent in Belgium. She'd lived an honorable life and had married five times, not counting her other boyfriends she'd had when she was young—though there's no need to talk about that now. She was the kind of woman who always wanted to be the first wife at church to make a donation to help the poor but would get angry and keep her money if any woman made a donation before she did. She rode her horse well and knew a lot about traveling because she'd been to so many foreign places. She'd been to Jerusalem three times, for example. She'd also been on religious pilgrimages to the cities of Rome and Bologne in Italy, to the shrine of St. James in Spain, and to Cologne, France. She was a good conversationalist and liked to laugh and gossip with the others. She could tell lots of stories, especially romantic ones, because she was an old pro when it came to love.

As brood as is a bokeler or a targe;
A foot-mantel aboute hir hipes large,
And on hir feet a paire of spores sharpe.
In felawschip wel coude she laughe and carpe.
Of remedyes of love she knew per-chaunce,
For she coude of that art the olde daunce.

A good man was ther of religioun, PERSOUN.
And was a povre PERSOUN of a toun;
But riche he was of holy thoght and werk.
480 He was also a lerned man, a clerk,
That Cristes gospel trewely wolde preche;
His parisshens devoutly wolde he teche.
Benigne he was, and wonder diligent,
And in adversitee ful pacient;
And swich he was y-preved ofte sythes.
Ful looth were him to cursen for his tythes,
But rather wolde he yeven, out of doute,
Unto his povre parisshens aboute
Of his offring, and eek of his substaunce.
490 He coude in litel thing han suffisaunce.
Wyd was his parisshe, and houses fer a-sonder,
But he ne lafte nat, for reyn ne thonder,
In siknes nor in meschief, to visyte
The ferreste in his parisshe, muche and lyte,
Upon his feet, and in his hand a staf.
This noble ensample to his sheep he yaf,
That first he wroghte, and afterward he taughte;
Out of the gospel he tho wordes caughte;
And this figure he added eek ther-to,
500 That if gold ruste, what shal iren do?
For if a preest be foul, on whom we truste,
No wonder is a lewed man to ruste;
And shame it is, if a preest take keep,
A shiten shepherde and a clene sheep.
Wel oghte a preest ensample for to yive,
By his clennesse, how that his sheep shold live.
He sette nat his benefice to hyre,

NO FEAR

477-528 There was also a poor PARSON, the priest of a rural county church. He was a good man, a person who thought only holy thoughts, and did only good deeds. He was very gentle, diligent, and always patient in the face of adversity. He wouldn't look down on any of his poor parishioners for not donating money to the church. In fact, he'd rather give them what little money he himself had, especially since he lived happily on very little. He didn't think himself better than others, but he would scold people for being too stubborn in their ways. The county where he lived was large and the houses were spread far apart, but that didn't stop him from visiting every one of his parishioners, rich or poor. With his walking stick in hand, he'd make his rounds from house to house no matter what, even if he was sick or it was raining. He truly was the embodiment of the teachings of Jesus Christ. He lived as he preached, which set the perfect example for his parishioners, his flock of sheep. He lived by the motto, "If gold rusts, what would iron do?" by which he meant, "The priest must live a holy life if he expects ordinary people to live holy lives; all hope is lost if he turns out to be corrupt." It's a shame whenever you see a filthy shepherd watching over clean sheep, which is why priests should live by example to show their sheep how to live. The parson remained loyal to his parishioners and would never think about leaving them for a more prestigious post in London or to make more money working for a church on a wealthy landowner's estate. He wasn't interested in wealth or status and wasn't obsessed with the philosophy of ethics or morality. No, he was merely a simple shepherd who sought to save the souls of his flock by living a good life himself and setting a good example. I believe he was the finest priest in the world.

Parson: The only devout churchman of the Canterbury

And leet his sheep encombred in the myre,
And ran to London, unto sëynt Poules,
510   To seken him a chaunterie for soules,
Or with a bretherhed to been withholde;
But dwelte at hoom, and kepte wel his folde,
So that the wolf ne made it nat miscarie;
He was a shepherde and no mercenarie.
And though he holy were, and vertuous,
He was to sinful man nat despitous,
Ne of his speche daungerous ne digne,
But in his teching discreet and benigne.
To drawen folk to heven by fairnesse
520   By good ensample, was his bisinesse:
But it were any persone obstinat,
What-so he were, of heigh or lowe estat,
Him wolde he snibben sharply for the nones.
A bettre preest, I trowe that nowher noon is.
He wayted after no pompe and reverence,
Ne maked him a spyced conscience,
But Cristes lore, and his apostles twelve,
He taughte, and first he folwed it him-selve.

With him ther was a PLOWMAN, was his brother,
530   That hadde y-lad of dong ful many a fother,
A trewe swinker and a good was he,
Livinge in pees and parfit charitee.
God loved he best with al his hole herte
At alle tymes, thogh him gamed or smerte,
And thanne his neighebour right as him-selve.
He wolde thresshe, and ther-to dyke and delve,
For Cristes sake, for every povre wight,
Withouten hyre, if it lay in his might.
His tythes payed he ful faire and wel,
540   Bothe of his propre swink and his catel.
In a tabard he rood upon a mere.

NO FEAR

529-541   There was also a PLOWMAN in our group, who was actually the parson's brother. He wore a simple shirt and rode upon a horse. He was a lowly laborer who worked with his hands. His love for God was always foremost in his thoughts, when he was both happy and sad. He also thought about the needs and wants of other people and had just as much love for others as he had for himself. He had carted many loads of manure and would dig and work hard, all for the love of God and humanity if he could. He donated a good percentage of his income and the value of his other property to the Church on a regular basis. He was a good and loyal man who lived in happiness and peace.

Ther was also a Reve and a Millere,
A Somnour and a Pardoner also,
A Maunciple, and my-self; ther were namo.

The MILLER was a stout carl, for the nones,
Ful big he was of braun, and eek of bones;
That proved wel, for over-al ther he cam,
At wrastling he wolde have alwey the ram.
He was short-sholdred, brood, a thikke knarre,
550   Ther nas no dore that he nolde heve of harre,
Or breke it, at a renning, with his heed.
His berd as any sowe or fox was reed,
And ther-to brood, as though it were a spade.
Upon the cop right of his nose he hade
A werte, and ther-on stood a tuft of heres,
Reed as the bristles of a sowes eres;
His nose-thirles blake were and wyde.
A swerd and bokeler bar he by his syde;
His mouth as greet was as a greet forneys.
560   He was a Ianglere and a goliardeys,
And that was most of sinne and harlotryes.
Wel coude he stelen corn, and tollen thryes;
And yet he hadde a thombe of gold, pardee.
A whyt cote and a blew hood wered he.
A baggepype wel coude he blowe and sowne,
And ther-with-al he broghte us out of towne.

A gentil MAUNCIPLE was ther of a temple,
Of which achatours mighte take exemple
For to be wyse in bying of vitaille.
570   For whether that he payde, or took by taille,
Algate he wayted so in his achat,
That he was ay biforn and in good stat.

542-544 There were six other people in our group too. There was a reeve, an overseer who looked after his master's property. There was also a miller, who owned a mill that turned grain into flour. There were also two court officials—a summoner, who was a bailiff in the court, and a manciple, who was in charge of buying food and provisions for the court. And finally, there was a pardoner, an official who sold formal pardons to criminals after they'd confessed their sins to God. And then, of course, there was me. And that was all of us.

545-566 The MILLER was short, but he was still a pretty big guy—muscular, broad, and big boned. He liked to prove how strong he was by wrestling other people wherever he went, and he always won the matches. There wasn't a door he couldn't either rip off its hinges or break down with a running headbutt. He wore a white coat with a blue hood and carried a sword and small shield at his side. He loved to talk, and he could tell the best bar stories, most of them about sex and sin. He would steal corn and then sell it for three times its worth. He had a beard that was as red as a fox and about the same size and shape as a gardening spade. He had a wide mouth; deep, gaping nostrils; and a wart on the tip of his nose that bristled with red hairs that looked like they grew out of a pig's ears. He could play the bagpipes well, and he played for us as we left town.

567-586 There was also a MANCIPLE, a clerk in charge of buying food and provisions for the Inner Temple, one of the courts in London. Other manicples could really learn from this guy, who was so careful about what he purchased and what he spent that he always saved a lot of money. He worked for thirty lawyers, all of whom were very smart and educated in the law. At least a dozen of them managed

Now is nat that of God a ful fair grace,
That swich a lewed mannes wit shal pace
The wisdom of an heep of lerned men?
Of maistres hadde he mo than thryes ten,
That were of lawe expert and curious;
Of which ther were a doseyn in that hous,
Worthy to been stiwardes of rente and lond
580 Of any lord that is in Engelond,
To make him live by his propre good,
In honour dettelees, but he were wood,
Or live as scarsly as him list desire;
And able for to helpen al a shire
In any cas that mighte falle or happe;
And yit this maunciple sette hir aller cappe.

The REVE was a sclendre colerik man,
His berd was shave as ny as ever he can.
His heer was by his eres round y-shorn.
590 His top was dokked lyk a preest biforn.
Ful longe were his legges, and ful lene,
Y-lyk a staf, ther was no calf y-sene.
Wel coude he kepe a gerner and a binne;
Ther was noon auditour coude on him winne.
Wel wiste he, by the droghte, and by the reyn,
The yelding of his seed, and of his greyn.
His lordes sheep, his neet, his dayerye,
His swyn, his hors, his stoor, and his pultrye,
Was hoolly in this reves governing,
600 And by his covenaunt yaf the rekening,
Sin that his lord was twenty yeer of age;
Ther coude no man bringe him in arrerage.
Ther nas baillif, ne herde, ne other hyne,
That he ne knew his sleighte and his covyne;
They were adrad of him, as of the deeth.
His woning was ful fair upon an heeth,
With grene treës shadwed was his place.
He coude bettre than his lord purchace.
Ful riche he was astored prively,

the wealth and lands of some of the most powerful aristocrats in England. Their job was to help the lords save money and help keep them out debt. And yet the manciple was wiser with money than all of them! It's proof of God's grace that an uneducated man with natural intelligence, such as this manciple, can be smarter and more successful than some of the most educated men.

587-622 Then there was the REEVE, an overseer who looked after his master's lands and property in the town of Bawdeswell in Norfolk, England. He was a bad-tempered guy who got angry easily. The hair on his head was clipped very short like a priest's and nearly shaved clean around his ears. He also had a neatly trimmed beard, which was also shaved pretty close. He was tall and slender and had gangly legs that looked like sticks—you couldn't even see his calves. He'd been in charge of his master's estate since he was twenty years old. He was very meticulous about his job, and no one could fault him for being inaccurate. He always knew how much grain was in the granary and could figure out crop yields in advance based on solely on how much rain had fallen that year. He knew every one of his lord's horses, chickens, cows, sheep, and pigs. All the other peasants who worked for the landlord were terrified of the reeve because he could tell when they were lying or trying to cheat him. He'd been a carpenter when he was younger and was still pretty good at it. He had a house underneath some shade trees in the middle of a meadow. He knew more about money and property than his master, which is how he was able to save up a small fortune over the years. It also helped that he'd been quietly tricking his master all along, by lending him things he already owned, for example, and then taking the master's thank-you gifts in return. He rode a sturdy plow horse, a dappled grey named Scot, and wore a rusty sword. He wore a long

610 His lord wel coude he plesen subtilly,
To yeve and lene him of his owne good,
And have a thank, and yet a cote and hood.
In youthe he lerned hadde a good mister;
He was a wel good wrighte, a carpenter.
This reve sat upon a ful good stot,
That was al pomely grey, and highte Scot.
A long surcote of pers upon he hade,
And by his syde he bar a rusty blade.
Of Northfolk was this reve, of which I telle,
620 Bisyde a toun men clepen Baldeswelle.
Tukked he was, as is a frere, aboute,
And ever he rood the hindreste of our route.

A SOMNOUR was ther with us in that place,
That hadde a fyr-reed cherubinnes face,
For sawcefleem he was, with eyen narwe.
As hoot he was, and lecherous, as a sparwe;
With scalled browes blake, and piled berd;
Of his visage children were aferd.
Ther nas quik-silver, litarge, ne brimstoon,
630 Boras, ceruce, ne oille of tartre noon,
Ne oynement that wolde dense and byte,
That him mighte helpen of his whelkes whyte,
Nor of the knobbes sitting on his chekes.
Wel loved he garleek, oynons, and eek lekes,
And for to drinken strong wyn, reed as blood.
Thanne wolde he speke, and crye as he were wood.
And whan that he wel dronken hadde the wyn,
Than wolde he speke no word but Latyn.
A fewe termes hadde he, two or three,
640 That he had lerned out of som decree;
No wonder is, he herde it al the day;
And eek ye knowen wel, how that a Iay
Can clepen 'Watte,' as well as can the pope.
But who-so coude in other thing him grope,
Thanne hadde he spent al his philosophye;
Ay 'Questio quid iuris' wolde he crye.

blue coat that he wore draped around him, which made him look like the friar. He rode last in our group.

623-668 There was also a SUMMONER traveling with us, a man who worked as a bailiff in a religious court. He had a fire-red face just like a little angel's because he had so many pimples. He was a pretty sketchy guy who scared little kids because of his scabby black eyebrows and his scraggily beard. There wasn't a medicine or ointment in the world that could get rid of the pimples and boils on his face. He liked to eat garlic, onions, and leeks and drink wine that was as red as blood. And when he'd get good and drunk, he'd go about shouting like crazy in Latin. He really only knew a few words in Latin, only because he heard the judges say them day in and day out in the courtroom. He'd repeat them over and over like a parrot. And if anyone challenged him by asking to say something else in Latin, he'd simply repeat the same question over and over: *"Questio quid juris?"* which meant, "I wonder which law applies in this situation?" He was a friendly guy who'd loan his girlfriend to you for a year for a bottle of wine, probably because he knew he could secretly find another girl on the side. He had all the ladies of the court wrapped around his little finger And if he caught another man cheating, he'd tell him not to worry about being punished by the Church because all he had to do was pay a bribe. On this subject, though, I know he was lying. Everyone should fear excommunication. He was riding around with a garland on his head to be funny, and he carried around a cake that he pretended to be his shield.

He was a gentil harlot and a kinde;
A bettre felawe sholde men noght finde.
He wolde suffre, for a quart of wyn,
650 A good felawe to have his concubyn
A twelf-month, and excuse him atte fulle:
Ful prively a finch eek coude he pulle.
And if he fond o-wher a good felawe,
He wolde techen him to have non awe,
In swich cas, of the erchedeknes curs,
But-if a mannes soule were in his purs;
For in his purs he sholde y-punisshed be.
'Purs is the erchedeknes helle,' seyde he.
But wel I woot he lyed right in dede;
660 Of cursing oghte ech gilty man him drede—
For curs wol slee, right as assoilling saveth—
And also war him of a *significavit*.
In daunger hadde he at his owne gyse
The yonge girles of the diocyse,
And knew hir counseil, and was al hir reed.
A gerland hadde he set upon his heed,
As greet as it were for an ale-stake;
A bokeler hadde he maad him of a cake.

With him ther rood a gentil PARDONER.
670 Of Rouncival, his freend and his compeer,
That streight was comen fro the court of Rome.
Ful loude he song, 'Com hider, love, to me.'
This somnour bar to him a stif burdoun,
Was never trompe of half so greet a soun.
This pardoner hadde heer as yelow as wex,
But smothe it heng, as dooth a strike of flex;
By ounces henge his lokkes that he hadde,
And ther-with he his shuldres overspradde;
But thinne it lay, by colpons oon and oon;
680 But hood, for Iolitee, ne wered he noon,
For it was trussed up in his walet.
Him thoughte, he rood al of the newe Iet;
Dischevele, save his cappe, he rood al bare.

NO FEAR

669-714 With the summoner rode a PARDONER from the hospital at Rouncivalle near London, a man who sold official pardons to criminals after hearing their confessions to God. He had eyes that popped out of his head like a rabbit's and a voice that sounded like the bleating of a goat. He didn't have a beard either, and I don't think he ever will have one. His face was always as smooth as if he had just shaven. His thin blond hair was as yellow as wax and hung in straight, stringy wisps from his head. Just for fun, he kept his hood packed up in his bag, thinking that without it he'd look cooler and more stylish with his hair falling over his shoulders. Instead, he wore only a cap that had a patch sewn on it, showing that he'd been to Rome to see the veil of St. Veronica with Jesus' face on it. In fact, he'd just come back from Rome, and the bag he carried on his lap was stuffed full of letters of pardon for him to sell. He and the summoner were close friends and together would belt out rounds

Swiche glaringe eyen hadde he as an hare.
A vernicle hadde he sowed on his cappe.
His walet lay biforn him in his lappe,
Bret-ful of pardoun come from Rome al hoot.
A voys he hadde as smal as hath a goot.
No berd hadde he, ne never sholde have,
As smothe it was as it were late y-shave;
I trowe he were a gelding or a mare.
But of his craft, fro Berwik into Ware,
Ne was ther swich another pardoner.
For in his male he hadde a pilwe-beer,
Which that, he seyde, was our lady veyl:
He seyde, he hadde a gobet of the seyl
That sëynt Peter hadde, whan that he wente
Upon the see, til Iesu Crist him hente.
He hadde a croys of latoun, ful of stones,
And in a glas he hadde pigges bones.
But with thise relikes, whan that he fond
A povre person dwelling upon lond,
Upon a day he gat him more moneye
Than that the person gat in monthes tweye.
And thus, with feyned flaterye and Iapes,
He made the person and the peple his apes.
But trewely to tellen, atte laste,
He was in chirche a noble ecclesiaste.
Wel coude he rede a lessoun or a storie,
But alderbest he song an offertorie;
For wel he wiste, whan that song was songe,
He moste preche, and wel affyle his tonge,
To winne silver, as he ful wel coude;
Therefore he song so meriely and loude.

Now have I told you shortly, in a clause,
Thestat, tharray, the nombre, and eek the cause
Why that assembled was this companye
In Southwerk, at this gentil hostelrye,
That highte the Tabard, faste by the Belle.
But now is tyme to yow for to telle

of the song "Come here, my love." Not even a trumpet was half as loud as the summoner. I'm pretty sure the pardoner was either a eunuch or gay. Still, he was one of the most interesting pardoners in all of England. He carried a pillowcase in his bag that he claimed contained a bunch of holy objects, including Mary's veil, a piece of canvas from the sails of Saint Peter's fishing boat, a crucifix made of brass and jewels, and even a jar of pig bones. He could make more money in a day charging country bumpkins and priests to see these "relics" than those priests could earn in two months. And so, through flattery and deceit he'd make fools out of the countryfolk and their priests. But, to give him credit, he took churchgoing seriously and could read lessons and stories from the Bible well. And he was best at singing the offertory song because he knew he had to sing loudly and happily if he wanted people to donate their money.

715-746 So now I've told you as best I can everything about the people in our little group—who they were, what they looked like, what they wore, and why we were all together in the Tabard Inn in the city of Southwark, England. Next, I'm going to tell you about what we all did that night after we'd checked into the hotel, and after that I'll tell you about the rest of our pilgrimage to Canterbury. But first, I

How that we baren us that ilke night,
Whan we were in that hostelrye alight.
And after wol I telle of our viage,
And al the remenaunt of our pilgrimage.
But first I pray yow, of your curteisye,
That ye narette it nat my vileinye,
Thogh that I pleynly speke in this matere,
To telle yow hir wordes and hir chere;
Ne thogh I speke hir wordes properly.
730 For this ye knowen al-so wel as I,
Who-so shal telle a tale after a man,
He moot reherce, as ny as ever he can,
Everich a word, if it be in his charge,
Al speke he never so rudeliche and large;
Or elles he moot telle his tale untrewe,
Or feyne thing, or finde wordes newe.
He may nat spare, al-thogh he were his brother;
He moot as wel seye o word as another.
Crist spak him-self ful brode in holy writ,
740 And wel ye woot, no vileinye is it.
Eek Plato seith, who-so that can him rede,
The wordes mote be cosin to the dede.
Also I prey yow to foryeve it me,
Al have I nat set folk in hir degree
Here in this tale, as that they sholde stonde;
My wit is short, ye may wel understonde.

Greet chere made our hoste us everichon,
And to the soper sette he us anon;
And served us with vitaille at the beste.
750 Strong was the wyn, and wel to drinke us leste.
A semely man our hoste was with-alle
For to han been a marshal in an halle;
A large man he was with eyen stepe,
A fairer burgeys is ther noon in Chepe:
Bold of his speche, and wys, and wel y-taught,
And of manhod him lakkede right naught.
Eek therto he was right a mery man,

have to ask for your forgiveness and not think me vulgar when I tell you what these people said and did. I've got to tell you these things exactly how they happened and repeat these stories word for word as best I can so that you get the facts straight without any of my interpretation. Jesus Christ told it like it is in the scriptures, and that wasn't considered to be vulgar. And Plato says (to the people who can read Greek anyway) that words must match the actions as closely as possible. I also beg your forgiveness if my storytelling changes your perception of the kinds of people these travelers were: I'm really not that clever, you see.

747-768   Our HOST, the owner of the Tabard Inn, welcomed all of us and served us dinner right away. The food was really good and the wine really strong, which we all were grateful for. The host seemed like he was a good enough innkeeper to have even been a butler in some great house. He was 100% man, big and with bulging eyes—bigger than any of the merchants in the markets of London, that's for sure. He spoke in a straightforward manner that conveyed his wisdom and his learning. He was also pretty jolly, and after dinner he started telling jokes and funny stories—after we'd paid the bill, of course— and said, "Gentlemen, I welcome you from the bottom of my heart. To tell you the truth, we haven't had as large a group of people all

And after soper pleyen he bigan,
And spak of mirthe amonges othere thinges,
760 Whan that we hadde maad our rekeninges;
And seyde thus: 'Now, lordinges, trewely,
Ye been to me right welcome hertely:
For by my trouthe, if that I shal nat lye,
I ne saugh this yeer so mery a companye
At ones in this herberwe as is now.
Fayn wolde I doon yow mirthe, wiste I how.
And of a mirthe I am right now bithoght,
To doon yow ese, and it shal coste noght.

Ye goon to Caunterbury; God yow spede,
770 The blisful martir quyte yow your mede.
And wel I woot, as ye goon by the weye,
Ye shapen yow to talen and to pleye;
For trewely, confort ne mirthe is noon
To ryde by the weye doumb as a stoon;
And therfore wol I maken yow disport,
As I seyde erst, and doon yow som confort.
And if yow lyketh alle, by oon assent,
Now for to stonden at my Iugement,
And for to werken as I shal yow seye,
780 To-morwe, whan ye ryden by the weye,
Now, by my fader soule, that is deed,
But ye be merye, I wol yeve yow myn heed.
Hold up your hond, withouten more speche.'

Our counseil was nat longe for to seche;
Us thoughte it was noght worth to make it wys,
And graunted him withouten more avys,
And bad him seye his verdit, as him leste.

'Lordinges,' quod he, 'now herkneth for the beste;
But tak it not, I prey yow, in desdeyn;
790 This is the poynt, to speken short and pleyn,
That ech of yow, to shorte with your weye,
In this viage, shal telle tales tweye,

year who seem as happy as you. I wish I could think of some way to entertain you, and—oh, wait! I've thought of something and, best of all, it won't cost you a penny!

769-783 "You are all going to Canterbury, where the martyr, Thomas Becket will hear your prayers and bless you. God be with you and speed you on your way! Well, I figure that you'll probably tell stories and whatnot to pass the time during your journey because it'd be pretty boring otherwise. I said before that I want to entertain you, so with your permission, I ask that you listen to what I have to say. And I swear on my father's grave that if you aren't entertained as you ride off to Canterbury tomorrow, you can have my own head! Now hold up your hands, and don't say another word!"

784-787 I didn't take long for us to decide to do as he asked, and we told him to just tell us what to do.

788-809 "Gentlemen," he said, "listen carefully, and try to understand what I'm about to propose. I'll make this short and sweet. I propose that each of you tell us two stories to help pass the time on the way to Canterbury, and then tell two more stories about the olden days on the way back. And whichever one of you tells the most informative

To Caunterbury-ward, I mene it so,
And hom-ward he shal tellen othere two,
Of aventures that whylom han bifalle.
And which of yow that bereth him best of alle,
That is to seyn, that telleth in this cas
Tales of best sentence and most solas,
Shal have a soper at our aller cost
800 Here in this place, sitting by this post,
Whan that we come agayn fro Caunterbury.
And for to make yow the more mery,
I wol my-selven gladly with yow ryde,
Right at myn owne cost, and be your gyde.
And who-so wol my Iugement withseye
Shal paye al that we spenden by the weye.
And if ye vouche-sauf that it be so,
Tel me anon, with-outen wordes mo,
And I wol erly shape me therfore.'

810 This thing was graunted, and our othes swore
With ful glad herte, and preyden him also
That he wold vouche-sauf for to do so,
And that he wolde been our governour,
And of our tales Iuge and reportour,
And sette a soper at a certeyn prys;
And we wold reuled been at his devys,
In heigh and lowe; and thus, by oon assent,
We been acorded to his Iugement.
And ther-upon the wyn was fet anon;
820 We dronken, and to reste wente echon,
With-outen any lenger taryinge.

A-morwe, whan that day bigan to springe,
Up roos our host, and was our aller cok,
And gadrede us togidre, alle in a flok,
And forth we riden, a litel more than pas,
Unto the watering of seint Thomas.
And there our host bigan his hors areste,
And seyde; 'Lordinges, herkneth, if yow leste.

or funny story will get a free dinner paid by the rest of us right here in my hotel when you all get back. And, to make sure you enjoy the journey, I'll pay my own way to go with you and be your guide. I'll also decide who tells the best story. And anyone who questions my judgment can pay the entire cost of the trip for everyone. Let me know if this sounds like a good idea to you, and I'll go get ready."

810-821   We all loved the idea and promised that we'd follow the rules of the bet and asked him to come with us to Canterbury and be the judge of the contest. We all ordered some wine and drank a toast, then immediately went to bed.

822-841   Our host got up the next morning at dawn and woke all of us up. We set out at a normal walking pace and rode to a stream where a lot of pilgrims on the way to Canterbury stop for a rest. Our host stopped his horse and said to us, "Gentlemen, your attention please. Remember our agreement from last night? Well, let's find out who's going to tell the first story. Remember that I'll be the judge and that anyone who disagrees with me will have to pay the cost of the entire

Ye woot your forward, and I it yow recorde.
830 If even-song and morwe-song acorde,
Lat se now who shal telle the firste tale.
As ever mote I drinke wyn or ale,
Who-so be rebel to my Iugement
Shal paye for al that by the weye is spent.
Now draweth cut, er that we ferrer twinne;
He which that hath the shortest shal biginne.
Sire knight,' quod he, 'my maister and my lord,
Now draweth cut, for that is myn acord.
Cometh neer,' quod he, 'my lady prioresse;
840 And ye, sir clerk, lat be your shamfastnesse,
Ne studieth noght; ley hond to, every man.'

Anon to drawen every wight bigan,
And shortly for to tellen, as it was,
Were it by aventure, or sort, or cas,
The sothe is this, the cut fil to the knight,
Of which ful blythe and glad was every wight;
And telle he moste his tale, as was resoun,
By forward and by composicioun,
As ye han herd; what nedeth wordes mo?
850 And whan this gode man saugh it was so,
As he that wys was and obedient
To kepe his forward by his free assent,
He seyde: 'Sin I shal biginne the game,
What, welcome be the cut, a Goddes name!
Now lat us ryde, and herkneth what I seye.'

And with that word we riden forth our weye;
And he bigan with right a mery chere
His tale anon, and seyde in this manere.

HERE ENDETH THE PROLOG OF THIS BOOK.

trip for everyone from here on out. Now, let's draw straws before we go any further, and whoever gets the shortest straw will go first. Mr. Knight, my good man, I've decided that you'll draw first, so please take a straw. Come on over, madame Prioress. And now you, Mr. Clerk—come on, don't be shy! Come on, everyone, grab a straw."

842-855 Everyone drew a straw, and—to make a long story short—somehow the knight drew the shortest straw, whether by fate or accident. Everyone was relieved that he would be the first to go. And that was that. The good knight, for his part, didn't complain at all, but sucked it up and said, "Looks like it's me. Must be God's will! Now let's get going, and listen to my story."

856-858 And with that, we set out on our way to Canterbury. The knight began his story immediately and said . . .

THIS IS THE END OF THE GENERAL PROLOGUE.

The Knight's Tale, Part One

Whylom, as olde stories tellen us,
Ther was a duk that highte Theseus;
Of Athenes he was lord and governour,
And in his tyme swich a conquerour,
That gretter was ther noon under the sonne.
Ful many a riche contree hadde he wonne;
What with his wisdom and his chivalrye,
He conquered al the regne of Femenye,
That whylom was y-cleped Scithia;
10　And weddede the quene Ipolita,
And broghte hir hoom with him in his contree
With muchel glorie and greet solempnitee,
And eek hir yonge suster Emelye.
And thus with victorie and with melodye
Lete I this noble duk to Athenes ryde,
And al his hoost, in armes, him bisyde.

And certes, if it nere to long to here,
I wolde han told yow fully the manere,
How wonnen was the regne of Femenye
20　By Theseus, and by his chivalrye;
And of the grete bataille for the nones
Bitwixen Athenës and Amazones;
And how asseged was Ipolita,
The faire hardy quene of Scithia;
And of the feste that was at hir weddinge,
And of the tempest at hir hoom-cominge;
But al that thing I moot as now forbere.
I have, God woot, a large feeld to ere,
And wayke been the oxen in my plough.
30　The remenant of the tale is long y-nough.
I wol nat letten eek noon of this route;
Lat every felawe telle his tale aboute,
And lat see now who shal the soper winne;
And ther I lefte, I wol ageyn biginne.

The Knight's Tale, Part One

1-16   Once upon a time, as they say in all the old fairy tales, there was a
        duke named Theseus who was the ruler of the kingdom of Athens
        in present-day Greece. His wisdom and his skill at fighting wars
        had made him the fiercest warrior of his generation. There was no
        one greater. He'd fought in many wars and conquered many other
        kingdoms, including even the women warriors of Amazonia, which
        used to be called Scythia. After defeating the Amazons, Theseus had
        married their queen, Hippolyta, and took her back to Athens with
        him along with her little sister, Emily. They traveled back to Athens
        in a boisterous victory march. And it's here, on their journey back to
        Athens, where my story begins.

17-46   Oh, I wish I had the time to tell you all about what the kingdom
        of Amazonia was like before Theseus arrived, and about the great
        battle between the Athenians and the Amazonians, and the capture
        of the beautiful and powerful Queen Hippolyta. And I wish I could
        tell you about their wedding feast and the parties and all the hub-
        bub that their return back to Athens caused along the way. But,
        God knows, I'm not a great storyteller, and the part I do want to
        tell you about is long enough without all that. Besides, I want to be
        fair and make sure that each of us gets a turn to tell a story on the
        way to Canterbury so that we can see who wins that free dinner! So,
        let me just start the story where I left a minute ago, with Theseus,
        Hippolyta, Emily, and the victorious Athenians marching back to
        Athens.

This duk, of whom I make mencioun,
When he was come almost unto the toun,
In al his wele and in his moste pryde,
He was war, as he caste his eye asyde,
Wher that ther kneled in the hye weye
40 A companye of ladies, tweye and tweye,
Ech after other, clad in clothes blake;
But swich a cry and swich a wo they make,
That in this world nis creature livinge,
That herde swich another weymentinge;
And of this cry they nolde never stenten,
Til they the reynes of his brydel henten.

'What folk ben ye, that at myn hoom-cominge
Perturben so my feste with cryinge?'
Quod Theseus, 'have ye so greet envye
50 Of myn honour, that thus compleyne and crye?
Or who hath yow misboden, or offended?
And telleth me if it may been amended;
And why that ye ben clothed thus in blak?'

The eldest lady of hem alle spak,
When she hadde swowned with a deedly chere,
That it was routhe for to seen and here,
And seyde: 'Lord, to whom Fortune hath yiven
Victorie, and as a conquerour to liven,
Noght greveth us your glorie and your honour;
60 But we biseken mercy and socour.
Have mercy on our wo and our distresse.
Som drope of pitee, thurgh thy gentillesse,
Upon us wrecched wommen lat thou falle.
For certes, lord, ther nis noon of us alle,
That she nath been a duchesse or a quene;
Now be we caitifs, as it is wel sene:
Thanked be Fortune, and hir false wheel,
That noon estat assureth to be weel.
And certes, lord, to abyden your presence,
70 Here in the temple of the goddesse Clemence

NO FEAR

Now, when the happy and victorious Athenians were just outside the city, Duke Theseus noticed out of the corner of his eye that there was a group of women kneeling in the middle of the road. They were arranged in two columns, dressed all in black, and were crying and wailing at the top of their lungs. You never heard anything like it. They continued wailing until one of them grabbed the bridle of Theseus's horse.

47-53 "Who are you people who dare to interrupt my victory march home?" asked Theseus. "Are you so jealous of me and my success that you're complaining like this? Or has someone else hurt or offended you? Tell me why you're all dressed in black and if there's any way we can make things better."

54-72 The oldest lady in the group nearly fainted at hearing this. She looked almost like Death itself, and she looked so miserable that everyone pitied her. When she recovered, she looked at Theseus and said, "My lord, Fortune has favored you and made you victorious. We aren't upset about your success at all. Rather, we ask for your kindness and your help. Even the tiniest drop of pity from you will make us poor women feel better. In fact, all of us women were once duchesses and queens. But now, as you clearly see, we are miserable nobodies. The goddess Fortune never promises anything to anyone, which is why we went from having everything to having nothing. We've been waiting for you in this temple for two weeks, and now that you're here, we're hoping you can help us since you have the power to do so.

We han ben waytinge al this fourtenight;
Now help us, lord, sith it is in thy might.

I wrecche, which that wepe and waille thus,
Was whylom wyf to king Capaneus,
That starf at Thebes, cursed be that day!
And alle we, that been in this array,
And maken al this lamentacioun,
We losten alle our housbondes at that toun,
Whyl that the sege ther-aboute lay.
80 And yet now the olde Creon, weylaway!
That lord is now of Thebes the citee,
Fulfild of ire and of iniquitee,
He, for despyt, and for his tirannye,
To do the dede bodyes vileinye,
Of alle our lordes, whiche that ben slawe,
Hath alle the bodyes on an heep y-drawe,
And wol nat suffren hem, by noon assent,
Neither to been y-buried nor y-brent,
But maketh houndes ete hem in despyt.'
90 And with that word, with-outen more respyt,
They fillen gruf, and cryden pitously,
'Have on us wrecched wommen som mercy,
And lat our sorwe sinken in thyn herte.'

This gentil duk doun from his courser sterte
With herte pitous, whan he herde hem speke.
Him thoughte that his herte wolde breke,
Whan he saugh hem so pitous and so mat,
That whylom weren of so greet estat.
And in his armes he hem alle up hente,
100 And hem conforteth in ful good entente;
And swoor his ooth, as he was trewe knight,
He wolde doon so ferforthly his might
Upon the tyraunt Creon hem to wreke,
That al the peple of Grece sholde speke
How Creon was of Theseus y-served,
As he that hadde his deeth ful wel deserved.

73-93 "I look wretched now because I've been crying and wailing so much. But I used to be the wife of King Capaneus, who died at the Battle of Thebes, damn it all! All of us miserable women you see here lost our husbands in that battle when the city was attacked. And just the other day, that good-for-nothing tyrant Creon—who defeated our husbands, conquered Thebes, and now rules the city—ordered that the dead bodies of our husbands be piled up so that he can let them rot like trash. He won't let us bury them or even burn them, but lets the dogs eat them out of spite." And at that moment the women started crying again and threw themselves face first on the ground, saying "Have mercy on us poor women, and take pity on us!"

94-106 The noble Theseus did feel sorry for them and thought his heart would break after hearing their story and seeing how poor and miserable these once royal women now were. He got off his horse and hugged them all and swore an oath to them that he would avenge their husbands' deaths and make the tyrant Creon pay for what he'd done. In fact, he promised the women that he would let everyone in Greece know what Creon had done and why Theseus had killed him in vengeance. He ordered Queen Hippolyta and Emily to wait for him in Athens. And right then and there he got back on his horse, turned around, and took his entire army to the city of Thebes. He didn't even make any stops along the way and would camp every night by the side of the road. It all happened just like that.

And right anoon, with-outen more abood,
His baner he desplayeth, and forth rood
To Thebes-ward, and al his host bisyde;
110   No neer Athenës wolde he go ne ryde,
Ne take his ese fully half a day,
But onward on his wey that night he lay;
And sente anoon Ipolita the quene,
And Emelye hir yonge suster shene,
Unto the toun of Athenës to dwelle;
And forth he rit; ther nis namore to telle.

The rede statue of Mars, with spere and targe,
So shyneth in his whyte baner large,
That alle the feeldes gliteren up and doun;
120   And by his baner born is his penoun
Of gold ful riche, in which ther was y-bete
The Minotaur, which that he slough in Crete.
Thus rit this duk, thus rit this conquerour,
And in his host of chivalrye the flour,
Til that he cam to Thebes, and alighte
Faire in a feeld, ther as he thoghte fighte.
But shortly for to speken of this thing,
With Creon, which that was of Thebes king,
He faught, and slough him manly as a knight
130   In pleyn bataille, and putte the folk to flight;
And by assaut he wan the citee after,
And rente adoun bothe wal, and sparre, and rafter;
And to the ladyes he restored agayn
The bones of hir housbondes that were slayn,
To doon obsequies, as was tho the gyse.
But it were al to long for to devyse
The grete clamour and the waymentinge
That the ladyes made at the brenninge
Of the bodyes, and the grete honour
140   That Theseus, the noble conquerour,
Doth to the ladyes, whan they from him wente;
But shortly for to telle is myn entente.

NO FEAR

117-146   The red symbol of Mars, the god of war, with his spear and shield, adorned Theseus's royal white flag. It gleamed in the sunlight, which made the surrounding fields glisten. And on Theseus's lance hung another banner, this one made of the finest gold, which bore the symbol of the Minotaur, the ferocious creature that was half-man, half-beast that he had killed on the island of Crete. Theseus rode off to the city of Thebes like this in full glory until he stopped in a field he thought would be a good place for a battle. And to cut to the chase, Theseus gave Creon an honorable death in battle and then chased Creon's army of out town. Then he captured the city of Thebes, tore down the city walls and beams and rafters, and returned the bones of the dead King Capaneus and noble Thebans to the wailing widows so that they could properly bury them. It'd take too long to tell you all about the great fuss and wailing that occurred at the burial or about how much the women thanked Theseus for helping them, so I'll skip all that. I really am trying to keep this story short.

Whan that this worthy duk, this Theseus,
Hath Creon slayn, and wonne Thebes thus,
Stille in that feeld he took al night his reste,
And dide with al the contree as him leste.

To ransake in the tas of bodyes dede,
Hem for to strepe of harneys and of wede,
The pilours diden bisinesse and cure,
150   After the bataille and disconfiture.
And so bifel, that in the tas they founde,
Thurgh-girt with many a grevous blody wounde,
Two yonge knightes ligging by and by,
Bothe in oon armes, wroght ful richely,
Of whiche two, Arcita hight that oon,
And that other knight hight Palamon.
Nat fully quike, ne fully dede they were,
But by hir cote-armures, and by hir gere,
The heraudes knewe hem best in special,
160   As they that weren of the blood royal
Of Thebes, and of sustren two y-born.
Out of the tas the pilours han hem torn,
And han hem caried softe unto the tente
Of Theseus, and he ful sone hem sente
To Athenës, to dwellen in prisoun
Perpetuelly, he nolde no raunsoun.
And whan this worthy duk hath thus y-don,
He took his host, and hoom he rood anon
With laurer crowned as a conquerour;
170   And there he liveth, in Ioye and in honour,
Terme of his lyf; what nedeth wordes mo?
And in a tour, in angwish and in wo,
Dwellen this Palamoun and eek Arcite,
For evermore, ther may no gold hem quyte.

This passeth yeer by yeer, and day by day,
Til it fil ones, in a morwe of May,
That Emelye, that fairer was to sene5
Than is the lilie upon his stalke grene,

And after he'd killed Creon and conquered Thebes, Theseus slept quietly in his tent on the battlefield that night and enjoyed the fruits of victory.

147-174 Meanwhile, looters ransacked the dead bodies on the battlefield looking for armor and weapons. And while they were searching they found two young knights lying side by side, badly wounded and on the brink of death. They wore matching clothing and armor that identified them as cousins—the sons of two sisters in the royal family of Thebes. One knight was named Arcite, and the other was named Palamon. The looters gently took the wounded knights to Theseus, who ordered that they be put in a prison in Athens. He decided that they should remain there for the rest of their lives, even if someone offered to pay a ransom for them. Soon after, Theseus himself returned to Athens a hero with a victory crown made of laurel. And there he lived happily and honorably for the rest of his life, with Arcite and Palamon stuck in prison for the rest of their miserable lives too.

175-197 This went on day-after-day, year-after-year. And then one day something happened. On a fine spring morning in the month of May, Emily—who'd become more beautiful than the finest flower and fresher than even spring itself—was walking through the garden at

And fressher than the May with floures newe—
180　For with the rose colour stroof hir hewe,
I noot which was the fairer of hem two—
Er it were day, as was hir wone to do,
She was arisen, and al redy dight;
For May wol have no slogardye a-night.
The sesoun priketh every gentil herte,
And maketh him out of his sleep to sterte,
And seith, 'Arys, and do thyn observaunce.'
This maked Emelye have remembraunce
To doon honour to May, and for to ryse.
190　Y-clothed was she fresh, for to devyse;
Hir yelow heer was broyded in a tresse,
Bihinde hir bak, a yerde long, I gesse.
And in the gardin, at the sonne up-riste,
She walketh up and doun, and as hir liste
She gadereth floures, party whyte and rede,
To make a sotil gerland for hir hede,
And as an aungel hevenly she song.

The grete tour, that was so thikke and strong,
Which of the castel was the chief dongeoun,
200　(Ther-as the knightes weren in prisoun,
Of whiche I tolde yow, and tellen shal)
Was evene Ioynant to the gardin-wal,
Ther as this Emelye hadde hir pleyinge.
Bright was the sonne, and cleer that morweninge,
And Palamon, this woful prisoner,
As was his wone, by leve of his gayler,
Was risen, and romed in a chambre on heigh,
In which he al the noble citee seigh,
And eek the gardin, ful of braunches grene,
210　Ther-as this fresshe Emelye the shene
Was in hir walk, and romed up and doun.
This sorweful prisoner, this Palamoun,
Goth in the chambre, roming to and fro,
And to him-self compleyning of his wo;
That he was born, ful ofte he seyde, 'alas!'

sunrise, singing like an angel and gathering flowers to make a garland that she could wear. She wore fresh new clothes, and her blond hair was tied in a single braid about a yard long down her back. Her cheeks were so rosy that I couldn't even say if they or the roses were a truer red. She'd woken up early because May itself had seemed to say, "Wake up! Get out of bed! Spring has sprung!"

198-233 Now, Arcite and Palamon were locked away at the top of a thick, strong dungeon tower, from which they could see the entire city below. It also happened to be next to the garden, where Emily was singing and picking flowers. It was a bright, clear sunny day, and Palamon, as usual, was pacing back and forth, feeling sorry for himself and wishing he'd never been born. And by chance, Palamon caught a glimpse of Emily through the thick bars of a tower window. He went pale and cried out as though he'd been stabbed in the heart. Arcite jumped up at the sound and rushed to Palamon, saying "Cousin, what's wrong? You're pale and look half dead. Why'd you cry out? Did someone hurt you? For the love of God, you know we can't do anything about being in this prison. That's just the way it is. Fortune has given us this fate, as has the god Saturn, who aligned the stars in the sky against us. This was our destiny from the moment we were born, and it would have turned out this way even if we had done everything in our lives differently. We just have to endure our imprisonment. It's as simple as that."

And so bifel, by aventure or cas,
That thurgh a window, thikke of many a barre5
Of yren greet, and square as any sparre,
He caste his eye upon Emelya,
220　And ther-with-al he bleynte, and cryde 'a!'
As though he stongen were unto the herte.
And with that cry Arcite anon up-sterte,
And seyde, 'Cosin myn, what eyleth thee,
That art so pale and deedly on to see?
Why crydestow? who hath thee doon offence?
For Goddes love, tak al in pacience
Our prisoun, for it may non other be;
Fortune hath yeven us this adversitee.
Som wikke aspect or disposicioun
230　Of Saturne, by sum constellacioun,
Hath yeven us this, al-though we hadde it sworn;
So stood the heven whan that we were born;
We moste endure it: this is the short and pleyn.'

This Palamon answerde, and seyde ageyn,
'Cosyn, for sothe, of this opinioun
Thou hast a veyn imaginacioun.
This prison caused me nat for to crye.
But I was hurt right now thurgh-out myn yë
In-to myn herte, that wol my bane be.
240　The fairnesse of that lady that I see
Yond in the gardin romen to and fro,
Is cause of al my crying and my wo.
I noot wher she be womman or goddesse;
But Venus is it, soothly, as I gesse.'
And ther-with-al on kneës doun he fil,
And seyde: 'Venus, if it be thy wil
Yow in this gardin thus to transfigure5
Bifore me, sorweful wrecche creature,
Out of this prisoun help that we may scapen.
250　And if so be my destinee be shapen
By eterne word to dyen in prisoun,
Of our linage have som compassioun,

234-264   "No, no, it's not that at all, Cousin," Palamon answered. "I didn't yell because we're stuck in this prison. I shouted because of what I just saw that struck my heart and will surely be the death of me—a beautiful maiden wandering in the garden below. I'm not sure if she's a woman or a goddess, but she must be the goddess of beauty, Venus herself." Palamon dropped to his knees and said, "Venus, if you really have decided to take the shape of this beautiful woman and show yourself to me, the wretched creation that I am, then help us escape this prison. But if it's my fate to die in this prison, show some compassion to us, a family ruined by tyranny." And at that moment, Arcite also caught sight of lady Emily through the window as she walked back and forth in the garden. Her beauty shocked Arcite just as much as it had stung Palamon, if not more so. He sighed rather piteously and said, "That lady is so beautiful it's killing me. All I know is that if she doesn't even allow me to see her any more, I'm going to die."

That is so lowe y-broght by tirannye.'
And with that word Arcite gan espye
Wher-as this lady romed to and fro.
And with that sighte hir beautee hurte him so,
That, if that Palamon was wounded sore,
Arcite is hurt as muche as he, or more.
And with a sigh he seyde pitously:
260 'The fresshe beautee sleeth me sodeynly
Of hir that rometh in the yonder place;
And, but I have hir mercy and hir grace,
That I may seen hir atte leeste weye,
I nam but deed; ther nis namore to seye.'

This Palamon, whan he tho wordes herde,
Dispitously he loked, and answerde:
'Whether seistow this in ernest or in pley?'

'Nay,' quod Arcite, 'in ernest, by my fey!
God help me so, me list ful yvele pleye.'

270 This Palamon gan knitte his browes tweye:
'It nere,' quod he, 'to thee no greet honour
For to be fals, ne for to be traytouro
To me, that am thy cosin and thy brother
Y-sworn ful depe, and ech of us til other,
That never, for to dyen in the peyne,
Til that the deeth departe shal us tweyne,
Neither of us in love to hindren other,
Ne in non other cas, my leve brother;
But that thou sholdest trewely forthren me
280 In every cas, and I shal forthren thee.
This was thyn ooth, and myn also, certeyn;
I wot right wel, thou darst it nat withseyn.
Thus artow of my counseil, out of doute.
And now thou woldest falsly been aboute
To love my lady, whom I love and serve,
And ever shal, til that myn herte sterve.
Now certes, fals Arcite, thou shalt nat so.

NO FEAR

265-267   Palamon, upon hearing this, turned to Arcite angrily and said, "You're kidding me, right?"

268-269   "No," answered Arcite, "No joke, I swear. God help me, you don't joke about stuff like this."

700-293   Palamon furrowed his brow and said, "You really shouldn't joke around like that or kick me while I'm down. I'm your cousin, your blood brother. We swore a serious oath that, even upon pain of death, we'd never let a woman or anything else come between us until the day we died. We both promised that we'd always be there to help each other out in anything the other chose to do. I know that you know this too, which means you're supposed to support me in this matter. And now you're going to stab me in the back and try to steal the woman I love and would do anything for until the day my heart stops beating? No, Arcite, I won't let you! I fell in love with her first and confided in you, my brother who'd sworn to always help me. For that reason, you're under the obligation as a fellow knight to help me out. Otherwise, you're just full of crap!"

I loved hir first, and tolde thee my wo
As to my counseil, and my brother sworn
290   To forthre me, as I have told biforn.
For which thou art y-bounden as a knight
To helpen me, if it lay in thy might,
Or elles artow fals, I dar wel seyn.'

This Arcitĕ ful proudly spak ageyn,
'Thou shalt,' quod he, 'be rather fals than I;
But thou art fals, I telle thee utterly;
For par amour I loved hir first er thow.
What wiltow seyn? thou wistest nat yet now
Whether she be a womman or goddesse!
300   Thyn is affeccioun of holinesse,
And myn is love, as to a creature;
For which I tolde thee myn aventure◦
As to my cosin, and my brother sworn.
I pose, that thou lovedest hir biforn;
Wostow nat wel the olde clerkes sawe,
That 'who shal yeve a lover any lawe?'
Love is a gretter lawe, by my pan,
Than may be yeve to any erthly man.
And therefore positif lawe and swich decree
310   Is broke al-day for love, in ech degree.
A man moot nedes love, maugree his heed.
He may nat fleen it, thogh he sholde be deed,
Al be she mayde, or widwe, or elles wyf.
And eek it is nat lykly, al thy lyf,
To stonden in hir grace; namore shal I;
For wel thou woost thy-selven, verraily,
That thou and I be dampned to prisoun◦
Perpetuelly; us gayneth no raunsoun.
We stryve as dide the houndes for the boon,
320   They foughte al day, and yet hir part was noon;
Ther cam a kyte, whyl that they were wrothe,
And bar awey the boon bitwixe hem bothe.
And therfore, at the kinges court, my brother,
Ech man for him-self, ther is non other.

NO FEAR

294-328   Arcite haughtily replied, "You're more of a traitor than I am. In fact, I'll be honest with you: You are a traitor. I loved her first before you even saw her, and you're not even sure whether she's a goddess or a flesh-and-blood woman! You're in love with a goddess! I, however, am in love with a woman, which is why I told you about her because I thought you were my cousin, my blood brother. And even if you'd fallen in love with her first, haven't you ever heard the saying 'All's fair in love and war?' I swear to God that love is more important than anything else in this world, especially anything that one man promises to another. Laws and promises are broken every day in the name of love by all kinds of men from all walks of life. Every man must love—even if it kills him—whether she's a young girl, a widow, or his wife. There isn't anything he can do about it. Besides, it's not like you or I will ever be able to meet this girl or do anything about our love for her anyway given the fact that we're locked in this tower. You and I both know we're stuck in this prison forever, without any possibility of anyone buying our freedom. You and I are like two dogs who spend all day fighting over a bone only to have a hawk swoop down and steal it from both of us. It's every man for himself out there, brother. That's just the way it is. You can be in love with her if you want. I know I will always be. That's really all there is to it. We've got to suck it up and take what we can get."

Love if thee list; for I love and ay shal;
And soothly, leve brother, this is al.
Here in this prisoun mote we endure,
And everich of us take his aventure.'

Greet was the stryf and long bitwixe hem tweye,
330　　If that I hadde leyser for to seye;
But to theffect. It happed on a day,
(To telle it yow as shortly as I may)o
A worthy duk that highte Perotheus,
That felawe was unto duk Theseus
Sin thilke day that they were children lyte,
Was come to Athenes, his felawe to visyte,
And for to pleye, as he was wont to do,
For in this world he loved no man so:
And he loved him as tendrely ageyn.
340　　So wel they loved, as olde bokes seyn,
That whan that oon was deed, sothly to telle,
His felawe wente and soghte him doun in helle;
But of that story list me nat to wryte.

Duk Perotheus loved wel Arcite,
And hadde him knowe at Thebes yeer by yere;
And fynally, at requeste and preyere
Of Perotheus, with-oute any raunsoun,
Duk Theseus him leet out of prisoun,
Freely to goon, wher that him liste over-al,
350　　In swich a gyse, as I you tellen shal.

This was the forward, pleynly for tendyte,
Bitwixen Theseus and him Arcite:
That if so were, that Arcite were y-founde
Ever in his lyf, by day or night or stounde
In any contree of this Theseus,
And he were caught, it was acorded thus,
That with a swerd he sholde lese his heed;
Ther nas non other remedye ne reed,

329-343 There was some pretty bad blood between these two guys for a long time, and I'd tell you all about it if I had time. But let me just cut to the chase and tell you the important thing that happened next. To make a longer story short, it happened one day that another duke named Perotheus came to Athens on vacation to visit Duke Theseus. The two had been best friends since they were little kids, and they were so tight that they'd do anything for each other. In fact, the story goes that when one of them finally died, the other journeyed all the way down to hell in search of him. Oh, but that's another story entirely.

344-350 Anyway, Duke Perotheus also happened to be good friends with Arcite, whom he'd known in the city of Thebes for a number of years. Perotheus begged Theseus to free Arcite, and after many requests and prayers, Theseus finally set him free. Perotheus didn't even have to pay him a ransom or anything. There was a catch, however, which is what I'm going to tell you about next.

351-360 To put it simply, Theseus freed Arcite on the condition that Arcite never return to Athens for the rest of his life, no matter what. If Thesus ever caught Arcite in Athens again, then he'd slice off his head with a sword. These terms were non-negotiable, and Arcite had no choice but to go back to Thebes and know that it'd be off-with-his-head if he ever came back!

But taketh his leve, and homward he him spedde;
360   Let him be war, his nekke lyth to wedde!

How greet a sorwe suffreth now Arcite!
The deeth he feleth thurgh his herte smyte;
He wepeth, wayleth, cryeth pitously;
To sleen him-self he wayteth prively.
He seyde, 'Allas that day that I was born!
Now is my prison worse than biforn;
Now is me shape eternally to dwelle5
Noght in purgatorie, but in helle.
Allas! that ever knew I Perotheus!
370   For elles hadde I dwelled with Theseus
Y-fetered in his prisoun ever-mo.
Than hadde I been in blisse, and nat in wo.
Only the sighte of hir, whom that I serve,
Though that I never hir grace may deserve,
Wolde han suffised right y-nough for me.
O dere cosin Palamon,' quod he,
'Thyn is the victorie of this aventure,
Ful blisfully in prison maistow dure;
In prison? certes nay, but in paradys!
380   Wel hath fortune y-turned thee the dys,
That hast the sighte of hir, and I thabsence.
For possible is, sin thou hast hir presence,
And art a knight, a worthy and an able,
That by som cas, sin fortune is chaungeable,
Thou mayst to thy desyr som-tyme atteyne.
But I, that am exyled, and bareyne
Of alle grace, and in so greet despeir,
That ther nis erthe, water, fyr, ne eir,
Ne creature, that of hem maked is,
390   That may me helpe or doon confort in this.
Wel oughte I sterve in wanhope and distresse;
Farwel my lyf, my lust, and my gladnesse!

Allas, why pleynen folk so in commune
Of purveyaunce of God, or of Fortune,

NO FEAR

361-392   It sucked for Arcite! He was so sad that he felt like he was going to die. He cried and wailed and screamed pitifully, and even thought about comitting suicide. "Curse the day I was born!" he cried out. "Being free is a worse kind of prison than being in that tower because now I'm forced to live not in purgatory but in hell itself. I wish I'd never met Perotheus! Then Theseus would never have set me free, and I could have lived in that prison for the rest of my life. That wouldn't have been bad. I'd have been so happy because then I could have seen that girl in the garden every day. And even though I would have never been able to see her, just seeing her is better than nothing, which is all I have now. You won in the end, Palamon, because you get to stay in that prison. Did I say prison? I meant paradise! The goddess Fortune has favored you because you get to see the girl every day, but I have to spend the rest of my life away from her. And who knows, you're brave and noble, and Fortune may take a turn so that by some twist of fate you might actually win Emily someday and have everything that you want—because you're actually there in Athens. But me, I'm banished from Athens forever with no chance of every getting back. I am so sad, and nothing—nothing and no one—can help me. All my hopes are ruined. I wish I were dead.

393-416   "Why is it that people complain so much about the will of God or Fortune when God and Fortune usually know what people want

That yeveth hem ful ofte in many a gyse
Wel bettre than they can hem-self devyse?
Som man desyreth for to han richesse,
That cause is of his mordre or greet siknesse.
And som man wolde out of his prison fayn,
400 That in his hous is of his meynee slayn.
Infinite harmes been in this matere;
We witen nat what thing we preyen here.
We faren as he that dronke is as a mous;
A dronke man wot wel he hath an hous,
But he noot which the righte wey is thider;
And to a dronke man the wey is slider.
And certes, in this world so faren we;
We seken faste after felicitee,
But we goon wrong ful often, trewely.
410 Thus may we seyen alle, and namely I,
That wende and hadde a greet opinioun,
That, if I mighte escapen from prisoun,
Than hadde I been in Ioye and perfit hele,
Ther now I am exyled fro my wele.
Sin that I may nat seen yow, Emelye,
I nam but deed; ther nis no remedye.'

Upon that other syde Palamon,
Whan that he wiste Arcite was agon,
Swich sorwe he maketh, that the grete tour
420 Resouneth of his youling and clamour.
The pure fettres on his shines grete
Weren of his bittre salte teres wete.
'Allas!' quod he, 'Arcita, cosin myn,
Of al our stryf, God woot, the fruyt is thyn.
Thow walkest now in Thebes at thy large,
And of my wo thou yevest litel charge.
Thou mayst, sin thou hast wisdom and manhede,
Assemblen alle the folk of our kinrede,
And make a werre so sharp on this citee,
430 That by som aventure, or som tretee,
Thou mayst have hir to lady and to wyf,

better than they know it themselves and give them far better things than they could have ever asked for? One guy, for example, wants to be rich, and his money ends up getting him murdered or sick. Or another man wants to escape from jail, and in his home is murdered by one of his own servants. I could go on and on with more examples. We simply don't know what we really want. We're no better than a man who's drunk off his rocker and knows he lives somewhere but can't seem to find his house and always gets lost along the way. That's life for you. We're all looking for happiness, but none of us really knows quite how to get there. Everyone thinks he knows what will make him happy, but he's usually wrong. I, for example, thought I knew that nothing would make me happier than to escape that prison, but now I'm free and am not happy at all. Because I can't see you, my beautiful Emily, I might as well be dead. And that's all there is to it."

417-454

Palamon, meanwhile, cried and screamed so loudly when he heard that Arcite had escaped that the whole tower shook with his howls, and he shed big, wet, salty tears. "Dammit, Arcite!" he said, "God knows you've won our little fight because now you're free to go back to Thebes, raise an army, attack Athens, and make fair Emily your wife by conquering Theseus or making a peace treaty with him. You'll go off and forget about me while I rot in this prison, and I'll lose Emily forever. And I can't do anything about the fact that I'm locked up and have lost the woman I love except pine away in this tower for the rest of my life." And with that realization, he became so jealous of Arcite that he burned with rage. "Cruel gods!" he screamed. "You rule the world with such cruel determination by writing the fate of men in stone so that they can't do anything about it! You make us cower before you, like sheep from a shepherd! All of us—

For whom that I mot nedes lese my lyf.
For, as by wey of possibilitee,
Sith thou art at thy large, of prison free,˚
And art a lord, greet is thyn avauntage,
More than is myn, that sterve here in a cage.
For I mot wepe and wayle, whyl I live,
With al the wo that prison may me yive,
And eek with peyne that love me yiveth also,
440 That doubleth al my torment and my wo.'
Ther-with the fyr of Ielousye up-sterte
With-inne his brest, and hente him by the herte˚
So woodly, that he lyk was to biholde
The box-tree, or the asshen dede and colde.
Tho seyde he; 'O cruel goddes, that governe
This world with binding of your word eterne,
And wryten in the table of athamaunt5
Your parlement, and your eterne graunt,
What is mankinde more unto yow holde
450 Than is the sheep, that rouketh in the folde?
For slayn is man right as another beste,
And dwelleth eek in prison and areste,
And hath siknesse, and greet adversitee,
And ofte tymes giltelees, pardee!

What governaunce is in this prescience,
That giltelees tormenteth innocence?
And yet encreseth this al my penaunce,
That man is bounden to his observaunce,
For Goddes sake, to letten of his wille,
460 Ther as a beest may al his lust fulfille.
And whan a beest is deed, he hath no peyne;
But man after his deeth moot wepe and pleyne,
Though in this world he have care and wo:
With-outen doute it may stonden so.
The answere of this I lete to divynis,
But wel I woot, that in this world gret pyne is.
Allas! I see a serpent or a theef,
That many a trewe man hath doon mescheef,

even the innocent men—are doomed to suffer hardships and adversity all our lives. And then we die like every other animal!

455-475   "What's the purpose of such pointless living, where man has no choice but to suffer before ultimately dying? And worse, why do people have to live good, moral lives and restrain their will in the name of the God if all the other animals can do whatever they want? And when an animal dies, that's it, it's dead and the pain is gone. But when a person dies, there's more sorrow to come, even though he's lived all his life in misery already. Priests and other thinkers can philosophize about life and death all they want, but that's pretty much what it comes down to. All I know is that an awful little snake has gotten away and is allowed to do whatever he pleases, while the gods' will has doomed me to waste away here in this dungeon. The god Saturn desires it, as does his vengeful wife, Juno, who's succeeded in dooming most of the royal house of Thebes after Saturn slept with some Theban women. And even Venus, the

Goon at his large, and wher him list may turne.
470 But I mot been in prison thurgh Saturne,
And eek thurgh Iuno, Ialous and eek wood,
That hath destroyed wel ny al the bloodo
Of Thebes, with his waste walles wyde.
And Venus sleeth me on that other syde
For Ielousye, and fere of him Arcite.'

Now wol I stinte of Palamon a lyte,
And lete him in his prison stille dwelle,
And of Arcita forth I wol yow telle.

The somer passeth, and the nightes longe
480 Encresen double wyse the peynes stronge
Bothe of the lovere and the prisoner.
I noot which hath the wofullere mester.
For shortly for to seyn, this Palamoun
Perpetuelly is dampned to prisoun,
In cheynes and in fettres to ben deed;
And Arcite is exyled upon his heed
For ever-mo as out of that contree,
Ne never-mo he shal his lady see.

Yow loveres axe I now this questioun,
490 Who hath the worse, Arcite or Palamoun?
That oon may seen his lady day by day,
But in prison he moot dwelle alway.
That other wher him list may ryde or go,
But seen his lady shal he never-mo.
Now demeth as yow liste, ye that can,
For I wol telle forth as I bigan.

EXPLICIT PRIMA PARS

goddess of love, is punishing me while she lets Arcite roam free to pursue Emily."

476-478 Well, let's leave Palamon rotting in his prison cell for a while and go back to Arcite, whom I'll tell you some more about in just a minute.

479-488 The summer passed and the nights grew longer, which made things worse for both Arcite and Palamon, one banished from Athens and from ever seeing Emily again, the other doomed to live the rest of his life in chains. In fact, I don't know which guy had it worse.

489-496 What do all you lovers think? Who had it worse, Arcite or Palamon? The one gets to see the woman he loves every day, even though he'll never leave the prison tower, while the other can go wherever he wants but can never see Emily again. You think about it, and I'll continue with my story.

END OF PART ONE

The Knight's Tale, Part Two

SEQUITUR PARS SECUNDA.

Whan that Arcite to Thebes comen was,
Ful ofte a day he swelte and seyde 'allas,'
For seen his lady shal he never-mo.
500 And shortly to concluden al his wo,
So muche sorwe had never creature
That is, or shal, whyl that the world may dure.
His sleep, his mete, his drink is him biraft,
That lene he wex, and drye as is a shaft.
His eyen holwe, and grisly to biholde;
His hewe falwe, and pale as asshen colde,
And solitarie he was, and ever allone,
And wailling al the night, making his mone.
And if he herde song or instrument,
510 Then wolde he wepe, he mighte nat be stent;
So feble eek were his spirits, and so lowe,
And chaunged so, that no man coude knoweo
His speche nor his vois, though men it herde.
And in his gere, for al the world he ferde
Nat oonly lyk the loveres maladye
Of Hereos, but rather lyk manye
Engendred of humour malencolyk,
Biforen, in his celle fantastyk.
And shortly, turned was al up-so-doun
520 Bothe habit and eek disposicioun
Of him, this woful lovere daun Arcite.

What sholde I al-day of his wo endyte?
Whan he endured hadde a yeer or two
This cruel torment, and this peyne and wo,
At Thebes, in his contree, as I seyde,
Upon a night, in sleep as he him leyde,
Him thoughte how that the winged god Mercuries
Biforn him stood, and bad him to be murye.

The Knight's Tale, Part Two

HERE'S THE SECOND PART OF THE KNIGHT'S TALE.

497-521   After Arcite made it back to Thebes, he wallowed in self-pity because he knew he'd never again see the woman he loved. He wasn't interested in food or sleep or wine, and he began wasting away until he was just a bony twig of a man. His skin became as pale as ashes, and his eyes sunk into his head. He spent all of his time alone, and he moaned to himself at night. Music would only make him cry unconsolably. He became so depressed that no one could recognize his voice anymore. And he was so lovesick that he didn't even look lovesick anymore, but looked like he'd gone completely insane. To put it simply, Arcite suffered more than anyone had ever suffered before or since and everything about him had changed completely.

522-540   Well, I could go on and on about how awful Arcite's life had become, but let me just get right to the point. After he'd been living like this for a year or two since coming back from Athens, he had a powerful dream one night. In the dream he saw the god Mercury, who was wearing a hat and carrying a staff. He stood before Arcite and told him to buck up and be happier. "Go to Athens," he said, "and all your misery will be gone." Arcite woke up instantly and said, "Okay. I can't take this any longer. No matter what happens, I'm going to

His slepy yerde in hond he bar uprighte;
530 An hat he werede upon his heres brighte.
Arrayed was this god (as he took keep)
As he was whan that Argus took his sleep;
And seyde him thus: 'To Athenes shaltou wende;
Ther is thee shapen of thy wo an ende.'
And with that word Arcite wook and sterte.
'Now trewely, how sore that me smerte,'
Quod he, 'to Athenes right now wol I fare;
Ne for the drede of deeth shal I nat spare
To see my lady, that I love and serve;
540 In hir presence I recche nat to sterve.'

And with that word he caughte a greet mirour,
And saugh that chaunged was al his colour,
And saugh his visage al in another kinde.
And right anoon it ran him in his minde,
That, sith his face was so disfigured
Of maladye, the which he hadde endured,
He mighte wel, if that he bar him lowe,
Live in Athenes ever-more unknowe,
And seen his lady wel ny day by day.
550 And right anon he chaunged his array,
And cladde him as a povre laborer,
And al allone, save oonly a squyer,
That knew his privetee and al his cas,
Which was disgysed povrely, as he was,
To Athenes is he goon the nexte way.
And to the court he wente upon a day,
And at the gate he profreth his servyse,
To drugge and drawe, what so men wol devyse.
And shortly of this matere for to seyn,
560 He fil in office with a chamberleyn,
The which that dwelling was with Emelye.
For he was wys, and coude soon aspye0
Of every servaunt, which that serveth here.
Wel coude he hewen wode, and water bere,
For he was yong and mighty for the nones,

set out for Athens and not stop until I see Emily, the woman I love, again. I don't care if it ends up killing me."

541-592 As he made this resolution, he caught sight of himself in a mirror and saw that he looked very different from the way he used to look. He realized immediately that his disfigurement from being so lovesick would allow him to disguise himself in Athens. And if he kept a really low profile, he might even be able to live the rest of his life there so that he could see Emily every day. He therefore changed his clothes and dressed himself as a poor worker before setting out for Athens. He took with him only a single servant who knew of his master's plan and had also disguised himself as a common worker. When he arrived in Athens, he went to Theseus's castle and offered up his services as a common laborer to do any work that needed to be done. He also told everyone that his name was Philostrato in order to hide his true identity. And to make a long story short, he eventually figured out the best way to get closest to Emily and got a job assisting her chamberlain. Arcite did whatever the chamberlain told him to do, whether it be collecting firewood or carrying water. He was young and strong. He worked as Emily's chamberlain's servant for a year or two, and he quickly became one of the most likeable people in the entire castle because of his good manners and personality. In fact, "Philostrato" became so well known and so well liked that people encouraged Theseus to promote him and find more noble work for him to do. And so Theseus made Philostrato his own assistant and paid him plenty of money to reflect his new status and position. Arcite also had, of course, his own yearly income from being a noble landlord back in Thebes, and he had this money

And ther-to be was strong and big of bones
To doon that any wight can him devyse.
A yeer or two he was in this servyse,
Page of the chambre of Emelye the brighte;
570 And 'Philostrate' he seide that he highte.
But half so wel biloved a man as he
Ne was ther never in court, of his degree;
He was so gentil of condicioun,
That thurghout al the court was his renoun.
They seyden, that it were a charitee
That Theseus wolde enhauncen his degree,
And putten him in worshipful servyse,
Ther as he mighte his vertu excercyse.
And thus, with-inne a whyle, his name is spronge
580 Bothe of his dedes, and his goode tonge,
That Theseus hath taken him so neer
That of his chambre he made him a squyer,
And yaf him gold to mayntene his degree;
And eek men broghte him out of his contree
From yeer to yeer, ful prively, his rente;
But honestly and slyly he it spente,
That no man wondred how that he it hadde.
And three yeer in this wyse his lyf he ladde,
And bar him so in pees and eek in werre,
590 Ther nas no man that Theseus hath derre.
And in this blisse lete I now Arcite,
And speke I wol of Palamon a lyte.

In derknesse and horrible and strong prisoun
This seven yeer hath seten Palamoun,
Forpyned, what for wo and for distresse;
Who feleth double soor and hevinesse
But Palamon? that love destreyneth so,
That wood out of his wit he gooth for wo;
And eek therto he is a prisoner
600 Perpetuelly, noght oonly for a yeer.
Who coude ryme in English proprely

secretly brought to him in Athens. He spent this money carefully, though, and lived pretty modestly so that no one noticed how well off he really was. He served Theseus at home and on the battlefield like this for three years, and he became the duke's most trusted advisor and friend. And with that, I'll leave Arcite and his adventures for a moment to talk a little more about Palamon.

593-603   For seven horrible years Palamon had been living locked up in the horrible darkness of the prison tower. In addition to having been imprisoned this entire time, he was also so lovesick that he'd nearly gone insane. Words can hardly describe his torment properly. I know I'm not doing a very good job myself at describing his misery, so I'm just going to get right to the point.

His martirdom? for sothe, it am nat I;
Therefore I passe as lightly as I may.

It fel that in the seventhe yeer, in May,
The thridde night, (as olde bokes seyn,
That al this storie tellen more pleyn,)
Were it by aventure or destinee,
(As, whan a thing is shapen, it shal be,)
That, sone after the midnight, Palamoun,
610 By helping of a freend, brak his prisoun,
And fleeth the citee, faste as he may go;
For he had yive his gayler drinke soo
Of a clarree, maad of a certeyn wyn,
With nercotikes and opie of Thebes fyn,
That al that night, thogh that men wolde him shake,
The gayler sleep, he mighte nat awake;
And thus he fleeth as faste as ever he may.
The night was short, and faste by the day,
That nedes-cost he moste him-selven hyde,
620 And til a grove, faste ther besyde,
With dredful foot than stalketh Palamoun.
For shortly, this was his opinioun,
That in that grove he wolde him hyde al day,
And in the night than wolde he take his way
To Thebes-ward, his freendes for to preye
On Theseus to helpe him to werreye;
And shortly, outher he wolde lese his lyf,
Or winnen Emelye unto his wyf;
This is theffect and his entente pleyn.

630 Now wol I torne unto Arcite ageyn,
That litel wiste how ny that was his care,
Til that Fortune had broght him in the snare.

The bisy larke, messager of day,
Saluëth in hir song the morwe gray;
And fyry Phebus ryseth up so brighte,
That al the orient laugheth of the lighte,

NO FEAR

604-629   Well, it so happened on the night of May third in the seventh year of his imprisonment (according to all the old books that tell this story anyway), whether by chance or by fate (which there's no escaping if it really was fate) that Palamon broke out of prison with a little help from a friend and fled Athens. His friend had spiked the prison guard's wine with a sweet drug made of opium from Thebes that made the poor guy sleep through the entire breakout. Palamon ran as fast as he could and hid in a grove of trees when the sun began to rise. He planned to hide in the grove all day then hightail it back to Thebes at night. There he would rally his friends and raise an army to attack Athens. To put it simply, he pledged to win Emily or die trying.

630-632   Okay, now back to Arcite, who'd thought he was living in the clear until the goddess Fortune put him in the hot seat once more.

633-669   Well, the fateful day began like all others, with the lark's song greeting the morning sun. Arcite, who was still Theseus's chief servant, woke up and looked out the window to take in the morning view. He decided to enjoy the spring air by saddling his horse and going for

And with his stremes dryeth in the greves5
The silver dropes, hanging on the leves.
And Arcite, that is in the court royal
640 With Theseus, his squyer principal,
Is risen, and loketh on the myrie day.
And, for to doon his observaunce to May,
Remembring on the poynt of his desyr,
He on a courser, sterting as the fyr,
Is riden in-to the feeldes, him to pleye,
Out of the court, were it a myle or tweye;
And to the grove, of which that I yow tolde,
By aventure, his wey he gan to holde,
To maken him a gerland of the greves,
650 Were it of wodebinde or hawethorn-leves,
And loude he song ageyn the sonne shene:
'May, with alle thy floures and thy grene,
Wel-come be thou, faire fresshe May,
I hope that I som grene gete may.'
And from his courser, with a lusty herte,
In-to the grove ful hastily he sterte,
And in a path he rometh up and doun,
Ther-as, by aventure, this Palamoun
Was in a bush, that no man mighte him see,
660 For sore afered of his deeth was he.
No-thing ne knew he that it was Arcite:
God wot he wolde have trowed it ful lyte.
But sooth is seyd, gon sithen many yeres,
That 'feeld hath eyen, and the wode hath eres.'
It is ful fair a man to bere him evene,
For al-day meteth men at unset stevene.
Ful litel woot Arcite of his felawe,
That was so ny to herknen al his sawe,
For in the bush he sitteth now ful stille.

670 Whan that Arcite had romed al his fille,
And songen al the roundel lustily,
In-to a studie he fil sodeynly,
As doon thise loveres in hir queynte geres,

a morning ride a mile or two away from the castle to the same grove where Palamon was hiding. He picked some flowers and wove a garland, all the while happily singing, "Welome fair, fresh May, with all your flowers and your green. These flowers are the loveliest I've seen!" And with a happy heart he strolled around the grove along the path that happened to run right past the bush that Palamon was hiding behind. Palamon, for his part, was terrified that he was going to die because he didn't realize that the man singing and walking through the grove was his cousin Arcite. Then again, how could he have possibly known since Arcite was supposedly exiled? Well, you know what they say: The fields have eyes and the trees talk. Arcite meanwhile had no idea that his old friend Palamon was lurking quietly in the bushes. People, though, should always keep their wits about them and be ready for the unexpected.

670-681   When Arcite got tired of strolling and singing, he fell into a solemn silence as he began thinking about how much he loved Emily. He grew moody as young people often do when thinking about love. Sometimes he felt great, other times awful, up, down, up, down, like

Now in the croppe, now doun in the breres,
Now up, now doun, as boket in a welle.
Right as the Friday, soothly for to telle,
Now it shyneth, now it reyneth faste,
Right so can gery Venus overcaste
The hertes of hir folk; right as hir day
680 Is gerful, right so chaungeth she array.
Selde is the Friday al the wyke y-lyke.

Whan that Arcite had songe, he gan to syke,
And sette him doun with-outen any more:
'Alas!' quod he, 'that day that I was bore!
How longe, Iuno, thurgh thy crueltee,
Woltow werreyen Thebes the citee?
Allas! y-broght is to confusioun
The blood royal of Cadme and Amphioun;
Of Cadmus, which that was the firste man
690 That Thebes bulte, or first the toun bigan,
And of the citee first was crouned king,
Of his linage am I, and his of-springo
By verray ligne, as of the stok royal:
And now I am so caitif and so thral,
That he, that is my mortal enemy,
I serve him as his squyer povrely.
And yet doth Iuno me wel more shame,
For I dar noght biknowe myn owne name;
But ther-as I was wont to highte Arcite,
700 Now highte I Philostrate, noght worth a myte.
Allas! thou felle Mars, allas! Iuno,
Thus hath your ire our kinrede al fordo,
Save only me, and wrecched Palamoun,
That Theseus martyreth in prisoun.
And over al this, to sleen me utterly,
Love hath his fyry dart so brenningly
Y-stiked thurgh my trewe careful herte,
That shapen was my deeth erst than my sherte.
Ye sleen me with your eyen, Emelye;
710 Ye been the cause wherfor that I dye.

a bucket in a well. Sometimes Venus, the goddess of love, makes it rain. Sometimes she makes it pour. There's never a dull day when you're in love.

682 716 Arcite sat down and sighed, "Damn the day I was born! How long are you going to continue punishing the city of Thebes and its people for your husband's infidelity, Juno? The royal family of Thebes is in complete disarray. Cadmus started the royal line, and I am his direct descendent! And here I am, practically slaving away for Theseus, the sworn enemy of Thebes. And did Juno stop there? No! I can't even let people know that I'm really Arcite! I have to pass myself off as 'Philostrato,' a nobody from nowhere. Dammit Mars, dammit Juno! You've completely wrecked the entire house of Thebes except for me and my poor cousin Palamon, who's still rotting away in that prison. And what's more, Love has struck me with his arrows. It's almost like I was fated to suffer before I was even born! You're killing me, Emily, you're killing me. Nothing else matters except pleasing you." And with that, he collapsed in a heap on the ground.

Of al the remenant of myn other care
Ne sette I nat the mountaunce of a tare,
So that I coude don aught to your plesaunce!'
And with that word he fil doun in a traunce
A longe tyme; and after he up-sterte.

This Palamoun, that thoughte that thurgh his herte
He felte a cold swerd sodeynliche glyde,
For ire he quook, no lenger wolde he byde.
And whan that he had herd Arcites tale,
720 As he were wood, with face deed and pale,
He sterte him up out of the buskes thikke,
And seyde: 'Arcite, false traitour wikke,
Now artow hent, that lovest my lady so,
For whom that I have al this peyne and wo,
And art my blood, and to my counseil sworn,
As I ful ofte have told thee heer-biforn,
And hast by-iaped here duk Theseus,
And falsly chaunged hast thy name thus;
I wol be deed, or elles thou shalt dye.
730 Thou shalt nat love my lady Emelye,
But I wol love hir only, and namo;
For I am Palamoun, thy mortal fo.
And though that I no wepne have in this place,
But out of prison am astert by grace,
I drede noght that outher thou shalt dye,
Or thou ne shalt nat loven Emelye.
Chees which thou wilt, for thou shalt nat asterte.' 5

This Arcitē, with ful despitous herte,
Whan he him knew, and hadde his tale herd,
740 As fiers as leoun, pulled out a swerd,
And seyde thus: 'by God that sit above,
Nere it that thou art sik, and wood for love,
And eek that thou no wepne hast in this place,
Thou sholdest never out of this grove pace,
That thou ne sholdest dyen of myn hond.
For I defye the seurtee and the bond

716-737 Palamon, who was still hiding in the bushes, shook with rage when he heard Arcite's little speech. He felt as if a cold sword were gliding through his heart. He jumped out from behind the bushes and screamed with deadly fury, "Arcite, you backstabbing son a bitch! I've caught you in your lies and deception! It's me, Palamon! I just escaped from that prison tower, and I'm going to kill you with my bare hands or die trying! You can either forget about Emily or die right here, right now, because she is mine and mine alone."

738-764 When he recognized Palamon and heard what he had to say, Arcite became equally furious. He rose and drew his sword and looked as fierce as a lion ready to fight. He said, "God knows that if it weren't for the fact that love has driven you mad, and you don't have a weapon on you, I'd never let you walk out of this grove alive. I'd kill you where you stand. Screw our friendship and the oath we made as blood brothers. Don't you know, dumbass, that I'm free to love anyone I want no matter how you feel? But we are knights, and we must behave like knights. Therefore, if you want to win Emily in

Which that thou seyst that I have maad to thee.
What, verray fool, think wel that love is free,
And I wol love hir, maugre al thy might!
750 But, for as muche thou art a worthy knight,
And wilnest to darreyne hir by batayle,
Have heer my trouthe, to-morwe I wol nat fayle,
With-outen witing of any other wight,
That here I wol be founden as a knight,
And bringen harneys right y-nough for thee;
And chees the beste, and leve the worste for me.
And mete and drinke this night wol I bringe5
Y-nough for thee, and clothes for thy beddinge.
And, if so be that thou my lady winne,
760 And slee me in this wode ther I am inne,
Thou mayst wel have thy lady, as for me.'
This Palamon answerde: 'I graunte it thee.'
And thus they been departed til a-morwe,
When ech of hem had leyd his feith to borwe.

O Cupide, out of alle charitee!
O regne, that wolt no felawe have with thee!
Ful sooth is seyd, that love ne lordshipe5
Wol noght, his thankes, have no felaweshipe;
Wel finden that Arcite and Palamoun.
770 Arcite is riden anon unto the toun,
And on the morwe, er it were dayes light,
Ful prively two harneys hath he dight,
Bothe suffisaunt and mete to darreyne
The bataille in the feeld bitwix hem tweyne.
And on his hors, allone as he was born,
He carieth al this harneys him biforn;
And in the grove, at tyme and place y-set,
This Arcite and this Palamon ben met.
Tho chaungen gan the colour in hir face;
780 Right as the hunter in the regne of Trace,
That stondeth at the gappe with a spere,
Whan hunted is the leoun or the bere,
And hereth him come russhing in the greves,

battle, then meet me here tomorrow and we'll settle this once and for all. Come alone. I give you my word as a knight that I'll come too—and with extra armor for you to wear. In fact, you can even take the better set of armor. Tonight I'll bring you food and wine and blankets to sleep on so that you're well rested for tomorrow. And if you should kill me tomorrow, then Emily is all yours." Palamon agreed, and they parted ways until they would meet the next day at the appointed time.

765-804   Cupid, you merciless god, who jealously rules mankind with love! It is true what they say, that nothing is as powerful as love, as Arcite and Palamon discovered for themselves. Arcite rode back to Athens and the next morning managed to secretly acquire two suits of armor for the upcoming battle. He took them out to the grove as he'd promised. And when they saw each other, their faces changed color and reflected their determination to meet their destiny, just as the face of the famous hunter from Thrace changed color when he hunted lions and bears with his spear. And just like that hunter that you hear about in all the old stories, both Arcite and Palamon thought, "There is my enemy. It all comes down to this: It's either going to be him or me." They didn't bother with any pleasantries— no "hellos" or "good mornings" or "How are you doings?" Instead, without a single word, each helped the other to put on his suit of armor, just as if they were brothers preparing for war. And then they grabbed their spears and began fighting, circling and jabbing each other for hours on end. Seeing them, you would've thought that Palamon was an angry lion and Arcite a ferocious tiger. They fought like wild dogs that froth at the mouth because they're so angry. They

And breketh bothe bowes and the leves,
And thinketh, 'heer cometh my mortel enemy,
With-oute faile, he moot be deed, or I;
For outher I mot sleen him at the gappe,
Or he mot sleen me, if that me mishappe:'
So ferden they, in chaunging of hir hewe,
790 As fer as everich of hem other knewe.
Ther nas no good day, ne no saluing;
But streight, with-outen word or rehersing,
Everich of hem halp for to armen other,
As freendly as he were his owne brother;
And after that, with sharpe speres stronge
They foynen ech at other wonder longe.
Thou mightest wene that this Palamoun5
In his fighting were a wood leoun,
And as a cruel tygre was Arcite:
800 As wilde bores gonne they to smyte,
That frothen whyte as foom for ire wood.
Up to the ancle foghte they in hir blood.
And in this wyse I lete hem fighting dwelle;
And forth I wol of Theseus yow telle.

The destinee, ministre general,
That executeth in the world over-al
The purveyaunce, that God hath seyn biforn,
So strong it is, that, though the world had sworn
The contrarie of a thing, by ye or nay,
810 Yet somtyme it shal fallen on a day
That falleth nat eft with-inne a thousand yere.
For certeinly, our appetytes here,
Be it of werre, or pees, or hate, or love,
Al is this reuled by the sighte above.
This mene I now by mighty Theseus,
That for to honten is so desirous,
And namely at the grete hert in May,
That in his bed ther daweth him no day,
That he nis clad, and redy for to ryde
820 With hunte and horn, and houndes him bisyde.

fought until the grass was soaked in blood up to their ankles. And it's here I'll stop and leave them in the middle of their battle to tell you a little more about Theseus.

805-824   Destiny—the hand of God that makes God's will happen throughout the world—is so powerful that no mere mortal can stop it. People might be able to postpone the inevitable, but ultimately God's will is always done. Even if it takes a thousand years because everything that people think and want and do has already been predetermined by God. I'll explain what I mean by telling you about Theseus. He loved hunting, you see—especially deer in May—and would wake at the crack of dawn every day to go hunting with his hunting horns and dogs. In this way he was not only a worshipper of the war god Mars, because he was so good in battle, but also a worshiper of Diana, the goddess of the hunt.

For in his hunting hath he swich delyt,
That it is al his Ioye and appetyto
To been him-self the grete hertes bane;
For after Mars he serveth now Diane.

Cleer was the day, as I have told er this,
And Theseus, with alle Ioye and blis,
With his Ipolita, the fayre quene,
And Emelye, clothed al in grene,
On hunting be they riden royally.
830 And to the grove, that stood ful faste by,
In which ther was an hert, as men him tolde,
Duk Theseus the streighte wey hath holde.
And to the launde he rydeth him ful right,
For thider was the hert wont have his flight,
And over a brook, and so forth on his weye.
This duk wol han a cours at him, or tweye,
With houndes, swiche as that him list comaunde.

And whan this duk was come unto the launde,
Under the sonne he loketh, and anon
840 He was war of Arcite and Palamon,
That foughten breme, as it were bores two;
The brighte swerdes wenten to and froo
So hidously, that with the leeste strook
It seemed as it wolde felle an ook;
But what they were, no-thing he ne woot.
This duk his courser with his spores smoot,
And at a stert he was bitwix hem two,
And pulled out a swerd and cryed, 'ho!
Namore, up peyne of lesing of your heed.
850 By mighty Mars, he shal anon be deed,
That smyteth any strook, that I may seen!
But telleth me what mister men ye been,
That been so hardy for to fighten here
With-outen Iuge or other officere,
As it were in a listes royally?'

825-837 Well, it was a bright, sunny day, and Theseus was out hunting with his wife Hippolyta and her sister Emily, who was wearing green from head to toe. They were on their way to the same clearing that I mentioned previously because Theseus had heard that a magnificent stag roamed around there. They'd taken quite a roundabout way to get there, through trees and across streams, because he wanted to extend the hunt as long as possible.

838-883 When they finally reached the grove, Theseus immediately spotted Arcite and Palamon duking it out in a vicious battle as if they were two wild beasts. They swung their swords so violently that it seemed like you could chop a thick oak tree with each blow. He had no idea who the men were or what was going on, but he spurred his horse and jumped in between the two of them to stop the battle. He drew his sword and yelled, "Stop! Enough already! I swear to Mars that I'll kill whoever swings next! Tell me what's going on here and why you two are dueling without a judge like a couple of ruffians."

This Palamon answerde hastily,
And seyde: 'sire, what nedeth wordes mo?
We have the deeth deserved bothe two.
Two woful wrecches been we, two caytyves,
860   That been encombred of our owne lyves;
And as thou art a rightful lord and Iuge,
Ne yeve us neither mercy ne refuge,
But slee me first, for seynte charitee;
But slee my felawe eek as wel as me.
Or slee him first; for, though thou knowe it lyte,
This is thy mortal fo, this is Arcite,
That fro thy lond is banished on his heed,
For which he hath deserved to be deed.
For this is he that cam unto thy gate,
870   And seyde, that he highte Philostrate.
Thus hath he Iaped thee ful many a yeer,
And thou has maked him thy chief squyer;
And this is he that loveth Emelye.
For sith the day is come that I shal dye,
I make pleynly my confessioun,
That I am thilke woful Palamoun,
That hath thy prison broken wikkedly.
I am thy mortal fo, and it am I
That loveth so hote Emelye the brighte,
880   That I wol dye present in hir sighte.
Therfore I axe deeth and my Iuwyse;
But slee my felawe in the same wyse,
For bothe han we deserved to be slayn.'

This worthy duk answerde anon agayn,
And seyde, 'This is a short conclusioun:
Youre owne mouth, by your confessioun,
Hath dampned you, and I wol it recorde,
It nedeth noght to pyne yow with the corde.
Ye shul be deed, by mighty Mars the rede!'

890   The quene anon, for verray wommanhede,
Gan for to wepe, and so dide Emelye,

NO FEAR

Palamon jumped in and said, "Sire, just let us keep fighting. Neither one of us is fit to live. We both live such awful lives that I beg you not to interfere or try to help us or anything and to just kill me now, for God's sake. And kill this guy too while you're at it. In fact, you may want to kill him first because this knight here—your friend and most trusted advisor, Philostrato—has been deceiving you all these years and is actually none other than your mortal enemy, Arcite, whom you banished from Athens so long ago. He is in love with Emily. And since it looks like I'm going to die here and now anyway, I might as well tell you that I am Palamon, your other enemy who has just escaped from your prison tower. I love Emily so much that I want to die in her presence, so I beg you to kill us here and now as punishment and to end our pain."

884-889 Without a bit of hesitation, Thesus said, "Well, you heard the man! He confessed his crimes, so that settles that. I condemn you to death!"

890-970 It was at that point that Queen Hyppolita, the best example of femininity, began crying, as did Emily and all the other women in

And alle the ladies in the companye.
Gret pitee was it, as it thoughte hem alle,
That ever swich a chaunce sholde falle;
For gentil men they were, of greet estat,
And no-thing but for love was this debat;
And sawe hir blody woundes wyde and sore;
And alle cryden, bothe lasse and more,
'Have mercy, lord, upon us wommen alle!'
900   And on hir bare knees adoun they falle,
And wolde have kist his feet ther-as he stood,
Til at the laste aslaked was his mood;
For pitee renneth sone in gentil herte.
And though he first for ire quook and sterte,
He hath considered shortly, in a clause,
The trespas of hem bothe, and eek the cause:
And al-though that his ire hir gilt accused,
Yet in his reson he hem bothe excused;
As thus, he thoghte wel, that every man
910   Wol helpe himself in love, if that he can,
And eek delivere him-self out of prisoun;
And eek his herte had compassioun
Of wommen, for they wepen ever in oon;
And in his gentil herte he thoghte anoon,
And softe unto himself he seyde: 'fy
Upon a lord that wol have no mercy,
But been a leoun, bothe in word and dede,
To hem that been in repentaunce and drede
As wel as to a proud despitous man
920   That wol maynteyne that he first bigan!
That lord hath litel of discrecioun,
That in swich cas can no divisioun,
But weyeth pryde and humblesse after oon.'
And shortly, whan his ire is thus agoon,
He gan to loken up with eyen lighte,
And spak thise same wordes al on highte:—
The god of love, a! *benedicite*,
How mighty and how greet a lord is he!
Ayeins his might ther gayneth none obstacles,

their hunting party. The whole situation seemed so tragic to them, and they couldn't believe that such handome, noble men would be willing to kill each other over their love. The women saw how bloody and bruised the knights were and dropped down on their knees and pleaded, "Please, Theseus, have mercy on these men for our sakes!" Seeing the women like this cooled Theseus's temper a little, and he thought the situation over with a more level-headed attitude. He figured that every person has the right to pursue love, and will do anything for it, even escape from prison. And as he looked at Arcite and Palamon standing there and the women kneeling before him, he said to himself, "Shame on me for having spoken so rashly and for acting pigheaded a moment ago. What kind of ruler would that make me if I didn't forgive them? And what kind of ruler would it make me if, now that I've realized my mistake, I choose not to change my mind? I'd be pretty foolish if I were too stubborn to be reasonable." Once his anger had fully passed, he looked at everyone watching him, and said, "How powerful and great the god of love must be! Nothing can stop him, and he has the power to change every heart. Just look at these two men here. Both of them got out of prison and could have returned to Thebes to live as kings, but they chose to be in Athens instead because of their love, in spite of knowing what would happen to them if they were caught. And yet their love has brought them here and is literally killing them. Crazy, isn't it? Or, then again, would they be crazy not to have followed their hearts and stayed in Athens? For God's sake, just look at them! Look at how battered they are! Love, I suppose, certainly has its price! And yet, those who follow their hearts believe they're the happiest people on earth no matter what happens. But the funniest thing about this whole mess is that Emily, the object of their love, didn't even know they were in love with her and fighting over here! On the other hand, what other options did these two men have? They had to do something about their feelings. I too was once as young and felt as passionately as they do now. So, since I know what these two men must be feeling, and since my wife and my sister-in-law are begging me to be merciful, I'm going to forgive Arcite and Palamon of their crimes. But both of you have to promise me that in exchange for my forgiveness you will never wage war upon Athens and will

930 He may be cleped a god for his miracles;
For he can maken at his owne gyse
Of everich herte, as that him list devyse.
Lo heer, this Arcite and this Palamoun,
That quitly weren out of my prisoun,
And mighte han lived in Thebes royally,
And witen I am hir mortal enemy,
And that hir deeth lyth in my might also,
And yet hath love, maugree hir eyen two,
Y-broght hem hider bothe for to dye!
940 Now loketh, is nat that an heigh folye?
Who may been a fool, but-if he love?
Bihold, for Goddes sake that sit above,
Se how they blede! be they noght wel arrayed?
Thus hath hir lord, the god of love, y-payed
Hir wages and hir fees for hir servyse!
And yet they wenen for to been ful wyse
That serven love, for aught that may bifalle!
But this is yet the beste game of alle,
That she, for whom they han this Iolitee,
950 Can hem ther-for as muche thank as me;
She woot namore of al this hote fare,
By God, than woot a cokkow or an hare!
But al mot been assayed, hoot and cold;
A man mot been a fool, or yong or old;
I woot it by myself ful yore agoon:
For in my tyme a servant was I oon.
And therfore, sin I knowe of loves peyne,
And woot how sore it can a man distreyne,
As he that hath ben caught ofte in his las,
960 I yow foryeve al hoolly this trespas,
At requeste of the quene that kneleth here,
And eek of Emelye, my suster dere.
And ye shul bothe anon unto me swere,
That never-mo ye shul my contree dere,
Ne make werre upon me night ne day,
But been my freendes in al that ye may;
I yow foryeve this trespas every del.'

be my allies instead." Arcite and Palamon thanked Theseus for his compassion and swore never to hurt the Athenian people.

And they him swore his axing fayre and wel,
And him of lordshipe and of mercy preyde,
970　And he hem graunteth grace, and thus he seyde:

'To speke of royal linage and richesse,
Though that she were a quene or a princesse,
Ech of yow bothe is worthy, doutelees,
To wedden whan tyme is, but nathelees
I speke as for my suster Emelye,
For whom ye have this stryf and Ielousye;
Ye woot yourself, she may not wedden twoS
At ones, though ye fighten evermo:
That oon of yow, al be him looth or leef,
980　He moot go pypen in an ivy-leef;
This is to seyn, she may nat now han bothe,
Al be ye never so Ielous, ne so wrothe.
And for-thy I yow putte in this degree,
That ech of yow shal have his destinee
As him is shape; and herkneth in what wyse;
Lo, heer your ende of that I shal devyse.

My wil is this, for plat conclusioun,
With-outen any replicacioun,
If that yow lyketh, tak it for the beste,
990　That everich of yow shal gon wher him leste
Frely, with-outen raunson or daunger;
And this day fifty wykes, fer ne ner,
Everich of yow shal bringe an hundred knightes,
Armed for listes up at alle rightes,
Al redy to darreyne hir by bataille.
And this bihote I yow, with-outen faille,
Upon my trouthe, and as I am a knight,
That whether of yow bothe that hath might,
This is to seyn, that whether he or thou
1000　May with his hundred, as I spak of now,
Sleen his contrarie, or out of listes dryve,
Him shal I yeve Emelya to wyve,
To whom that Fortune yeveth so fair a grace.

NO FEAR

971-986 Theseus then said, "But it looks like we still have the matter of your lovesickness to solve, don't we? Both of you are honorable and noble enough to marry any woman you please, even a queen or a princess. But you two happen to be in love with my own sister-in-law. You know that she can't marry you both at the same time, now matter how badly you want her. One of you is simply going to have to let her go no matter how you feel about the matter. So, to resolve this matter, this is what I propose:

987-1011 Both of you should think on the matter for a year. Go wherever you please, but both of you should return here in fifty weeks with a hundred knights each to participate in a great tournament that will decide which one of you will marry Emily. I'll be the judge, and the outcome of the tournament will be final: Whoever's team of knights manages to kill or defeat the other team will have Emily's hand in marriage. We'll hold the tournament here in Athens. What do you two think about my plan?

The listes shal I maken in this place,
And God so wisly on my soule rewe,
As I shal even Iuge been and trewe.
Ye shul non other ende with me maken,
That oon of yow ne shal be deed or taken.
And if yow thinketh this is wel y-sayd,
1010 Seyeth your avys, and holdeth yow apayd.
This is your ende and your conclusioun.'

Who loketh lightly now but Palamoun?
Who springeth up for Ioye but Arcite?
Who couthe telle, or who couthe it endyte,
The Ioye that is maked in the place
Whan Theseus hath doon so fair a grace?
But doun on knees wente every maner wight,
And thanked him with al her herte and might,
And namely the Thebans ofte sythe.
1020 And thus with good hope and with herte blythe
They take hir leve, and hom-ward gonne they ryde
To Thebes, with his olde walles wyde.

EXPLICIT SECUNDA PARS

1012 1022 Well, could anyone have been any happier than Palamon? Could anyone have ever smiled any bigger than Arcite? Everyone in the grove applauded Theseus for having shown both knights mercy and for coming up with such a brilliant solution. And with that, both Arcite and Palamon collected their things and set off for Thebes.

END OF PART TWO

The Knight's Tale, Part Three

EQUITUR PARS TERCIA.

I trowe men wolde deme it necligence,
If I foryete to tellen the dispence
Of Theseus, that goth so bisily
To maken up the listes royally;
That swich a noble theatre as it was,
I dar wel seyn that in this world ther nas.
The circuit a myle was aboute,
1030 Walled of stoon, and diched al with-oute.
Round was the shap, in maner of compas,
Ful of degrees, the heighte of sixty pas,
That, whan a man was set on o degree,
He letted nat his felawe for to see.

Est-ward ther stood a gate of marbel whyt,
West-ward, right swich another in the opposit.
And shortly to concluden, swich a place
Was noon in erthe, as in so litel space;
For in the lond ther nas no crafty man,
1040 That geometrie or ars-metrik can,
Ne purtreyour, ne kerver of images,
That Theseus ne yaf him mete and wages
The theatre for to maken and devyse.
And for to doon his ryte and sacrifyse,
He est-ward hath, upon the gate above,
In worship of Venus, goddesse of love,
Don make an auter and an oratorie;
And west-ward, in the minde and in memorie
Of Mars, he maked hath right swich another,
1050 That coste largely of gold a fother.
And north-ward, in a touret on the wal,
Of alabastre whyt and reed coral
An oratorie riche for to see,
In worship of Dyane of chastitee,
Hath Theseus don wroght in noble wyse.

The Knight's Tale, Part Three

HERE'S THE THIRD PART OF THE KNIGHT'S TALE.

23-1034 I guess I wouldn't do a good job of telling this story if I didn't tell you all about the magnificent stadium Theseus built to host the tournament between Arcite and Palamon and their teams of knights. The stadium was enormous. It was circular and made of stone and was a full mile in circumferance and sixty feet high. It also had stadium seating, which meant that if someone sat in front of you, you could still see the field clearly. There really was no finer stadium in the entire world.

35-1059 There was a white marble gate on both the eastern and western sides of the stadium. Theseus also had altars built on the eastern, western, and northern sides of the stadium where he could make sacrifices to the gods. The eastern altar was for making sacrifices to Venus, the goddess of love, while the expensive altar near the western gate was built to honor Mars, the god of war. On the northern side he built an oratory platform of white alabaster and red coral, from which people could address the audience. This he dedicated to Diana, the goddess of the moon and hunting. As I said, the stadium truly was one of a kind, in part because Theseus hired every single mathematician, construction worker, painter, or sculptor in the country.

But yet hadde I foryeten to devyse
The noble kerving, and the portreitures,
The shap, the countenaunce, and the figures,
That weren in thise oratories three.

1060 First in the temple of Venus maystow see
Wroght on the wal, ful pitous to biholde,
The broken slepes, and the sykes colde;
The sacred teres, and the waymenting;
The fyry strokes of the desiring,
That loves servaunts in this lyf enduren;
The othes, that hir covenants assuren;
Plesaunce and hope, desyr, fool-hardinesse,
Beautee and youthe, bauderie, richesse,
Charmes and force, lesinges, flaterye,
1070 Dispense, bisynesse, and Ielousye,
That wered of yelwe goldes a gerland,
And a cokkow sitting on hir hand;
Festes, instruments, caroles, daunces,
Lust and array, and alle the circumstaunces
Of love, whiche that I rekne and rekne shal,
By ordre weren peynted on the wal,
And mo than I can make of mencioun.
For soothly, al the mount of Citheroun,
Ther Venus hath hir principal dwelling,
1080 Was shewed on the wal in portreying,
With al the gardin, and the lustinesse.
Nat was foryeten the porter Ydelnesse,
Ne Narcisus the faire of yore agon,
Ne yet the folye of king Salamon,
Ne yet the grete strengthe of Hercules—
Thenchauntements of Medea and Circes—
Ne of Turnus, with the hardy fiers corage,
The riche Cresus, caytif in servage.
Thus may ye seen that wisdom ne richesse,
1090 Beautee ne sleighte, strengthe, ne hardinesse,
Ne may with Venus holde champartye;
For as hir list the world than may she gye.

NO FEAR

Oh, but before I forget, let me tell you a little bit more about the sculptures and paintings that adorned these three altars because they were truly amazing.

1060-1096 Well, first, if you look at the altar devoted to Venus, you'll see paintings of all sorts of people who personify everything that love has the ability to make people feel: Pleasure, Hope, Desire, Foolishness, Beauty, Youth, Lust, Wealth, Magic, Power, Deceit, Flattery, Opulence, Toil, and Jealousy, who wore a garland of golden flowers and had a cuckoo bird sitting on her hand. The paintings also depict parties, musical instruments, singers, dancing, happiness, and everything else that love has the power to create but that I don't have time to talk about. There was also a painting of beautiful Mount Cytheria, the home of Venus. There were also paintings of all sorts of people who've felt love's pleasure and pain, including Narcisus, the man who fell in love with his own reflection; King Solomon; Hercules; the sirens Medea and Circe; fierce Turnus; and wealthy Croesus. So, as you can see, no one is immune from Venus's powers of love, not even the wisest and richest and strongest men out there. I could go on and on, but you get the idea.

Lo, alle thise folk so caught were in hir las,
Til they for wo ful ofte seyde 'allas!'
Suffyceth heer ensamples oon or two,
And though I coude rekne a thousand mo.

The statue of Venus, glorious for to see,
Was naked fleting in the large see,
And fro the navele doun all covered was
1100   With wawes grene, and brighte as any glas.
A citole in hir right hand hadde she,
And on hir heed, ful semely for to see,
A rose gerland, fresh and wel smellinge;
Above hir heed hir dowves flikeringe.
Biforn hir stood hir sone Cupido,
Upon his shuldres winges hadde he two;
And blind he was, as it is ofte sene;
A bowe he bar and arwes brighte and kene.

Why sholde I noght as wel eek telle yow al
1110   The portreiture, that was upon the wal
With-inne the temple of mighty Mars the rede?
Al peynted was the wal, in lengthe and brede,
Lyk to the estres of the grisly place,
That highte the grete temple of Mars in Trace,
In thilke colde frosty regioun,
Ther-as Mars hath his sovereyn mansioun.

First on the wal was peynted a foreste,
In which ther dwelleth neither man ne beste,
With knotty knarry bareyn treës olde
1120   Of stubbes sharpe and hidous to biholde;
In which ther ran a rumbel and a swough,
As though a storm sholde bresten every bough:
And downward from an hille, under a bente,
Ther stood the temple of Mars armipotente,
Wroght al of burned steel, of which thentree
Was long and streit, and gastly for to see.
And ther-out cam a rage and such a vese,

NO FEAR

097-1108 The altarpiece was a glorius statue of Venus that depicted her naked, floating in the ocean so that she was covered from the waist down by green waves that sparkled like glass. She held a stringed lyre in her right hand and wore a garland made of beautiful and sweet-smelling roses on top of her head. Doves flew above her head while her son, Cupid, stood in front of her. Cupid had wings, carried a bow and arrows, and was blind, just as most other sculptures and paintings depict him.

109-1116 And while I'm at it, I should tell you all about the artwork inside the temple of Mars too. This temple was decorated with scenes of the horrors of war, the same scenes you'll find in the temple to him in the region of Thrace, where Mars lives.

117-1136 The first scene of the painting on the wall was that of a dark and scary forest on top of a hill that was filled not with people or animals, but with old, knotted trees and stumps. You could hear the creaking of the wood and the howling of the wind just by looking at the painting. A painting of a temple dedicated to Mars stood at the bottom of the hill, complete with a statue of the god dressed in a full suit of steel armor and ready for battle. It made him look pretty frightening. The temple gates were gaping, and you could imagine hearing the wind slam them shut. The columns holding up the roof were enormous and made of solid iron. The temple doors, which were made of the indestructible metal adamant, were shut and

That it made al the gates for to rese.
The northren light in at the dores shoon,
1130   For windowe on the wal ne was ther noon,
Thurgh which men mighten any light discerne.
The dores were alle of adamant eterne,
Y-clenched overthwart and endelong
With iren tough; and, for to make it strong,
Every piler, the temple to sustene,
Was tonne-greet, of iren bright and shene.

Ther saugh I first the derke imagining
Of felonye, and al the compassing;
The cruel ire, reed as any glede;
1140   The pykepurs, and eek the pale drede;
The smyler with the knyf under the cloke;
The shepne brenning with the blake smoke;
The treson of the mordring in the bedde;
The open werre, with woundes al bi-bledde;
Contek, with blody knyf and sharp manace;
Al ful of chirking was that sory place.
The sleere of him-self yet saugh I ther,
His herte-blood hath bathed al his heer;
The nayl y-driven in the shode a-night;
1150   The colde deeth, with mouth gaping up-right.
Amiddes of the temple sat meschaunce,
With disconfort and sory contenaunce.
Yet saugh I woodnesse laughing in his rage;
Armed compleint, out-hees, and fiers outrage.
The careyne in the bush, with throte y-corve:
A thousand slayn, and nat of qualm y-storve;
The tiraunt, with the prey by force y-raft;
The toun destroyed, ther was no-thing laft.
Yet saugh I brent the shippes hoppesteres;
1160   The hunte strangled with the wilde beres:
The sowe freten the child right in the cradel;
The cook y-scalded, for al his longe ladel.
Noght was foryeten by the infortune of Marte;
The carter over-riden with his carte,

locked up tightly. The north side of the temple was lit, but everything else was dark.

137-1182 As with the paintings honoring Venus, you could see all the emotions associated with war personified in the paintings in the temple of Mars. There was Treachery plotting and scheming, Anger glowing red, and Dread as well. There was the smiling character holding a knife underneath his cape, a barn burning with black smoke, murder, bloodshed, gaping wounds, misery, bloody knives, and piled bodies. You could almost hear the clash of steel and the screams of battle. There was a painting of a man who'd killed himself, his head lying in a pool of his own blood. Death himself stalked another man who had an iron stake poking through his head. Other figures representing personified emotions were nearby too. Misfortune, for example, sat in the middle of the temple looking forlorn, while Insanity laughed hysterically. Sadness and Outrage were there too, and Conquest sat high up in a tower overlooking the entire scene below. You could see a dead body lying in the bushes with its throat cut, and a thousand dead bodies all piled up, dead from war rather than old age or even disease. There were kidnappers and burning cities and sailing ships, hunters gored to death by their own prey, pigs gorging themselves on little babies lying in their cribs. Mars's servants were there too, including the battlefield surgeon, the butcher, and the blacksmith who makes weapons for war. You could see the scenes of the murders of Julius Caesar and the Roman emperors Nero and Caracalla, who'd all been murdered. Nothing was left out. All the horrors of war were there to see in the paintings inside the temple of Mars.

Under the wheel ful lowe he lay adoun.
Ther were also, of Martes divisioun,
The barbour, and the bocher, and the smith
That forgeth sharpe swerdes on his stith.
And al above, depeynted in a tour,
Saw I conquest sittinge in greet honour,
With the sharpe swerde over his heed
Hanginge by a sotil twynes threed.
Depeynted was the slaughtre of Iulius,
Of grete Nero, and of Antonius;
Al be that thilke tyme they were unborn,
Yet was hir deeth depeynted ther-biforn,
By manasinge of Mars, right by figure;
So was it shewed in that portreiture
As is depeynted in the sterres above,
Who shal be slayn or elles deed for love.
Suffyceth oon ensample in stories olde,
I may not rekne hem alle, thogh I wolde.

The statue of Mars upon a carte stood,
Armed, and loked grim as he were wood;
And over his he'ed ther shynen two figures
Of sterres, that been cleped in scriptures,
That oon Puella, that other Rubeus.
This god of armes was arrayed thus:—
A wolf ther stood biforn him at his feet
With eyen rede, and of a man he eet;
With sotil pencel was depeynt this storie,
In redoutinge of Mars and of his glorie.

Now to the temple of Diane the chaste
As shortly as I can I wol me haste,
To telle yow al the descripcioun.
Depeynted been the walles up and doun
Of hunting and of shamfast chastitee.
Ther saugh I how woful Calistopee,
Whan that Diane agreved was with here,
Was turned from a womman til a bere,

NO FEAR

183-1192 The statue of Mars inside the temple rode a chariot, and he looked as fierce and angry as ever. The constellations Puella and Rubeus that are often associated with him shone brightly over his head. A red-eyed wolf was at his feet, visciously tearing the flesh of a man. The painting was quite amazing and was a true tribute to Mars.

193-1230 And now, as quickly as I can, I'll tell you all about the temple devoted to the celibate goddess Diana. All up and down, the walls were painted with scenes of hunting and those depicting chastity. There were portraits of lots of hunters, including Callisto, who pissed Diana off and was transformed into a bear as punishment and later was placed in the sky as the North Star. Her son is a star too. There was also a painting of Daphne, whom Diana changed into a tree. You could also see a painting of Actaeon, the poor hunter

And after was she maad the lode-sterre;
Thus was it peynt, I can say yow no ferre;
Hir sone is eek a sterre, as men may see.
Ther saugh I Dane, y-turned til a tree,
I mene nat the goddesse Diane,
But Penneus doughter, which that highte Dane.
Ther saugh I Attheon an hert y-maked,
For vengeaunce that he saugh Diane al naked;
I saugh how that his houndes have him caught,
1210   And freten him, for that they knewe him naught.
Yet peynted was a litel forther-moor,
How Atthalante hunted the wilde boor,
And Meleagre, and many another mo,
For which Diane wroghte him care and wo.
Ther saugh I many another wonder storie,
The whiche me list nat drawen to memorie.
This goddesse on an hert ful hye seet,
With smale houndes al aboute hir feet;
And undernethe hir feet she hadde a mone,
1220   Wexing it was, and sholde wanie sone.
In gaude grene hir statue clothed was,
With bowe in honde, and arwes in a cas.
Hir eyen caste she ful lowe adoun,
Ther Pluto hath his derke regioun.
A womman travailinge was hir biforn,
But, for hir child so longe was unborn,
Ful pitously Lucyna gan she calle,
And seyde, 'help, for thou mayst best of alle.'
Wel couthe he peynten lyfly that it wroghte,
1230   With many a florin he the hewes boghte.

Now been thise listes maad, and Theseus,
That at his grete cost arrayed thus
The temples and the theatre every del,
Whan it was doon, him lyked wonder wel.
But stinte I wol of Theseus a lyte,
And speke of Palamon and of Arcite.

whom Diana changed into a deer after he'd seen her naked. The painting even showed his hunting dogs tearing him apart because they didn't realize that the deer was their master. You could also see Atalanta and Meleager, the couple who hunted the wild boar, and many paintings of other people too, none of which I can recall off the top of my head. The statue of Diana inside the temple featured her sitting on a deer with all her hunting dogs at her feet as well as the moon. She wore bright green clothes and held a bow and arrows in her hands. Her eyes were pointed toward the ground toward the underworld. There was a sculpture of a woman crying out for mercy in the middle of childbirth next to the statue of Diana. The artists who made these sculptures and paintings really knew how to make scenes come to life, and you could tell they spared no expense in creating the altar.

231-1236 And when the stadium had finally been completed, Theseus felt pretty happy with the results. But, before I talk any more about him, let me switch gears quickly and tell you more about Arcite and Palamon.

The day approcheth of hir retourninge,
That everich sholde an hundred knightes bringe,
The bataille to darreyne, as I yow tolde;
1240 And til Athenes, hir covenant for to holde,
Hath everich of hem broght an hundred knightes
Wel armed for the werre at alle rightes.
And sikerly, ther trowed many a man
That never, sithen that the world bigan,
As for to speke of knighthod of hir hond,
As fer as God hath maked see or lond,
Nas, of so fewe, so noble a companye.
For every wight that lovede chivalrye,
And wolde, his thankes, han a passant name,
1250 Hath preyed that he mighte ben of that game;
And wel was him, that ther-to chosen was.
For if ther fille to-morwe swich a cas,
Ye knowen wel, that every lusty knight,
That loveth paramours, and hath his might,
Were it in Engelond, or elles-where,
They wolde, hir thankes, wilnen to be there.
To fighte for a lady, *benedicite!*
It were a lusty sighte for to see.

And right so ferden they with Palamon.
1260 With him ther wenten knightes many oon;
Som wol ben armed in an habergeoun,
In a brest-plat and in a light gipoun;
And somme woln have a peyre plates large;
And somme woln have a Pruce sheld, or a targe;
Somme woln ben armed on hir legges weel,
And have an ax, and somme a mace of steel.
Ther nis no newe gyse, that it nas old.
Armed were they, as I have you told,
Everich after his opinioun.

1270 Ther maistow seen coming with Palamoun
Ligurge him-self, the grete king of Trace;
Blak was his berd, and manly was his face.

37-1258 Well, the day of the tournament came very quickly, and Arcite and Palamon assembled their one hundred battle-ready knights in the new stadium in Athens. God, a tournament fought for the love of a woman. That would definitely be a sight to see, now wouldn't it? Lots of Athenians said that never had so many of the world's most noble and valiant assembled in one place for such a tournament. Knights had come from far and wide and applied to fight for Arcite and Palamon, but only 200 men total were chosen to participate. Well, you know yourselves that if it was announced that this kind of tournament was going to be held tomorrow—either here in England or somewhere else—every knight who ever dreamt of honor and glory would come out of the woodwork to get a piece of the action.

259-1269 Well, the knights who fought for Palamon felt this way too. They all wanted to prove their honor. Some came dressed in chain mail, a tunic, and a breastplate. Others simply wore a couple of steel plates, one on the front and one on the back. Others carried a simple round shield, or made sure to wear leg armor. Some wanted to fight with a mace, while other knights brought axes. Each person came with the armor and weapons he thought would help him win.

270-1296 Lycurgus himself, the powerful king of Thrace, came with Palamon. He looked so manly with his jet-black beard and hair that fell down to his waist. The pupils of his eyes were somewhere between red and

The cercles of his eyen in his heed,
They gloweden bitwixe yelow and reed;
And lyk a griffon loked he aboute,
With kempe heres on his browes stoute;
His limes grete, his braunes harde and stronge,
His shuldres brode, his armes rounde and longe.
And as the gyse was in his contree,
1280　Ful hye upon a char of gold stood he,
With foure whyte boles in the trays.
In-stede of cote-armure over his harnays,
With nayles yelwe and brighte as any gold,
He hadde a beres skin, col-blak, for-old.
His longe heer was kembd bihinde his bak,
As any ravenes fether it shoon for-blak:
A wrethe of gold arm-greet, of huge wighte,
Upon his heed, set ful of stones brighte,
Of fyne rubies and of dyamaunts.
1290　Aboute his char ther wenten whyte alaunts,
Twenty and mo, as grete as any steer,
To hunten at the leoun or the deer,
And folwed him, with mosel faste y-bounde,
Colers of gold, and torets fyled rounde.
An hundred lordes hadde he in his route
Armed ful wel, with hertes sterne and stoute.

With Arcita, in stories as men finde,
The grete Emetreus, the king of Inde,
Upon a stede bay, trapped in steel,
1300　Covered in cloth of gold diapred weel,
Cam ryding lyk the god of armes, Mars.
His cote-armure was of cloth of Tars,
Couched with perles whyte and rounde and grete.
His sadel was of brend gold newe y-bete;
A mantelet upon his shuldre hanginge
Bret-ful of rubies rede, as fyr sparklinge.
His crispe heer lyk ringes was y-ronne,
And that was yelow, and glitered as the sonne.
His nose was heigh, his eyen bright citryn,

yellow. Those eyes and his big bushy eyebrows made him look like a griffin, half lion and half eagle. He had broad shoulders and strong, muscular arms. He wore an enormous black bearskin over his armor instead of a tunic, and its yellow claws shone like gold. A crown of gold studded with diamonds and rubies glittered on top of his head. Like most Thracian warriors, he arrived in a golden chariot pulled by four white bulls. Twenty giant white wolves circled around his chariot, tethered with gold collars and muzzles. He brought with him a hundred of his own knights for moral support.

297-1331   Meanwhile, Emetreus, the king of India, had come with Arcite. He had a large nose, bright eyes, a rosy complexion, and a voice that thundered like a trumpet. His curly blonde hair glittered like the sun. He had a few freckles too, and the combination of the freckles and golden locks made him look like a lion. He had the beginnings of a good beard, which makes me think he was around twenty-five years old. He wore a crown of green laurel and carried a hawk that was as white as snow. He rode a light-colored horse decked out with a steel bridle and covered in golden, woven cloth. His coat of arms was decorated with the most perfect large pearls, and his saddle shone like gold. His cape was lined with rubies that sparkled like fire. He too brought a hundred of his kinsmen with him, all wearing armor. Everyone made sure to look his best because they knew that

1310   His lippes rounde, his colour was sangwyn,
A fewe fraknes in his face y-spreynd,
Betwixen yelow and somdel blak y-meynd,
And as a leoun he his loking caste.
Of fyve and twenty yeer his age I caste.
His berd was wel bigonne for to springe;
His voys was as a trompe thunderinge.
Upon his heed he wered of laurer grene
A gerland fresh and lusty for to sene.
Upon his hand he bar, for his deduyt,
1320   An egle tame, as eny lilie whyt.
An hundred lordes hadde he with him there,
Al armed, sauf hir heddes, in al hir gere,
Ful richely in alle maner thinges.
For trusteth wel, that dukes, erles, kinges,
Were gadered in this noble companye,
For love and for encrees of chivalrye.
Aboute this king ther ran on every part
Ful many a tame leoun and lepart.
And in this wyse thise lordes, alle and some,
1330   Ben on the Sonday to the citee come
Aboute pryme, and in the toun alight.

This Theseus, this duk, this worthy knight,
Whan he had broght hem in-to his citee,
And inned hem, everich in his degree,
He festeth hem, and dooth so greet labour
To esen hem, and doon hem al honour,
That yet men weneth that no mannes wit
Of noon estat ne coude amenden it.
The minstralcye, the service at the feste,
1340   The grete yiftes to the moste and leste,
The riche array of Theseus paleys,
Ne who sat first ne last upon the deys,
What ladies fairest been or best daunsinge,
Or which of hem can dauncen best and singe,
Ne who most felingly speketh of love:
What haukes sitten on the perche above,

many of the most powerful people in the world were attending this tournament. Many kings even brought their tame lions and leopards. And it was in this way that these kings and dukes and princes and knights gathered together outside of Athens around nine on a Sunday morning.

332-1350   Theseus did all he could to make his many guests comfortable. He found rooms for everyone to stay in that matched each person's social standing, and he hosted feasts. He spent so much energy looking after his guests that everyone agreed that he couldn't have done any better had he tried. I could tell you all the details—the food, the wine, the songs, the beautiful women, the decorations, the parties, the dancing, the hunts, the shows—but that would take too long, and I should really just cut to the chase.

What houndes liggen on the floor adoun:
Of al this make I now no mencioun;
But al theffect, that thinketh me the beste;
1350 Now comth the poynt, and herkneth if yow leste.

The Sonday night, er day bigan to springe,
When Palamon the larke herde singe,
Although it nere nat day by houres two,
Yet song the larke, and Palamon also.
With holy herte, and with an heigh corage
He roos, to wenden on his pilgrimage
Unto the blisful Citherea benigne,
I mene Venus, honurable and digne.
And in hir houre he walketh forth a pas
1360 Unto the listes, ther hir temple was,
And doun he kneleth, and with humble chere
And herte soor, he seyde as ye shul here.

'Faireste of faire, o lady myn, Venus,
Doughter to Iove and spouse of Vulcanus,
Thou glader of the mount of Citheroun,
For thilke love thou haddest to Adoun,
Have pitee of my bittre teres smerte,
And tak myn humble preyer at thyn herte.
Allas! I ne have no langage to telle
1370 Theffectes ne the torments of myn helle;
Myn herte may myne harmes nat biwreye;
I am so confus, that I can noght seye.
But mercy, lady bright, that knowest weel
My thought, and seest what harmes that I feel,
Considere al this, and rewe upon my sore,
As wisly as I shal for evermore,
Emforth my might, thy trewe servant be,
And holden werre alwey with chastitee;
That make I myn avow, so ye me helpe.
1380 I kepe noght of armes for to yelpe,
Ne I ne axe nat to-morwe to have victorie,
Ne renoun in this cas, ne veyne glorie

NO FEAR

351-1362 Well, on Sunday morning before dawn, Palamon woke up when he heard the birds singing (it was still two hours before the sun would rise, but for some reason, the birds were singing early that day) and prepared to go to the temple of Venus at the new stadium to pray to the goddess before the tournament began. He knelt before the statue of Venus and said:

363-1402 "My lady Venus, most beautiful of all the gods, daughter of Jupiter and wife of Vulcan, keeper of Mt. Cytheria, hear my prayers. There are no words to describe how much I've suffered for love these past years, and there's nothing I can really ask except for your pity and mercy. I will always be your humble servant and will do everything in my power to serve you if you help me tomorrow. I'll always pray at your temples and make sacrifices to you all the time, no matter where I am, for the rest of my life. I'm not going to brag about my abilities on the battlefield, and I'm not even asking you to help me win or to turn me into a famous warrior tomorrow. I don't care whether I win or lose. All I want is Emily. I could pray to Mars, the god of war, to bless me and help me win, but I know that the power of love is greater and that I'll have Emily if you help make it happen. Please find a way to help make this happen. And if you can't give me Emily, then please just let Arcite kill me with his spear. When I'm dead I won't feel this pain anymore and won't care whether Arcite marries Emily. Please help me if you can, my lady."

Of pris of armes blowen up and doun,
But I wolde have fully possessioun
Of Emelye, and dye in thy servyse;
Find thou the maner how, and in what wyse.
I recche nat, but it may bettre be,
To have victorie of hem, or they of me,
So that I have my lady in myne armes.
1390 For though so be that Mars is god of armes,
Your vertu is so greet in hevene above,
That, if yow list, I shal wel have my love,
Thy temple wol I worshipe evermo,
And on thyn auter, wher I ryde or go,
I wol don sacrifice, and fyres bete.
And if ye wol nat so, my lady swete,
Than preye I thee, to-morwe with a spere
That Arcita me thurgh the herte bere.
Thanne rekke I noght, whan I have lost my lyf,
1400 Though that Arcita winne hir to his wyf.
This is theffect and ende of my preyere,
Yif me my love, thou blisful lady dere.'

Whan thorisoun was doon of Palamon,
His sacrifice he dide, and that anon
Ful pitously, with alle circumstaunces,
Al telle I noght as now his observaunces.
But atte laste the statue of Venus shook,
And made a signe, wher-by that he took
That his preyere accepted was that day.
1410 For thogh the signe shewed a delay,
Yet wiste he wel that graunted was his bone;
And with glad herte he wente him hoom ful sone.

The thridde houre inequal that Palamon
Bigan to Venus temple for to goon,
Up roos the sonne, and up roos Emelye,
And to the temple of Diane gan hye.
Hir maydens, that she thider with hir ladde,
Ful redily with hem the fyr they hadde,

1403-1412 Palamon then offered sacrifices to Venus and made sure that he did them absolutely perfectly, without missing a single ritual. And a few moments after he finished, the statue of Venus in the temple shook, which Palamon interpreted as a sign that Venus had heard his prayers and would grant his request. He left the temple in a happy mood and prepared for the coming tournament.

1413-1438 A couple hours after Palamon had gone to the temple of Venus, Emily woke up at dawn and made her own way to the temple of the goddess Diana. She brought several servant girls with her, who brought all the stuff they needed to make a proper sacrifice to Diana, including the incense, fire, ceremonial clothing, and bull's horns filled with mead. When the fires and incense had been lit and every-

Thencens, the clothes, and the remenant al
1420   That to the sacrifyce longen shal;
The hornes fulle of meth, as was the gyse;
Ther lakked noght to doon hir sacrifyse.
Smoking the temple, ful of clothes faire,
This Emelye, with herte debonaire,
Hir body wessh with water of a welle;
But how she dide hir ryte I dar nat telle,
But it be any thing in general;
And yet it were a game to heren al;
To him that meneth wel, it were no charge:
1430   But it is good a man ben at his large.
Hir brighte heer was kempt, untressed al;
A coroune of a grene ook cerial
Upon hir heed was set ful fair and mete.
Two fyres on the auter gan she bete,
And dide hir thinges, as men may biholde
In Stace of Thebes, and thise bokes olde.
Whan kindled was the fyr, with pitous chere
Unto Diane she spak, as ye may here.

'O chaste goddesse of the wodes grene,
1440   To whom bothe hevene and erthe and see is sene,
Quene of the regne of Pluto derk and lowe,
Goddesse of maydens, that myn herte hast knowe
Ful many a yeer, and woost what I desire,
As keep me fro thy vengeaunce and thyn ire,
That Attheon aboughte cruelly.
Chaste goddesse, wel wostow that I
Desire to been a mayden al my lyf,
Ne never wol I be no love ne wyf.
I am, thou woost, yet of thy companye,
1450   A mayde, and love hunting and venerye,
And for to walken in the wodes wilde,
And noght to been a wyf, and be with childe.
Noght wol I knowe companye of man.
Now help me, lady, sith ye may and can,
For tho thre formes that thou hast in thee.

one had put on the prayer clothing, Emily went to the well and washed herself with the sacred water. And while I could tell you all the details about how she prayerd to Diana and made sacrifices—it really would be quite interesting to hear about all this—it's always good to keep stories focused on just the essentials, you know. Ah, well, Emily had her beautiful glossy hair down, and she wore a simple crown made of twigs and leaves from an oak tree. She built two fires on the alter and starting performing all the rituals necessary to pray to Diana, which you can read about in the ancient scholar Statius's book Thebaid, as well as other very old books. And when everything was ready, she said:

1439-1472 "Oh virgin goddess of the forest, queen of the underworld, and keeper of my heart, bless me, and please don't be angry with me as you been have with others in the past. You know that I want to remain a virgin all my life and be one of your faithful virgin followers who hunt in the forest just as you do. I never want to have sex with a man, get married, or have children. Diana—goddess of the moon, the underworld, and the hunt—please help me to keep this tournament from happening. Please make Palamon and Arcite stop fighting over me. Make them not love me any more so that they can move on with their lives instead of wasting them fighting over me. And if you can't help me stay a virgin forever, then let me marry whoever wants me more. Look at the tears on my cheeks, Diana, goddess of virginity. I beg of you to help me, one of your devoted followers, and preserve my virginity for the rest of my life so that I may continue to worship and serve you."

And Palamon, that hath swich love to me,
And eek Arcite, that loveth me so sore,
This grace I preye thee with-oute more,
As sende love and pees bitwixe hem two;
And fro me turne awey hir hertes so,
That al hir hote love, and hir desyr,
And al hir bisy torment, and hir fyr
Be queynt, or turned in another place;
And if so be thou wolt not do me grace,
Or if my destinee be shapen so,
That I shal nedes have oon of hem two,
As sende me him that most desireth me.
Bihold, goddesse of clene chastitee,
The bittre teres that on my chekes falle.
Sin thou are mayde, and keper of us alle,
My maydenhede thou kepe and wel conserve,
And whyl I live a mayde, I wol thee serve.'

The fyres brenne upon the auter clere,
Whyl Emelye was thus in hir preyere;
But sodeinly she saugh a sighte queynte,
For right anon oon of the fyres queynte,
And quiked agayn, and after that anon
That other fyr was queynt, and al agon;
And as it queynte, it made a whistelinge,
As doon thise wete brondes in hir brenninge,
And at the brondes ende out-ran anoon
As it were blody dropes many oon;
For which so sore agast was Emelye,
That she was wel ny mad, and gan to crye,
For she ne wiste what it signifyed;
But only for the fere thus hath she cryed,
And weep, that it was pitee for to here.
And ther-with-al Diane gan appere,
With bowe in hond, right as an hunteresse,
And seyde: 'Doghter, stint thyn hevinesse.
Among the goddes hye it is affermed,
And by eterne word write and confermed,

NO FEAR

When Emily finished her prayer, she saw something very strange. One of the two fires burning on the altar flicked, went out, then sparked back to life. Then other fire did the same thing and snapped back to life, just like wet branches do when they burn. This scared Emily so much that she screamed and started crying because she didn't know what was going on. She was so frightened that the goddess Diana, dressed as a hunter and with her bow in hand, appeared before Emily and said, "Stop crying, my child. The gods in the heavens have already decided that you're going to marry either Arcite or Palamon, both of whom have suffered so much pain because of you. I'm sorry, but I'm not allowed to tell you which of them it will be. I'm also sorry that I can't stay, but pay attention to the fires burning on the altar because they will tell you what the future holds if you interpret the signs correctly. And with a bang, Diana disappeared again. Emily was so shocked by what had just happened that she said, "God, what does this all mean? Diana, I give myself over to you. Do with me as you see fit." And when she was done, she returned back to the palace.

Thou shalt ben wedded unto oon of tho
That han for thee so muchel care and wo;
But unto which of hem I may nat telle.
Farwel, for I ne may no lenger dwelle.
The fyres which that on myn auter brenne
Shul thee declaren, er that thou go henne,
Thyn aventure of love, as in this cas.'
1500   And with that word, the arwes in the cas
Of the goddesse clateren faste and ringe,
And forth she wente, and made a vanisshinge;
For which this Emelye astoned was,
And seyde, 'What amounteth this, allas!
I putte me in thy proteccioun,
Diane, and in thy disposicioun.'
And hoom she gooth anon the nexte weye.
This is theffect, ther is namore to seye.

The nexte houre of Mars folwinge this,
1510   Arcite unto the temple walked is
Of fierse Mars, to doon his sacrifyse,
With alle the rytes of his payen wyse.
With pitous herte and heigh devocioun,
Right thus to Mars he seyde his orisoun:

'O strange god, that in the regnes colde
Of Trace honoured art, and lord y-holde,
And hast in every regne and every lond
Of armes al the brydel in thyn hond,
And hem fortunest as thee list devyse,
1520   Accept of me my pitous sacrifyse.
If so be that my youthe may deserve,
And that my might be worthy for to serve
Thy godhede, that I may been oon of thyne,
Than preye I thee to rewe upon my pyne.
For thilke peyne, and thilke hote fyr,
In which thou whylom brendest for desyr,
Whan that thou usedest the grete beautee
Of fayre yonge fresshe Venus free,

NO FEAR

509-1514   Soon after this, Arcite went to the stadium to offer sacrifices at the temple of Mars, the god of war. With genuine devotion, he prayed:

1515-1562   "Oh Mars, patron of Thrace and god of all war throughout the entire world, please accept my humble sacrifice. If I am strong enough and not too young to receive your blessing and be one of your devoted followers, I ask you to have mercy on me. I have suffered for my desire for a beautiful woman, just as you once suffered for Venus when you slept with her (even though you were caught by Vulcan, her husband). Remember how you felt then and then think of me, who suffers just as much. You know as well as I do that I'm young and naïve, just as you were, but I'm suffering love's pains more than anyone has ever suffered before. The woman whom I love makes me suffer like this, not caring what happens to me. I know that I have to win her if I'm ever to have her, and in order to do that, I'll need some help because I'm not strong enough to do it on my own. Mars, remember the love you once felt for Venus and help me tomorrow

And haddest hir in armes at thy wille,
1530   Al-though thee ones on a tyme misfille
Whan Vulcanus had caught thee in his las,
And fond thee ligging by his wyf, allas!
For thilke sorwe that was in thyn herte,
Have routhe as wel upon my peynes smerte.
I am yong and unkonning, as thou wost,
And, as I trowe, with love offended most,
That ever was any lyves creature;
For she, that dooth me al this wo endure,
Ne reccheth never wher I sinke or flete.
1540   And wel I woot, er she me mercy hete,
I moot with strengthe winne hir in the place;
And wel I woot, withouten help or grace
Of thee, ne may my strengthe noght availle.
Than help me, lord, to-morwe in my bataille,
For thilke fyr that whylom brente thee,
As wel as thilke fyr now brenneth me;
And do that I to-morwe have victorie.
Myn be the travaille, and thyn be the glorie!
Thy soverein temple wol I most honouren
1550   Of any place, and alwey most labouren
In thy plesaunce and in thy craftes stronge,
And in thy temple I wol my baner honge,
And alle the armes of my companye;
And evere-mo, unto that day I dye,
Eterne fyr I wol biforn thee finde.
And eek to this avow I wol me binde:
My berd, myn heer that hongeth long adoun,
That never yet ne felte offensioun
Of rasour nor of shere, I wol thee yive,
1560   And ben thy trewe servant whyl I live.
Now lord, have routhe upon my sorwes sore,
Yif me victorie, I aske thee namore.'

The preyere stinte of Arcita the stronge,
The ringes on the temple-dore that honge,
And eek the dores, clatereden ful faste,

in battle. For this I will be forever indebted to you and will pray to you more than any other god and wage war to please you and burn a fire at your alter from now until the day I die. This I promise you with my whole heart. I swear I'll even chop off my beard and hair— neither of which has ever been cut—for you. I'll be your devoted servant as long as I'm alive and will never ask anything else of you ever again."

563-1579   When Arcite had finished saying his prayer, the doors to the temple slammed shut with a bang all by themselves. The altar fires grew stronger so that they lit up the whole temple, while a sweet fra-

Of which Arcita som-what him agaste.
The fyres brende upon the auter brighte,
That it gan al the temple for to lighte;
And swete smel the ground anon up-yaf,
1570 And Arcita anon his hand up-haf,
And more encens in-to the fyr he caste,
With othere rytes mo; and atte laste
The statue of Mars bigan his hauberk ringe.
And with that soun he herde a murmuringe
Ful lowe and dim, that sayde thus, 'Victorie:'
For which he yaf to Mars honour and glorie.
And thus with Ioye, and hope wel to fare,
Arcite anon unto his inne is fare,
As fayn as fowel is of the brighte sonne.

1580 And right anon swich stryf ther is bigonne
For thilke graunting, in the hevene above,
Bitwixe Venus, the goddesse of love,
And Mars, the sterne god armipotente,
That Iupiter was bisy it to stente;
Til that the pale Saturnus the colde,
That knew so manye of aventures olde,
Fond in his olde experience an art,
That he ful sone hath plesed every part.
As sooth is sayd, elde hath greet avantage;
1590 In elde is bothe wisdom and usage;
Men may the olde at-renne, and noght at-rede.
Saturne anon, to stinten stryf and drede,
Al be it that it is agayn his kynde,
Of al this stryf he gan remedie fynde.

'My dere doghter Venus,' quod Saturne,
'My cours, that hath so wyde for to turne,
Hath more power than wot any man.
Myn is the drenching in the see so wan;
Myn is the prison in the derke cote;
1600 Myn is the strangling and hanging by the throte;
The murmure, and the cherles rebelling,

grance began wafting up from the floor. Frightened a little, Arcite threw more incense into the fires and began reciting prayers. And then suddenly the chain mail on the statue of Mars began to clank as a low voice murmured, "Victory." Grateful for the omen, Arcite said more prayers and made more sacrifices to Mars. And when he was finished, he left the temple, happy that Mars had heard his prayers.

1580-1594   Arcite may have been happy, but Venus was furious when she heard that Mars had promised his favored Theban warrior victory. She and Mars got into a big fight, which Jupiter tried unsuccessfully to resolve. Finally, old Saturn, who'd seen so many other squabbles between gods in his time, stepped in with a compromise that would make everyone happy. I guess it's true that we get wiser as we get older. Anyway, Saturn turned to them both, and said:

1595-1620   "My dear daughter Venus, my planetary orbit is wide and gives me more power over men and the course of human events than anyone really knows. I am the waves that drown you in the ocean, the darkness that imprisons you with fear, the noose around the condemned man's neck, the rebellion of the common folk, dissatisfaction and poison and disease and treason. I am vengeful and punishing when in the constellation Leo. I've brought down kingdoms and castle

The groyning, and the pryvee empoysoning:
I do vengeance and pleyn correccioun
Whyl I dwelle in the signe of the leoun.
Myn is the ruine of the hye halles,
The falling of the toures and of the walles
Upon the mynour or the carpenter.
I slow Sampsoun in shaking the piler;
And myne be the maladyes colde,
1610   The derke tresons, and the castes olde;
My loking is the fader of pestilence.
Now weep namore, I shal doon diligence
That Palamon, that is thyn owne knight,
Shal have his lady, as thou hast him hight.
Though Mars shal helpe his knight, yet nathelees
Bitwixe yow ther moot be som tyme pees,
Al be ye noght of o complexioun,
That causeth al day swich divisioun.
I am thin ayel, redy at thy wille;
1620   Weep thou namore, I wol thy lust fulfille.'

Now wol I stinten of the goddes above,
Of Mars, and of Venus, goddesse of love,
And telle yow, as pleynly as I can,
The grete effect, for which that I bigan.

EXPLICIT TERCIA PARS

walls. I killed Samson when I created the earthquake that brought the pillar down. My gaze can even infect people with the plague all by itself. Now please stop crying, Venus. I'll make sure that Palamon wins the woman he loves, just as you promised him. Even if Mars is going to help Arcite and even if you don't see eye to eye, you two still shouldn't fight anymore. Listen to me, and I'll make sure you get what you want."

1621-1624   Well, now I'm going to stop talking about Mars and Venus and the gods in the heavens, and I'll tell you all about the most important and exciting part of the story, which is why I wanted to tell you this story in the first place.

END OF PART THREE

The Knight's Tale, Part Four

SEQUITUR PARS QUARTA.

Greet was the feste in Athenes that day,
And eek the lusty seson of that May
Made every wight to been in swich plesaunce,
That al that Monday Iusten they and daunce,
And spenden it in Venus heigh servyse.
1630 But by the cause that they sholde ryse
Erly, for to seen the grete fight,
Unto hir reste wente they at night.
And on the morwe, whan that day gan springe,
Of hors and harneys, noyse and clateringe
Ther was in hostelryes al aboute;
And to the paleys rood ther many a route
Of lordes, upon stedes and palfreys.
Ther maystow seen devysing of herneys
So uncouth and so riche, and wroght so weel
1640 Of goldsmithrie, of browding, and of steel;
The sheeldes brighte, testers, and trappures;
Gold-hewen helmes, hauberks, cote-armures;
Lordes in paraments on hir courseres,
Knightes of retenue, and eek squyeres
Nailinge the speres, and helmes bokelinge,
Gigginge of sheeldes, with layneres lacinge;
Ther as need is, they weren no-thing ydel;
The fomy stedes on the golden brydel
Gnawinge, and faste the armurers also
1650 With fyle and hamer prikinge to and fro;
Yemen on fote, and communes many oon
With shorte staves, thikke as they may goon;
Pypes, trompes, nakers, clariounes,
That in the bataille blowen blody sounes;
The paleys ful of peples up and doun,
Heer three, ther ten, holding hir questioun,
Divyninge of thise Thebane knightes two.
Somme seyden thus, somme seyde it shal be so;

The Knight's Tale, Part Four

HERE'S THE FOURTH PART OF THE KNIGHT'S TALE.

625-1664 Well, there was a magnificent festival on Monday to celebrate the beginning of the tournament and the arrival of spring. All of Athens danced and jousted and feasted that day. And when night fell, everyone went to bed early so that they could get up early on Tuesday morning to watch the tournament. By sunrise the next morning, the whole city was already up and about. The noise was tremendous as knights rode to and fro, horses stamped their feet, and blacksmiths fine-tuned weapons and armor. You could see all sorts of interesting armor, helmets, chain mail, shields, swords, spears, and other weapons lying about, some of them very fancy and expensive, others just plain bizarre. Squires, servants, and other men were running here and there as they gathered their knights' weapons and gear, while the horses chomped at their bits, anxious from all the commotion. The commonfolk crowded in with every kind of noisemaker you can imagine, from trumpets and horns to drums and pipes and pots. And, of course, everyone was talking about Arcite and Palamon, and which of them would win. Some people said Palamon didn't stand a chance, while others thought that Arcite wouldn't live to see tomorrow. Others favored the knight with the black beard, or the one with the bald head, or the one with bushy hair. You could hear people saying things such as, "Well, that guy has a mace that weighs a good twenty pounds, so he's sure to win."

Somme helden with him with the blake berd,
1660   Somme with the balled, somme with the thikke-herd;
Somme sayde, he loked grim and he wolde fighte;
He hath a sparth of twenty pound of wighte.
Thus was the halle ful of divyninge,
Longe after that the sonne gan to springe.

The grete Theseus, that of his sleep awaked
With minstralcye and noyse that was maked,
Held yet the chambre of his paleys riche,
Til that the Thebane knightes, bothe y-liche
Honoured, were into the paleys fet.
1670   Duk Theseus was at a window set,
Arrayed right as he were a god in trone.
The peple preesseth thider-ward ful sone
Him for to seen, and doon heigh reverence,
And eek to herkne his hest and his sentence.

An heraud on a scaffold made an ho,
Til al the noyse of the peple was y-do;
And whan he saugh the peple of noyse al stille,
Tho showed he the mighty dukes wille.

'The lord hath of his heigh discrecioun
1680   Considered, that it were destruccioun
To gentil blood, to fighten in the gyse
Of mortal bataille now in this empryse;
Wherfore, to shapen that they shul not dye,
He wol his firste purpos modifye.
No man therfor, up peyne of los of lyf,
No maner shot, ne pollax, ne short knyf
Into the listes sende, or thider bringe;
Ne short swerd for to stoke, with poynt bytinge,
No man ne drawe, ne bere it by his syde.
1690   Ne no man shal unto his felawe ryde
But o cours, with a sharp y-grounde spere;
Foyne, if him list, on fote, him-self to were.
And he that is at meschief, shal be take,

NO FEAR

65-1674 All that noise and clatter from the streets below woke up Theseus, who decided to remain inside his bedroom in the palace until Arcite and Palamon arrived at the palace to begin the tournament. He sat on a chair that looked out a window upon the chaotic scene below as if he were one of the gods on high sitting in his throne. The crowds surged forward beneath his window so that people could get a look at him and pay their respects, and to hear the announcement that he was about to make.

75-1678 When the time was right, a palace servant shouted, "Listen, listen, everyone!" to shush the crowd. When everyone had quieted down, he said:

79-1702 "Our lord, Theseus, has been thinking things over and has come to the conclusion that it would be an awful waste if so many honorable knights died in the tournament today. Therefore, he's decided to change the terms of the original agreement he struck between Palamon and Arcite by declaring that the participants can't kill each other in the fight. That means knights are only allowed to bring non-lethal weapons with them, such as broad swords and maces. Deadly weapons, including short swords made for stabbing, battleaxes, daggers, or arrows are prohibited. And knights can use their spears only one time against each opponent so as not to kill them when they're down. The official referees, meanwhile, will take fallen knights—by force, if it comes to that—to their respective penalty boxes, where they'll wait out the rest of the tournament. If either Arcite or Palamon is taken to a penalty box, however, then the tournament will be finished immediately. Now, fight hard, good luck, and God be with you."

And noght slayn, but be broght unto the stake
That shal ben ordeyned on either syde;
But thider he shal by force, and ther abyde.
And if so falle, the chieftayn be take
On either syde, or elles slee his make,
No lenger shal the turneyinge laste.

1700 God spede yow; goth forth, and ley on faste.
With long swerd and with maces fight your fille.
Goth now your wey; this is the lordes wille.'

The voys of peple touchede the hevene,
So loude cryden they with mery stevene:
'God save swich a lord, that is so good,
He wilneth no destruccioun of blood!'
Up goon the trompes and the melodye.
And to the listes rit the companye
By ordinaunce, thurgh-out the citee large,

1710 Hanged with cloth of gold, and nat with sarge.

Ful lyk a lord this noble duk gan ryde,
Thise two Thebanes upon either syde;
And after rood the quene, and Emelye,
And after that another companye
Of oon and other, after hir degree.
And thus they passen thurgh-out the citee,
And to the listes come they by tyme.
It nas not of the day yet fully pryme,
Whan set was Theseus ful riche and hye,

1720 Ipolita the quene and Emelye,
And other ladies in degrees aboute.
Unto the seetes preesseth al the route.
And west-ward, thurgh the gates under Marte,
Arcite, and eek the hundred of his parte,
With baner reed is entred right anon;
And in that selve moment Palamon
Is under Venus, est-ward in the place,
With baner whyt, and hardy chere and face.
In al the world, to seken up and doun,

03-1710 The crowd below shouted for joy at hearing that no one would die in the tournament. People said things such as, "God bless Theseus, who's so wise and kind!" Then the trumpets and the music began, which signaled the beginning of the parade of knights marching through the banner-filled city toward the stadium.

11-1736 Theseus rode in the parade looking very noble. Palamon and Arcite rode next to him, one on either side. Behind him rode Queen Hippolyta and then her sister Emily, followed by a large group of noble Athenians. They rode all the way through Athens until they arrived at the stadium Theseus had constructed for just this occasion just before nine in the morning. After Theseus, Hippolyta, Emily, and other noble ladies had seated themselves in the seats with the best views, the crowd surged forward and rushed to find their seats. Then Arcite and his hundred knights flying a red flag strode into the stadium through the western gate of Mars, while Palamon and his hundred knights simultaneously entered through the eastern gate of Venus flying a white flag. The knights formed single-file lines on each side of the stadium. Both sides were so equally matched in honor, nobility, age, and skill that no one could really say which side would win.

1730   So even with-outen variacioun,
       Ther nere swiche companyes tweye.
       For ther nas noon so wys that coude seye,
       That any hadde of other avauntage
       Of worthinesse, ne of estaat, ne age,
       So even were they chosen, for to gesse.
       And in two renges faire they hem dresse.

       Whan that hir names rad were everichoon,
       That in hir nombre gyle were ther noon,
       Tho were the gates shet, and cryed was loude:
1740   'Do now your devoir, yonge knightes proude!'

       The heraudes lefte hir priking up and doun;
       Now ringen trompes loude and clarioun;
       Ther is namore to seyn, but west and est
       In goon the speres ful sadly in arest;
       In goth the sharpe spore in-to the syde.
       Ther seen men who can Iuste, and who can ryde;
       Ther shiveren shaftes upon sheeldes thikke;
       He feleth thurgh the herte-spoon the prikke.
       Up springen speres twenty foot on highte;
1750   Out goon the swerdes as the silver brighte.
       The helmes they to-hewen and to-shrede;
       Out brest the blood, with sterne stremes rede.
       With mighty maces the bones they to-breste.
       He thurgh the thikkeste of the throng gan threste.
       Ther stomblen stedes stronge, and doun goth al.
       He rolleth under foot as dooth a bal.
       He foyneth on his feet with his tronchoun,
       And he him hurtleth with his hors adoun.
       He thurgh the body is hurt, and sithen y-take,
1760   Maugree his heed, and broght unto the stake,
       As forward was, right ther he moste abyde;
       Another lad is on that other syde.

       And som tyme dooth hem Theseus to reste,
       Hem to refresshe, and drinken if hem leste.

NO FEAR

737-1740 After each knight's name had been read aloud—so that everyone knew that both sides had a hundred men each—the gates to the stadium grounds were closed, and the announcer said, "Let the battle begin!"

741-1762 And with that, the trumpets blared, and the battle began! Knights galloped on their horses left and right, spears went flying into the air and clattering against the shields as they flew back down. You could hear the sounds of metal clashing against metal and the sound of crunching bones. You could see the glimmer of the steel as swords swung to and fro, bits of metal flying everywhere, and red blood spurting into the air. Men fell down and horses rolled to the ground in a heap as if they were standing on balls instead of the earth. One knight shoves another's spear away with his foot. Another is wounded in the abdomen and pulled away by the referees to the penalty box as he struggles to get back into the fight. They all know the rules, but none of them wants to give up so easily.

763-1777 Every now and then Theseus calls for a break so that the knights still fighting can rest and get something to drink if they want. Arcite and

Ful ofte a-day han thise Thebanes two
Togidre y-met, and wroght his felawe wo;
Unhorsed hath ech other of hem tweye.
Ther nas no tygre in the vale of Galgopheye,
Whan that hir whelp is stole, whan it is lyte,
1770   So cruel on the hunte, as is Arcite
For Ielous herte upon this Palamoun:
Ne in Belmarye ther nis so fel leoun,
That hunted is, or for his hunger wood,
Ne of his praye desireth so the blood,
As Palamon to sleen his fo Arcite.
The Ielous strokes on hir helmes byte;
Out renneth blood on bothe hir sydes rede.

Som tyme an ende ther is of every dede;
For er the sonne unto the reste wente,
1780   The stronge king Emetreus gan hente
This Palamon, as he faught with Arcite,
And made his swerd depe in his flesh to byte;
And by the force of twenty is he take
Unyolden, and y-drawe unto the stake.
And in the rescous of this Palamoun
The stronge king Ligurge is born adoun;
And king Emetreus, for al his strengthe,
Is born out of his sadel a swerdes lengthe,
So hitte him Palamon er he were take;
1790   But al for noght, he was broght to the stake.
His hardy herte mighte him helpe naught;
He moste abyde, whan that he was caught
By force, and eek by composicioun.

Who sorweth now but woful Palamoun,
That moot namore goon agayn to fighte?
And whan that Theseus had seyn this sighte,
Unto the folk that foghten thus echoon
He cryde, 'Ho! namore, for it is doon!
I wol be trewe Iuge, and no partye.
1800   Arcite of Thebes shal have Emelye,

Palamon have found each other in the melee a few times, and both of them have wounded the other and knocked each other off their horses twice. Arcite's jealousy of Palamon makes him fight harder than a mother tiger looking after her threatened cubs, while Palamon's desire to kill Arcite makes him more ferocious than the hungriest lion. Both are after blood, which streams down both their faces.

778-1793   Well, you know what they say: Everything eventually comes to an end. Before sunset, King Emetreus of India slashed Palamon so badly that the referees came out and dragged him away to a penalty box. Palamon knew that he'd lose Emily if he left the battle, so he fought off the referees as hard as he could—in fact, it took twenty of them to pull him off the field. The referees knocked down King Lycurgas from Thrace in their struggle to grab Palamon, who also managed to knock Emetreus off his horse and slug him as he was being dragged in the dirt. None of it made any difference, though, not even the burning in his heart because the referees managed to drag him to the penalty box.

794-1804   No one has ever been sadder than Palamon, who knew he'd lost the fight—and Emily—forever. When Theseus saw Palamon enter the penalty box, he looked at the knights still fighting below, and shouted, "Stop! Stop immediately! The tournament is over! I have been an unbiased judge in this contest, and Arcite has won. Therefore, Emily will mary Arcite, knight of Thebes, because he has won the tournament fairly." The crowd shouted and cheered so loudly that it seemed the stadium itself would collapse.

That by his fortune hath hir faire y-wonne.'
Anon ther is a noyse of peple bigonne
For Ioye of this, so loude and heigh with-alle,
It semed that the listes sholde falle.

What can now faire Venus doon above?
What seith she now? what dooth this quene of love?
But wepeth so, for wanting of hir wille,
Til that hir teres in the listes fille;
She seyde: 'I am ashamed, doutelees.'
1810 Saturnus seyde: 'Doghter, hold thy pees.
Mars hath his wille, his knight hath al his bone,
And, by myn heed, thou shalt ben esed sone.'
The trompes, with the loude minstralcye,
The heraudes, that ful loude yolle and crye,
Been in hir wele for Ioye of daun Arcite.
But herkneth me, and stinteth now a lyte,
Which a miracle ther bifel anon.

This fierse Arcite hath of his helm y-don,
And on a courser, for to shewe his face,
1820 He priketh endelong the large place,
Loking upward upon this Emelye;
And she agayn him caste a freendlich yë,
(For wommen, as to speken in comune,
They folwen al the favour of fortune),
And she was al his chere, as in his herte.
Out of the ground a furie infernal sterte,
From Pluto sent, at requeste of Saturne,
For which his hors for fere gan to turne,
And leep asyde, and foundred as he leep;
1830 And, er that Arcite may taken keep,
He pighte him on the pomel of his heed,
That in the place he lay as he were deed,
His brest to-brosten with his sadel-bowe.
As blak he lay as any cole or crowe,
So was the blood y-ronnen in his face.
Anon he was y-born out of the place

NO FEAR

305-1817 And what did Venus, the goddess of love, have to say about this as she watched the tournament from the heavens? She cried bitterly because Palamon had lost and she hadn't gotten her way. She cried so hard, in fact, that her tears rained down on the crowd in the stadium below. She said, "I am so ashamed that Palamon and I have lost." The god Saturn said, "Stop crying, Venus. Mars and his knight Arcite have won this battle, but I promise you that you'll feel better soon enough. Everyone is cheering in celebration of Arcite's victory, but take my advice and don't be too sad just yet."

818-1841 The victorious Arcite, meanwhile, had ripped off his helmet to show his face to Emily as he galloped across the batteflied. Emily looked down on him with admiration (because women, generally speaking, always favor the winners), which filled his heart with happiness. Suddenly, an earthquake caused by Saturn shook the ground, which caused Arcite's horse to trip and collapse. Before he had time to react, Arcite slammed into the horn of his saddle, breaking his sternum. He then flew forward so violently that he lay still on the ground just as if he were dead, his face covered completely in blood. Theseus's men immediately took Arcite to the palace, where they cut off his armor and put him to bed. He was barely alive, but conscious, and cried out continually for Emily.

With herte soor, to Theseus paleys.
Tho was he corven out of his harneys,
And in a bed y-brought ful faire and blyve,
1840   For he was yet in memorie and alyve,
And alway crying after Emelye.

Duk Theseus, with al his companye,
Is comen hoom to Athenes his citee,
With alle blisse and greet solempnitee.
Al be it that this aventure was falle,
He nolde noght disconforten hem alle.
Men seyde eek, that Arcite shal nat dye;
He shal ben heled of his maladye.
And of another thing they were as fayn,
1850   That of hem alle was ther noon y-slayn,
Al were they sore y-hurt, and namely oon,
That with a spere was thirled his brest-boon.
To othere woundes, and to broken armes,
Some hadden salves, and some hadden charmes;
Fermacies of herbes, and eek save
They dronken, for they wolde hir limes have.
For which this noble duk, as he wel can,
Conforteth and honoureth every man,
And made revel al the longe night,
1860   Unto the straunge lordes, as was right.
Ne ther was holden no disconfitinge,
But as a Iustes or a tourneyinge;
For soothly ther was no disconfiture,
For falling nis nat but an aventure;
Ne to be lad with fors unto the stake
Unyolden, and with twenty knightes take,
O persone allone, with-outen mo,
And haried forth by arme, foot, and to,
And eek his stede driven forth with staves,
1870   With footmen, bothe yemen and eek knaves,
It nas aretted him no vileinye,
Ther may no man clepen it cowardye.

842-1872 Duke Theseus returned home to Athens amidst the cheering and celebrating throngs of happy Athenians. He didn't say anything about Arcite's accident because he didn't want to darken the cheerful mood. Besides, his servants had told him that Arcite's wounds weren't serious and that he would live. The people were especially happy that none of the knights in the tournament had died, even though a few had been badly injured, one guy in particular whose chest had been punctured by a spear. Others had suffered from bruises and broken bones, but they were being treated with ointments and herbal medicines, prayers, and all sorts of other treatments. Theseus personally visted and congratulated every wounded knight, and hosted a magnificent banquet for all the foreign dignitaries as was the custom. Everyone could celebrate because there were no real losers in this tournament since everyone had lived. Even those who'd been wounded were still winners because they'd all fought tooth and nail to remain in the battle and not be dragged to the penalty box. Not even Palamon's defeat was considered cowardly or dishonorable since he'd fought harder than anyone to remain in the fight.

For which anon duk Theseus leet crye,
To stinten alle rancour and envye,
The gree as wel of o syde as of other,
And either syde y-lyk, as otheres brother;
And yaf hem yiftes after hir degree,
And fully heeld a feste dayes three;
And conveyed the kinges worthily
1880 Out of his toun a Iournee largely.
And hoom wente every man the righte way.
Ther was namore, but 'far wel, have good day!'
Of this bataille I wol namore endyte,
But speke of Palamon and of Arcite.

Swelleth the brest of Arcite, and the sore
Encreesseth at his herte more and more.
The clothered blood, for any lechecraft,
Corrupteth, and is in his bouk y-laft,
That neither veyne-blood, ne ventusinge,
1890 Ne drinke of herbes may ben his helpinge.
The vertu expulsif, or animal,
Fro thilke vertu cleped natural
Ne may the venim voyden, ne expelle.
The pypes of his longes gonne to swelle,
And every lacerte in his brest adoun
Is shent with venim and corrupcioun.
Him gayneth neither, for to gete his lyf,
Vomyt upward, ne dounward laxatif;
Al is to-brosten thilke regioun,
1900 Nature hath now no dominacioun.
And certeinly, ther nature wol nat wirche,
Far-wel, phisyk! go ber the man to chirche!
This al and som, that Arcita mot dye,
For which he sendeth after Emelye,
And Palamon, that was his cosin dere;
Than seyde he thus, as ye shul after here.

'Naught may the woful spirit in myn herte
Declare o poynt of alle my sorwes smerte

NO FEAR

To make sure that everyone attending the festivities felt good about the results of the tournament, Theseus announced that both sides had fought honorably and had won the tournament. Then he gave gifts to all the participants on both sides and invited them to a feast that lasted for three days. And when it was time to leave, he helped pay for the journey home for all the visiting kings. And that's how the tournament ended, with warm goodbyes and farewells.

Even though Theseus's servants had told him that Arcite would live, poor Arcite was actually getting worse. His chest swelled up with blood from his wound, which caused more and more pain. Theseus's doctors tried everything they could think of to save him, but they couldn't stop the internal bleeding or prevent the blood poisoning. None of their medicines would work, not the ones that made him throw up or the ones that gave him diarrhea. His breathing soon became affected from all the blood in his chest—his whole upper body was a complete mess. To put it simply, Arcite was dying, and there was nothing anyone could do to save him. Arcite, still awake, asked to see Emily and his dear cousin Palamon so that he could talk to them both before he died. When they arrived, he said:

"I can't tell you how sad I am, my Emily, my love. God, the hurt and the pain I felt because of you for so long… And now that I have you,

To yow, my lady, that I love most;
1910 But I biquethe the service of my gost
To yow aboven every creature,
Sin that my lyf may no lenger dure.
Allas, the wo! allas, the peynes stronge,
That I for yow have suffred, and so longe!
Allas, the deeth! allas, myn Emelye!
Allas, departing of our companye!
Allas, myn hertes quene! allas, my wyf!
Myn hertes lady, endere of my lyf!
What is this world? what asketh men to have?
1920 Now with his love, now in his colde grave
Allone, with-outen any companye.
Far-wel, my swete fo! myn Emelye!
And softe tak me in your armes tweye,
For love of God, and herkneth what I seye.

I have heer with my cosin Palamon
Had stryf and rancour, many a day a-gon,
For love of yow, and for my Ielousye.
And Iupiter so wis my soule gye,
To speken of a servant proprely,
1930 With alle circumstaunces trewely,
That is to seyn, trouthe, honour, and knighthede,
Wisdom, humblesse, estaat, and heigh kinrede,
Fredom, and al that longeth to that art,
So Iupiter have of my soule part,
As in this world right now ne knowe I non
So worthy to ben loved as Palamon,
That serveth yow, and wol don al his lyf.
And if that ever ye shul been a wyf,
Foryet nat Palamon, the gentil man.'

1940 And with that word his speche faille gan,
For from his feet up to his brest was come
The cold of deeth, that hadde him overcome.
And yet more-over, in his armes two
The vital strengthe is lost, and al ago.

I'm going to die and go away from you. Oh my beautiful Emily, my beautiful wife, love of my life! Why? Why does it have to be this way? What does a guy have to do to be happy? One moment he has everthing he's ever wanted, and then the next moment he's dead and alone. Goodbye, my Emily, who's caused so much joy and ache. Now, for the love of God, hold me in your arms and listen to what I'm about to tell you.

925-1939 "I've been fighting with my cousin Palamon over you for a long time, because of my love for you and because of my jealousy. Now, may Jupiter, who guides my soul so wisely, help me to articulate the fidelity, honor, knighthood, wisdom, humility, nobility, noble birth, generosity, and everything else that a worthy lover needs. Just as I hope Jupiter to bear my soul away to the next life, I know that Palamon deserves you more than anyone else alive, and will protect and look after her until the day he dies. If you're ever thinking of marrying again, my Emily, please consider Palamon.

1940-1958 And with those last words, Arcite began to lose his voice as death swept over him from the tip of his toes to the top of his head. He lost strength throughout his entire body until all that was left was his consciousness—and even that too failed when his heart finally stopped beating. The light began to leave his eyes and his breath

Only the intellect, with-outen more,
That dwelled in his herte syk and sore,
Gan faillen, when the herte felte deeth,
Dusked his eyen two, and failled breeth.
But on his lady yet caste he his yē;
1950   His laste word was, 'mercy, Emelye!'
His spirit chaunged hous, and wente ther,
As I cam never, I can nat tellen wher.
Therfor I stinte, I nam no divinistre;
Of soules finde I nat in this registre,
Ne me ne list thilke opiniouns to telle
Of hem, though that they wryten wher they dwelle.
Arcite is cold, ther Mars his soule gye;
Now wol I speken forth of Emelye.

Shrighte Emelye, and howleth Palamon,
1960   And Theseus his suster took anon
Swowninge, and bar hir fro the corps away.
What helpeth it to tarien forth the day,
To tellen how she weep, bothe eve and morwe?
For in swich cas wommen have swich sorwe,
Whan that hir housbonds been from hem ago,
That for the more part they sorwen so,
Or elles fallen in swich maladye,
That at the laste certeinly they dye.

Infinite been the sorwes and the teres
1970   Of olde folk, and folk of tendre yeres,
In al the toun, for deeth of this Theban;
For him ther wepeth bothe child and man;
So greet a weping was ther noon, certayn,
Whan Ector was y-broght, al fresh y-slayn,
To Troye; allas! the pitee that was ther,
Cracching of chekes, rending eek of heer.
'Why woldestow be deed,' thise wommen crye,
'And haddest gold y-nough, and Emelye?'
No man mighte gladen Theseus,
1980   Savinge his olde fader Egeus,

became shallow in the final moments, but he looked toward Emily and managed to speak one last time: "Mercy, Emily." And then his soul left his body to a place I'ver never been before and can't really tell you much about. I'm no priest, so I'm not going to waste our time philosophizing about the meaning of death. Arcite died, and Mars, the god of war, took care of his soul.

1959-1968   Emily screamed as Arcite passed, while Palamon howled. Theseus took Emily in his arms and pulled her away from Arcite's body. It wouldn't be any use for me to tell you how she pined for him all day and all night because you know how it is when women lose their husbands—they mourn and grieve or else wither away and die from sadness.

1969-1984   The entire city of Athens cried over Arcite's death—men, women, children, old people, everyone. The people of the ancient city of Troy didn't even cry as much when the Greek warrior Achilles killed Hector, their chosen son. The Athenians scratched their cheeks and pulled their hair as they grieved, asking each other such questions as, "Why did he have to die? He was so noble and had just won Emily!" Even Theseus was glum, and no one could cheer him up at all except for his aging father Aegeus, who was wise enough to know that both pleasure and pain comes and goes with the passing of time. He tried to brighten Theseus's mood by saying:

That knew this worldes transmutacioun,
As he had seyn it chaungen up and doun,
Ioye after wo, and wo after gladnesse:
And shewed hem ensamples and lyknesse.

'Right as ther deyed never man,' quod he,
'That he ne livede in erthe in som degree,
Right so ther livede never man,' he seyde,
'In al this world, that som tyme he ne deyde.
This world nis but a thurghfare ful of wo,
1990   And we ben pilgrimes, passinge to and fro;
Deeth is an ende of every worldly sore.'
And over al this yet seyde he muchel more
To this effect, ful wysly to enhorte
The peple, that they sholde hem reconforte.

Duk Theseus, with al his bisy cure,
Caste now wher that the sepulture
Of good Arcite may best y-maked be,
And eek most honurable in his degree.
And at the laste he took conclusioun,
2000   That ther as first Arcite and Palamoun
Hadden for love the bataille hem bitwene,
That in that selve grove, swote and grene,
Ther as he hadde his amorous desires,
His compleynt, and for love his hote fires,
He wolde make a fyr, in which thoffice
Funeral he mighte al accomplice;
And leet comaunde anon to hakke and hewe
The okes olde, and leye hem on a rewe
In colpons wel arrayed for to brenne;
2010   His officers with swifte feet they renne
And ryde anon at his comaundement.
And after this, Theseus hath y-sent
After a bere, and it al over-spradde
With cloth of gold, the richest that he hadde.
And of the same suyte he cladde Arcite;
Upon his hondes hadde he gloves whyte;

NO FEAR

"No man can die if he never was born to live life on this earth, and nobody can live on this earth without having to die someday. Life is a highway filled with pain and sadness, and we're travelers on that highway, going back and forth. Death is merely the final destination of many painful journeys." He said lots of things like this in order to help make Theseus and the people feel better.

Theseus then made the arrangements for a suitable funeral that would honor the noble Arcite. He put a lot of thought into all the details of the funeral and ultimately decided that he would hold the ceremony in the grove where he'd first seen Arcite and Palamon dueling exactly a year ago. Theseus instructed his men to cut down several of the largest oak trees in the grove and lay them next to each other in the clearing in order to make a funeral pyre. He then bought a coffin to the grove, which he draped with the best golden clothes that he owned. He also made sure that his men dressed the body of Arcite in the finest clothing, including white gloves, a crown made of laurel, and a brand new sword. Theseus kept the coffin open and placed it inside the hall of his palace so that the people could see his body, mourn, and pay their respects. Theseus himself cried bitterly over Arcite's body.

Eek on his heed a croune of laurer grene,
And in his hond a swerd ful bright and kene.
He leyde him bare the visage on the bere,
2020   Therwith he weep that pitee was to here.
And for the peple sholde seen him alle,
Whan it was day, he broghte him to the halle,
That roreth of the crying and the soun.

Tho cam this woful Theban Palamoun,
With flotery berd, and ruggy asshy heres,
In clothes blake, y-dropped al with teres;
And, passing othere of weping, Emelye,
The rewfulleste of al the companye.
In as muche as the service sholde be
2030   The more noble and riche in his degree,
Duk Theseus leet forth three stedes bringe,
That trapped were in steel al gliteringe,
And covered with the armes of daun Arcite.
Upon thise stedes, that weren grete and whyte,
Ther seten folk, of which oon bar his sheeld,
Another his spere up in his hondes heeld;
The thridde bar with him his bowe Turkeys,
Of brend gold was the cas, and eek the harneys;
And riden forth a pas with sorweful chere
2040   Toward the grove, as ye shul after here.
The nobleste of the Grekes that ther were
Upon hir shuldres carieden the bere,
With slakke pas, and eyen rede and wete,
Thurgh-out the citee, by the maister-strete,
That sprad was al with blak, and wonder hye
Right of the same is al the strete y-wrye.
Upon the right hond wente old Egeus,
And on that other syde duk Theseus,
With vessels in hir hand of gold ful fyn,
2050   Al ful of hony, milk, and blood, and wyn;
Eek Palamon, with ful greet companye;
And after that cam woful Emelye,

NO FEAR

After Theseus came Palamon, dressed all in black, his hair and beard matted and tangled from crying. Emily followed him, and cried more than anyone else there. Three white horses arrived with shiny steel bridles and draped in cloth bearing Arcite's coat of arms. Theseus had ordered these to pay special tribute to Arcite. On one horse sat a man who carried Arcite's shield, while another man on the second horse carried his spear. The third rider carried Arcite's golden bow and arrows, which had been made far away in Turkey. They led the funeral proession at a slow and steady pace toward the grove. The most noble of the Athenians carried Arcite's body on their shoulders through Athens, which the people had draped in black cloth to express their sadness. Theseus's father, Aegeus, walked to the right of Arcite's body, while Theseus walked on the left and carried golden vessels filled with honey, milk, blood, and wine. Palamon followed close behind, as did Emily, who carried a burning torch in her hand, which was how they did things back then.

With fyr in honde, as was that tyme the gyse,
To do thoffice of funeral servyse.

Heigh labour, and ful greet apparaillinge
Was at the service and the fyr-makinge,
That with his grene top the heven raughte,
And twenty fadme of brede the armes straughte;
This is to seyn, the bowes were so brode.
2060 Of stree first ther was leyd ful many a lode.
But how the fyr was maked up on highte,
And eek the names how the treës highte,
As ook, firre, birch, asp, alder, holm, popler,
Wilow, elm, plane, ash, box, chasteyn, lind, laurer,
Mapul, thorn, beech, hasel, ew, whippeltree,
How they weren feld, shal nat be told for me;
Ne how the goddes ronnen up and doun,
Disherited of hir habitacioun,
In which they woneden in reste and pees,
2070 Nymphes, Faunes, and Amadrides;
Ne how the bestes and the briddes alle
Fledden for fere, whan the wode was falle;
Ne how the ground agast was of the light,
That was nat wont to seen the sonne bright;
Ne how the fyr was couched first with stree,
And than with drye stokkes cloven a three,
And than with grene wode and spycerye,
And than with cloth of gold and with perrye,
And gerlandes hanging with ful many a flour,
2080 The mirre, thencens, with al so greet odour;
Ne how Arcite lay among al this,
Ne what richesse aboute his body is;
Ne how that Emelye, as was the gyse,
Putte in the fyr of funeral servyse;
Ne how she swowned whan men made the fyr,
Ne what she spak, ne what was hir desyr;
Ne what Ieweles men in the fyr tho caste,
Whan that the fyr was greet and brente faste;
Ne how som caste hir sheeld, and som hir spere,

NO FEAR

055-2108 A lot of work had gone into making this funeral pyre. It was very tall and about 120 feet long because it was made out of such tall trees. Theseus's men had placed straw all over it to help make it light. I'm not going to go into all the details about exactly how it was built, though, or what other kinds of trees they used such as fir, birch, aspen, alder, poplar, willow, elm, plane, ash, chestnut, laurel, maple, thorn, beech, hazel, yew, dogwood, or talk about how all the magical forest creatures such as the fauns and the tree nymphs and birds and animals all ran away when their trees were cut down. I don't want to talk about how the plants on the forest floor were shocked to suddenly see the light of day when the trees above had been cut down, or how Emily first set fire to the straw, which then caught the smaller branches on fire, and then the bigger branches. I don't really want to go into how everyone sprinkled gold and jewels and spices and milk and honey and incense on Arcite's body. I'm not going to tell you how Emily fainted after the fire started, and what she said when she woke up, or how some knights tossed in weapons and bits of their armor to pay tribute. I don't want to talk about how the Athenians circled clockwise around the raging inferno three times as they shouted and made as much noise as they could or how the women howled out loud three times or how they played funeral sports and who won and who lost or that they were out there all night until the next morning when they finally went home. I'm also not going to mention how Arcite's body burned until there was nothing left but ashes. I'm just going to plow on and try to finish up this long story.

2090
And of hir vestiments, whiche that they were,
And cuppes ful of wyn, and milk, and blood,
Into the fyr, that brente as it were wood;
Ne how the Grekes with an huge route
Thryës riden al the fyr aboute
Upon the left hand, with a loud shoutinge,
And thryës with hir speres clateringe;
And thryës how the ladies gonne crye;
Ne how that lad was hom-ward Emelye;
Ne how Arcite is brent to asshen colde;
2100
Ne how that liche-wake was y-holde
Al thilke night, ne how the Grekes pleye
The wake-pleyes, ne kepe I nat to seye;
Who wrastleth best naked, with oille enoynt,
Ne who that bar him best, in no disioynt.
I wol nat tellen eek how that they goon
Hoom til Athenes, whan the pley is doon;
But shortly to the poynt than wol I wende,
And maken of my longe tale an ende.

By processe and by lengthe of certeyn yeres
2110
Al stinted is the moorning and the teres
Of Grekes, by oon general assent.
Than semed me ther was a parlement
At Athenes, upon certeyn poynts and cas;
Among the whiche poynts y-spoken was
To have with certeyn contrees alliaunce,
And have fully of Thebans obeisaunce.
For which this noble Theseus anon
Leet senden after gentil Palamon,
Unwist of him what was the cause and why;
2120
But in his blake clothes sorwefully
He cam at his comaundement in hye.
Tho sente Theseus for Emelye.
Whan they were set, and hust was al the place,
And Theseus abiden hadde a space
Er any word cam from his wyse brest,
His eyen sette he ther as was his lest,

109-2128   Well, several years passed, enough so that the most painful memories of Arcite's death had begun to pass too. And around this time it just so happened that the Athenian nobles had gotten together to talk about politics and affairs of state. They talked about the need to make new alliances, particularly an alliance with Thebes so that there wouldn't be war between the two kingdoms. An idea dawned on Theseus, and he immediately sent for Palamon to visit him in the palace. Palamon wasn't sure why Theseus had summoned him, but he went to Athens, still wearing black mourning clothes. Theseus also asked Emily to come see him. After both Palamon and Emily had arrived and had been quieting sitting with Theseus for awhile, Theseus sadly said:

And with a sad visage he syked stille,
And after that right thus he seyde his wille.

'The firste moevere of the cause above,
2130   Whan he first made the faire cheyne of love,
Greet was theffect, and heigh was his entente;
Wel wiste he why, and what ther-of he mente;
For with that faire cheyne of love he bond
The fyr, the eyr, the water, and the lond
In certeyn boundes, that they may nat flee;
That same prince and that moevere,' quod he,
'Hath stablissed, in this wrecched world adoun,
Certeyne dayes and duracioun
To al that is engendred in this place,
2140   Over the whiche day they may nat pace,
Al mowe they yet tho dayes wel abregge;
Ther needeth non auctoritee allegge,
For it is preved by experience,
But that me list declaren my sentence.
Than may men by this ordre wel discerne,
That thilke moevere stable is and eterne.
Wel may men knowe, but it be a fool,
That every part deryveth from his hool.
For nature hath nat take his beginning
2150   Of no partye ne cantel of a thing,
But of a thing that parfit is and stable,
Descending so, til it be corrumpable.
And therfore, of his wyse purveyaunce,
He hath so wel biset his ordinaunce,
That speces of thinges and progressiouns
Shullen enduren by successiouns,
And nat eterne be, with-oute lye:
This maistow understonde and seen at eye.

'Lo the ook, that hath so long a norisshinge
2160   From tyme that it first biginneth springe,
And hath so long a lyf, as we may see,
Yet at the laste wasted is the tree.

NO FEAR

129-2158   "The Maker first created the chain of love to bind the heavens and the earth together, the water and the fire and the air, and it was good. That same Maker, however, has put death and suffering in the world too, which place limitations on what we can and cannot do. You don't need to read books to teach you all this—experience alone does that. Well, the Maker is eternal, and anyone who pays attention can see that everything is part of something bigger because nature didn't come from nothing, you know. Ah, listen to me babble: What I'm trying to say is that something comes from everything, even the worst events.

159-2168   "Take, for example, that oak tree over there. See how tall and old it is—it's been a long time since it was just a little sapling. And yet, one day it'll be dead and gone. Or look at the rocks underneath our feet: It's hard and solid, but will someday no longer be part of the road

'Considereth eek, how that the harde stoon
Under our feet, on which we trede and goon,
Yit wasteth it, as it lyth by the weye.
The brode river somtyme wexeth dreye.
The grete tounes see we wane and wende.
Than may ye see that al this thing hath ende.

'Of man and womman seen we wel also,
2170   That nedeth, in oon of thise termes two,
This is to seyn, in youthe or elles age,
He moot ben deed, the king as shal a page;
Som in his bed, som in the depe see,
Som in the large feeld, as men may se;
Ther helpeth noght, al goth that ilke weye.
Thanne may I seyn that al this thing moot deye.
What maketh this but Iupiter the king?
The which is prince and cause of alle thing,
Converting al unto his propre welle,
2180   From which it is deryved, sooth to telle.
And here-agayns no creature on lyve
Of no degree availleth for to stryve.

'Thanne is it wisdom, as it thinketh me,
To maken vertu of necessitee,
And take it wel, that we may nat eschue,
And namely that to us alle is due.
And who-so gruccheth ought, he dooth folye,
And rebel is to him that al may gye.
And certeinly a man hath most honour
2190   To dyen in his excellence and flour,
Whan he is siker of his gode name;
Than hath he doon his freend, ne him, no shame.
And gladder oghte his freend ben of his deeth,
Whan with honour up-yolden is his breeth,
Than whan his name apalled is for age;
For al forgeten is his vasselage.
Than is it best, as for a worthy fame,
To dyen whan that he is best of name.

NO FEAR

we walk on. Rivers eventually dry up, great cities become towns and eventually ruins—everything has an end.

169-2182 "The same is true of people, whether they be men or women, young or old, king or commoner—everyone will die. Some will die in bed, others in war, some out in their fields. There really isn't anything any one can do about it because that's just the way it is. The god Jupiter decides that everything will return to the place from which it came no matter how hard you or I or anyone else tries to prevent it.

183-2198 "So, I've come to the conclusion that we just have to accept that death is inevitable. People who complain about it are just plain stupid and set themselves against the Maker who demands it. Besides, it's better for a person to die honorably and with dignity that to ruin one's good name foolishly trying to stop death. And this also means that the friends of those who have died need to do honor to their memory by not grieving forever until no one can remember whom they're grieving for in the first place.

The contrarie of al this is wilfulnesse.
2200   Why grucchen we? why have we hevinesse,
That good Arcite, of chivalrye flour
Departed is, with duetee and honour,
Out of this foule prison of this lyf?
Why grucchen heer his cosin and his wyf
Of his wel-fare that loved hem so weel?
Can he hem thank? nay, God wot, never a deel,
That bothe his soule and eek hem-self offende,
And yet they mowe hir lustes nat amende.

'What may I conclude of this longe serie,
2210   But, after wo, I rede us to be merie,
And thanken Iupiter of al his grace?
And, er that we departen from this place,
I rede that we make, of sorwes two,
O parfyt Ioye, lasting ever-mo;
And loketh now, wher most sorwe is her-inne,
Ther wol we first amenden and biginne.

'Suster,' quod he, 'this is my fulle assent,
With al thavys heer of my parlement,
That gentil Palamon, your owne knight,
2220   That serveth yow with wille, herte, and might,
And ever hath doon, sin that ye first him knewe,
That ye shul, of your grace, upon him rewe,
And taken him for housbonde and for lord:
Leen me your hond, for this is our acord.
Lat see now of your wommanly pitee.
He is a kinges brother sone, pardee;
And, though he were a povre bacheler,
Sin he hath served yow so many a yeer,
And had for yow so greet adversitee,
2230   It moste been considered, leveth me;
For gentil mercy oghte to passen right.'

Than seyde he thus to Palamon ful right;
'I trowe ther nedeth litel sermoning

199-2208 "To try and do anything else is just plain stubborn. We shouldn't whine and complain, and we shouldn't still be mourning for Arcite, that noble knight who left us honorably and escaped the burdens of this world. Why is it that his wife and his cousin are still mourning his passing so many years later? Can he thank them? No, he's dead and gone. Besides, they're sullying his memory by continuing to grieve for him.

209-2216 I've said pretty much everything there is to say about this matter except that we need to move on and thank Jupiter for what we have instead of being sorry for what we don't have. And before you two go, I suggest that we turn your two, solitary sorrows into a single joy that will last forever.

217-2231 "Emily, my sister-in-law," Theseus continued, "My advisors and I all agree that you would do well if you took Palamon here—a knight who's served you from afar so faithfully since the day he first laid eyes on you—to be your husband and lord. Put your hand in mine and make this agreement with me—show me how merciful women are by taking him as your husband. He is the nephew of the king of Thebes, but would be worthy of you even if he were a poor squire since he's doted on you—and definitely suffered for his love for you—for so many long years, and that's more noble than blood."

232-2250 Then Theseus turned to Palamon and said, "I suppose I don't have to say much to convince you to marry Emily. Come over here, and

To make yow assente to this thing.
Com neer, and tak your lady by the hond.'
Bitwixen hem was maad anon the bond,
That highte matrimoine or mariage,
By al the counseil and the baronage.
And thus with alle blisse and melodye
2240   Hath Palamon y-wedded Emelye.
And God, that al this wyde world hath wroght,
Sende him his love, that hath it dere a-boght.
For now is Palamon in alle wele,
Living in blisse, in richesse, and in hele;
And Emelye him loveth so tendrely,
And he hir serveth al-so gentilly,
That never was ther no word hem bitwene
Of Ielousye, or any other tene.
Thus endeth Palamon and Emelye;
2250   And God save al this faire companye!—Amen.

HERE IS ENDED THE KNIGHTES TALE.

take Emily by the hand." And then, in front of the entire Athenian council of nobles, Theseus married them so that they finally became husband and wife. And God, creator of the world, bless Palamon with happiness and health and success. And Emily loved him deeply and he loved her equally for the rest of their lives together, so much in fact that they never fought or suffered from jealousy or anything. And that's the story of how Palamon finally won Emily, his lady love. God bless them all—Amen.

THE END.

Prologue to the Miller's Tale

HERE FOLWEN THE WORDES BITWENE THE HOST AND
THE MILLERE.

Whan that the Knight had thus his tale y-told,
In al the route nas ther yong ne old
That he ne seyde it was a noble storie,
And worthy for to drawen to memorie;
And namely the gentils everichoon.
Our Hoste lough and swoor, 'so moot I goon,
This gooth aright; unbokeled is the male;
Lat see now who shal telle another tale:
For trewely, the game is wel bigonne.
10   Now telleth ye, sir Monk, if that ye conne,
Sumwhat, to quyte with the Knightes tale.'
The Miller, that for-dronken was al pale,
So that unnethe upon his hors he sat,
He nolde avalen neither hood ne hat,
Ne abyde no man for his curteisye,
But in Pilates vois he gan to crye,
And swoor by armes and by blood and bones,
'I can a noble tale for the nones,
With which I wol now quyte the Knightes tale.'

20   Our Hoste saugh that he was dronke of ale,
And seyde: 'abyd, Robin, my leve brother,
Som bettre man shal telle us first another:
Abyd, and lat us werken thriftily.'

'By Goddes soul,' quod he, 'that wol nat I;
For I wol speke, or elles go my wey.'
Our Hoste answerde: 'tel on, a devel wey!
Thou art a fool, thy wit is overcome.'

'Now herkneth,' quod the Miller, 'alle and some!
But first I make a protestacioun
30   That I am dronke, I knowe it by my soun;

Prologue to the Miller's Tale

THIS WAS THE CONVERSATION BETWEEN THE MILLER AND
THE HOST:

1-19   When the Knight finished talking, everyone agreed that he'd told
a great story, one that was good enough to tell again sometime in
the future. The classier people in the group particularly liked the
story. Our Host laughed and swore, then said, "All right, all right,
not bad! That was a great way to break the ice and begin our story-
telling contest. Okay, let's see . . . who's going to tell the next story?
How about you, Mr. Monk? Can you tell us anything as good as the
Knight's story?" But the Miller, who was pale and drunk and nearly
falling off his horse, interrupted without even an apology. With a
booming voice like Pontius Pilate's, he drunkenly swore and blurted
out, "By God's bloody bones, I got one for you that's better than the
Knight's story!"

20-23   Our Host saw that the Miller was drunk from having had too much
ale and said, "Hold on there, Robin, my brother. Let someone else
who's in better shape tell the next story. Wait a little bit, and you'll
get your chance."

25-27   "I swear to God, I won't wait," answered the Miller. "I'm gonna tell
my story right now, or else ditch you guys and go on by myself."
"Go on then, dammit, and tell your story," our Host said. "You're a
drunken fool and don't know what you're saying."

28-35   "Listen up, everybody," started the Miller. "I'm gonna tell you a true
story about a carpenter and his wife and how a young student made
a fool outta the carpenter. But first you gotta know that I'm pretty

And therfore, if that I misspeke or seye,
Wyte it the ale of Southwerk, I yow preye;
For I wol telle a legende and a lyf
Bothe of a Carpenter, and of his wyf,
How that a clerk hath set the wrightes cappe.'

The Reve answerde and seyde, 'stint thy clappe,
Lat be thy lewed dronken harlotrye.
It is a sinne and eek a greet folye
To apeiren any man, or him diffame,
40   And eek to bringen wyves in swich fame.
Thou mayst y-nogh of othere thinges seyn.'

This dronken Miller spak ful sone ageyn,
And seyde, 'leve brother Osewold,
Who hath no wyf, he is no cokewold.
But I sey nat therfore that thou art oon;
Ther been ful gode wyves many oon,
And ever a thousand gode ayeyns oon badde,
That knowestow wel thy-self, but-if thou madde.
Why artow angry with my tale now?
50   I have a wyf, pardee, as well as thou,
Yet nolde I, for the oxen in my plogh,
Taken upon me more than y-nogh,
As demen of my-self that I were oon;
I wol beleve wel that I am noon.
An housbond shal nat been inquisitif
Of Goddes privetee, nor of his wyf.
So he may finde Goddes foyson there,
Of the remenant nedeth nat enquere.'

What sholde I more seyn, but this Millere
60   He nolde his wordes for no man forbere,
But tolde his cherles tale in his manere;
Me thinketh that I shal reherce it here.
And ther-fore every gentil wight I preye,
For Goddes love, demeth nat that I seye
Of evel entente, but that I moot reherce

NO FEAR

drunk. I can tell by the sound of my own voice. So if I make a mistake or anything, blame it on that ale we drank back in Southwark, not me."

36-41 The Reeve interrupted and said, "Stop your drunken babbling! It's a sin and bad form to hurt another man's reputation with such stories, especially when you drag their wives through the mud with them. Tell us a story about something else."

42-58 The drunken Miller shot back, "Why're you so pissed off, huh? My dear friend Oswald, we all know that unmarried men can't be the victims of adultery. I'm not saying that your wife cheats on you or anything. There are lots of respectable women out there, at least a thousand faithful ones to every adulteress. I'm married too, you know, just like you, but I wouldn't take it upon myself to suspect her of cheating. I think she's been faithful. Husbands shouldn't go around digging in God's secrets or in their wives'. You just gotta enjoy the pleasures God gives you and keep your nose outta the rest."

59-78 Well, there really isn't a whole lot more to say except that this Miller wouldn't take no for an answer. He was determined to tell his raunchy story no matter what. I'm sorry that I'm including it here with the other stories in this collection, but, as I told you before, I promised to tell you exactly what happened on our trip—for better or worse. I wouldn't be much of a storyteller myself if I left out some parts, now would I? So, I ask you well-mannered folk for your for-

Hir tales alle, be they bettre or werse,
Or elles falsen som of my matere.
And therfore, who-so list it nat y-here,
Turne over the leef, and chese another tale;
70   For he shal finde y-nowe, grete and smale,
Of storial thing that toucheth gentillesse,
And eek moralitee and holinesse;
Blameth nat me if that ye chese amis.
The Miller is a cherl, ye knowe wel this;
So was the Reve, and othere many mo,
And harlotrye they tolden bothe two.
Avyseth yow and putte me out of blame;
And eek men shal nat make ernest of game.

HERE ENDETH THE PROLOGE.

giveness. And for the love of God, don't blame me for what I'm about to tell you. In fact, those of you who think you might be offended by this story, just go ahead and skip to another one. There are plenty of other long and short stories about nicer things, such as nobility and morality and holiness. But if you stick with this one, well, don't say I didn't warn you. The Miller and the Reeve and some of the others were pretty trashy, as were their stories. Be well advised and don't blame me. And don't take seriously what was said in fun.

THE PROLOGUE ENDS HERE.

The Miller's Tale

HERE BIGINNETH THE MILLERE HIS TALE.

Whylom ther was dwellinge at Oxenford
A riche gnof, that gestes heeld to bord,
And of his craft he was a Carpenter.
With him ther was dwellinge a povre scoler,
Had lerned art, but al his fantasye
Was turned for to lerne astrologye,
And coude a certeyn of conclusiouns
To demen by interrogaciouns,
If that men axed him in certein houres,
10 Whan that men sholde have droghte or elles shoures,
Or if men axed him what sholde bifalle
Of every thing, I may nat rekene hem alle.

This clerk was cleped hende Nicholtas;
Of derne love he coude and of solas;
And ther-to be was sleigh and ful privee,
And lyk a mayden meke for to see.
A chambre hadde he in that hostelrye
Allone, with-outen any companye,
Ful fetisly y-dight with herbes swote;
20 And he him-self as swete as is the rote
Of licorys, or any cetewale.
His Almageste and bokes grete and smale,
His astrelabie, longinge for his art,
His augrim-stones layen faire a-part
On shelves couched at his beddes heed:
His presse y-covered with a falding reed.
And al above ther lay a gay sautrye,
On which he made a nightes melodye
So swetely, that al the chambre rong;
30 And *Angelus ad virginem* he song;
And after that he song the kinges note;
Ful often blessed was his mery throte.

The Miller's Tale

THE MILLER'S TALE STARTS HERE.

1-12 Once upon a time, there was a wealthy but oafish carpenter named John who owned a house in the town of Oxford. A poor young student Nicholas lived with him and was renting one of the empty rooms. This student had already finished some of his liberal arts courses but was entirely consumed by his passion for learning astrology. He knew how to calculate which course of action to take if you asked him if it were going to rain or shine, or if you asked about the future in all sorts of matters. I could go on and on, but you get the idea.

13-34 Now, this student went by the nickname Tricky Nicky because he was pretty clever and knew all about love and pleasure and sweet talk. He was pretty crafty and very cautious but looked as innocent as a little girl. He lived in a room by himself, which he kept neat and clean. He even used potpurri to keep it smelling fresh. He kept his astrology books, astrolabe, and counting stones—all crucial instruments for astrologers—on some shelves next to the head of his bed. A piece of red cloth covered his clothes chest, and on top of that he kept his guitar, which he often played beautifully in the evenings. He liked to play the holy song "*Angelus ad Virginem*" followed by a song called "The King's Tune." People loved to hear the sound of his voice because he sang so well. And that's how Nicholas spent his time, getting by and making ends meet with a little financial help from his friends.

And thus this swete clerk his tyme spente
After his freendes finding and his rente.

This Carpenter had wedded newe a wyf
Which that he lovede more than his lyf;
Of eightetene yeer she was of age.
Ialous he was, and heeld hir narwe in cage,
For she was wilde and yong, and he was old
40 And demed him-self ben lyk a cokewold.
He knew nat Catoun, for his wit was rude,
That bad man sholde wedde his similitude.
Men sholde wedden after hir estaat,
For youthe and elde is often at debaat.
But sith that he was fallen in the snare,
He moste endure, as other folk, his care.

Fair was this yonge wyf, and ther-with-al
As any wesele hir body gent and smal.
A ceynt she werede barred al of silk,
50 A barmclooth eek as whyt as morne milk
Upon hir lendes, ful of many a gore.
Whyt was hir smok, and brouded al bifore
And eek bihinde, on hir coler aboute,
Of col-blak silk, with-inne and eek with-oute.
The tapes of hir whyte voluper
Were of the same suyte of hir coler;
Hir filet brood of silk, and set ful hye:
And sikerly she hadde a likerous yë.
Ful smale y-pulled were hir browes two,
60 And tho were bent, and blake as any sloo.
She was ful more blisful on to see
Than is the newe pere-ionette tree;
And softer than the wolle is of a wether.
And by hir girdel heeng a purs of lether
Tasseld with silk, and perled with latoun.
In al this world, to seken up and doun,
There nis no man so wys, that coude thenche
So gay a popelote, or swich a wenche.

35-46   Now, this carpenter had just gotten married to a girl he loved more than life itself. He kept her in the house all the time, though, because she was wild and only eighteen years old. He was much older, and he worried that if he didn't keep a close eye on her, she'd make him a cuckold. I guess he was too ignorant to have heard of the Roman philosopher Cato, who said that people should marry someone at the same stage in life as themselves because young people and older people often want different things. But since he'd already made this mistake, there was nothing he could do but live with it.

Cuckold: A man whose wife has cheated on him.

47-84   Anyway, this young wife—whose name was Alison—was beautiful, with a body as small and slim as a weasel's. She wore an apron around her waist that was as white as milk. She also wore a blouse embroidered in black silk all the way around the collar. She had matching ribbons in her hair as well as a headband on the crown of her head. She wore a leather purse at her waist that had dangling tassles made of silk and shiny metal beads. She also had a large brooch pinned to her collar, and her shoes were laced high up her legs. She had a flirtatious look in her eyes. She trimmed her eyebrows, too, which were black as coal and arched. Her skin, meanwhile, was as soft as sheep's wool, and her lips were as sweet as wine made from honey and as red as the reddest apple. She sparkled like a newly minted coin from the royal treasury. This girl was more beautiful to look at than an orchard full of spring blossoms. She was so beautiful, in fact, that you'd never be able to find someone who could even *conceive* of such beauty. Plus, she was happy and always smiling and playing or singing with that enchanting voice of hers. She was a rose, pure and simple, and fit for any king to sleep with—or any good man to make his wife.

Ful brighter was the shyning of hir hewe
70　Than in the tour the noble y-forged newe.
But of hir song, it was as loude and yerne
As any swalwe sittinge on a berne.
Ther-to she coude skippe and make game,
As any kide or calf folwinge his dame.
Hir mouth was swete as bragot or the meeth,
Or hord of apples leyd in hey or heeth.
Winsinge she was, as is a Ioly colt,
Long as a mast, and upright as a bolt.
A brooch she baar upon hir lowe coler,
80　As brood as is the bos of a bocler.
Hir shoes were laced on hir legges hye;
She was a prymerole, a pigges-nye
For any lord to leggen in his bedde,
Or yet for any good yeman to wedde.

Now sire, and eft sire, so bifel the cas,
That on a day this hende Nicholas
Fil with this yonge wyf to rage and pleye,
Whyl that hir housbond was at Oseneye,
As clerkes ben ful subtile and ful queynte;
90　And prively he caughte hir by the queynte,
And seyde, 'y-wis, but if ich have my wille,
For derne love of thee, lemman, I spille.'
And heeld hir harde by the haunche-bones,
And seyde, 'lemman, love me al at-ones,
Or I wol dyen, also God me save!'
And she sprong as a colt doth in the trave,
And with hir heed she wryed faste awey,
And seyde, 'I wol nat kisse thee, by my fey,
Why, lat be,' quod she, 'lat be, Nicholas,
100　Or I wol crye out "harrow" and "allas."
Do wey your handes for your curteisye!'

This Nicholas gan mercy for to crye,
And spak so faire, and profred hir so faste,
That she hir love him graunted atte laste,

NO FEAR

85-101   Well now, it just so happened one day that Tricky Nicky was playing
and teasing with Alison while the carpenter was away in the city of
Osney on business. Those college boys can be pretty forward, you
know, and in no time at all he had his hand on her crotch. He said,
"I'm going to die if I can't have my way with you, my love." Then he
grabbed her butt and said, "Make love to me right now, or, by God,
I'm going to die!" She pulled away from him and twisted out of his
grasp as she turned to him and said, "Stop it! I wouldn't even kiss
you, let alone do anything else! Quit it, Nicholas, or I'll cry 'rape!'
Now get your hands off me, you creep!"

102-111   Nicholas begged her for forgiveness and calmed her fears with sweet
words, but he continued hitting on her all the same so that in no
time at all, she'd fallen for him too. She swore on St. Thomas of

And swoor hir ooth, by seint Thomas of Kent,
That she wol been at his comandement,
Whan that she may hir leyser wel espye.
'Myn housbond is so ful of Ialousye,
That but ye wayte wel and been privee,
110   I woot right wel I nam but deed,' quod she.
'Ye moste been ful derne, as in this cas.'

'Nay ther-of care thee noght,' quod Nicholas,
'A clerk had litherly biset his whyle,
But-if he coude a carpenter bigyle.'
And thus they been acorded and y-sworn
To wayte a tyme, as I have told biforn.
Whan Nicholas had doon thus everydeel,
And thakked hir aboute the lendes weel,
He kist hir swete, and taketh his sautrye,
120   And pleyeth faste, and maketh melodye.

Than fil it thus, that to the parish-chirche,
Cristes owne werkes for to wirche,
This gode wyf wente on an haliday;
Hir forheed shoon as bright as any day,
So was it wasshen whan she leet hir werk.

Now was ther of that chirche a parish-clerk,
The which that was y-cleped Absolon.
Crul was his heer, and as the gold it shoon,
And strouted as a fanne large and brode;
130   Ful streight and even lay his Ioly shode.
His rode was reed, his eyen greye as goos;
With Powles window corven on his shoos,
In hoses rede he wente fetisly.
Y-clad he was ful smal and proprely,
Al in a kirtel of a light wachet;
Ful faire and thikke been the poyntes set.
And ther-upon he hadde a gay surplys
As whyt as is the blosme upon the rys.
A mery child he was, so God me save,

Becket himself that she'd let him have his way with her as soon as they could safely get away with it. "My husband is so jealous that he'll kill me if he finds out," she explained to him. "This has to stay between you and me, and we have to be careful."

112-120   "Oh don't worry about that," Nicholas replied. "All that time I spent studying would be a waste if I couldn't fool a simple carpenter." And so they promised each other to bide their time and wait for the right opportunity to sleep with each other. And when everything was settled, he kissed her sweetly and caressed her a while between her legs before playing a fast but sweet song on his guitar.

121-125   Well, one day this young, good wife went to church on a holy day to pray. Her face was so radiant because she'd done herself up nicely before leaving the house.

126-152   Now, the parish clerk at this church was a guy named Absalom. He had curly blond hair that shone like gold, and he kept it parted down the middle of his head so that large locks fell down from his head like a fan. He had a ruddy complexion and eyes as grey as a goose. He wore red leggings with latticed shoes that went high up his leg and a light blue shirt that fit him smartly. On top of this he wore a surplice, which is a long white tunic that parish clerks often wear. God knows he was as giddy as a schoolboy. He was also pretty knowledgeable, though: He could cut hair well and give good shaves, and he was good at bloodletting too. He could also write legal contracts for property sales or other agreements. And he knew how to sing, dance all the new songs and styles that were all the rage with the students at Oxford, and play the fiddle. He also knew how to fid-

Parish clerk: Generally a trusted young man in his twenties who performed a variety of minor tasks for the presiding clergyman.

140 Wel coude he laten blood and clippe and shave,
And make a chartre of lond or acquitaunce.
In twenty manere coude he trippe and daunce
After the scole of Oxenforde tho,
And with his legges casten to and fro,
And pleyen songes on a small rubible;
Ther-to he song som-tyme a loud quinible;
And as wel coude he pleye on his giterne.
In al the toun nas brewhous ne taverne
That he ne visited with his solas,
150 Ther any gaylard tappestere was.
But sooth to seyn, he was somdel squaymous
Of farting, and of speche daungerous.

This Absolon, that Iolif was and gay,
Gooth with a sencer on the haliday,
Sensinge the wyves of the parish faste;
And many a lovely look on hem he caste,
And namely on this carpenteres wyf.
To loke on hir him thoughte a mery lyf,
She was so propre and swete and likerous.
160 I dar wel seyn, if she had been a mous,
And he a cat, he wolde hir hente anon.

This parish-clerk, this Ioly Absolon,
Hath in his herte swich a love-longinge,
That of no wyf ne took he noon offringe;
For curteisye, he seyde, he wolde noon.
The mone, whan it was night, ful brighte shoon,
And Absolon his giterne hath y-take,
For paramours, he thoghte for to wake.
And forth he gooth, Iolif and amorous,
170 Til he cam to the carpenteres hous
A litel after cokkes hadde y-crowe;
And dressed him up by a shot-windowe
That was upon the carpenteres wal.
He singeth in his vois gentil and smal,
'Now, dere lady, if thy wille be,

dle around with the ladies, if you know what I mean. In fact, there wasn't a bar or tavern in town where he wouldn't play, especially if they had cute little waitresses there. Truth be told, though, he was a little too prim and proper and squeamish, especially when it came to farting or loose speech.

153-161 So anyway, this priest named Absalom would go around town burning incense on holy days. Absalom especially liked to cense the women, while looking lovingly into their eyes. He particularly liked Alison, the carpenter's wife. She was so pretty and delightful that just looking at her would make his heart skip a beat. If she'd have been a mouse and he a cat, there'd be no doubt that he would have snatched her up right away.

162-183 Absalom liked her so much that he wouldn't take offerings from any of the other women in town because he thought it would be like cheating on her. One night, he grabbed his guitar and went to the carpenter's house in the middle of the night. The moon shone brightly, and he was feeling very lovesick. When he got to the house, he stood under a shuttered window and sang in a high-pitched voice as he strummed his guitar, "Now, dear lady, please take pity on me if you will." The carpenter woke up to the sound of the music, and he turned to Alison and said, "What is that? Alison, do you hear singing? Is that Absalom singing outside our house?" "Yes, God knows, John, I hear it very well," she snapped.

I preye yow that ye wol rewe on me,'
Ful wel acordaunt to his giterninge.
This carpenter awook, and herde him singe,
And spak unto his wyf, and seyde anon,
180   'What! Alison! herestow nat Absolon
That chaunteth thus under our boures wal?'
And she answerde hir housbond ther-with-al,
'Yis, God wot, Iohn, I here it every-del.'

This passeth forth; what wol ye bet than wel?
Fro day to day this Ioly Absolon
So woweth hir, that him is wo bigon.
He waketh al the night and al the day;
He kempte hise lokkes brode, and made him gay;
He woweth hir by menes and brocage,
190   And swoor he wolde been hir owne page;
He singeth, brokkinge as a nightingale;
He sente hir piment, meeth, and spyced ale,
And wafres, pyping hote out of the glede;
And for she was of toune, he profred mede.
For som folk wol ben wonnen for richesse,
And som for strokes, and som for gentillesse.

Somtyme, to shewe his lightnesse and maistrye,
He pleyeth Herodes on a scaffold hye.
But what availleth him as in this cas?
200   She loveth so this hende Nicholas,
That Absolon may blowe the bukkes horn;
He ne hadde for his labour but a scorn;
And thus she maketh Absolon hir ape,
And al his ernest turneth til a Iape.
Ful sooth is this proverbe, it is no lye,
Men seyn right thus, 'alwey the nye slye
Maketh the ferre leve to be looth.'
For though that Absolon be wood or wrooth,
By-cause that he fer was from hir sighte,
210   This nye Nicholas stood in his lighte.

NO FEAR

This went on for a long time, however, but Absalom had no luck. Pretty soon he became depressed. He tried everything he could think of: dressing up for her and combing his hair neatly, swearing to her that he'd do anything for her, singing like a nightingale, having his friends say nice things about him to her, sending her wine and treats and fresh pies. He even tried to buy her love. Some women like money, they say, some like kindness, and others like soft touches, but none of those seemed to work for Absalom.

One time, to impress Alison with his acting abilities, Absalom even stood on a makeshift stage and put on a little play in which he pretended to be King Herod from the Bible. But did it do him any good? No. Alison loved Tricky Nicky and thought that Absalom should take a hike. She gave him nothing but dirty looks in return and made a buffoon out of him so that he was the laughing stock of the town. You know, it really is true what they say: People want what they can't have and ignore what's right in front of them. No matter how hard Absalom tried, Alison showered all her affection on Nicholas.

Now bere thee wel, thou hende Nicholas!
For Absolon may waille and singe 'allas.'
And so bifel it on a Saterday,
This carpenter was goon til Osenay;
And hende Nicholas and Alisoun
Acorded been to this conclusioun,
That Nicholas shal shapen him a wyle
This sely Ialous housbond to bigyle;
And if so be the game wente aright,
220   She sholde slepen in his arm al night,
For this was his desyr and hir also.
And right anon, with-outen wordes mo,
This Nicholas no lenger wolde tarie,
But doth ful softe unto his chambre carie
Bothe mete and drinke for a day or tweye,
And to hir housbonde bad hir for to seye,
If that he axed after Nicholas,
She sholde seye she niste where he was,
Of al that day she saugh him nat with yĕ;
230   She trowed that he was in maladye,
For, for no cry, hir mayde coude him calle;
He nolde answere, for no-thing that mighte falle.

This passeth forth al thilke Saterday,
That Nicholas stille in his chambre lay,
And eet and sleep, or dide what him leste,
Til Sonday, that the sonne gooth to reste.

This sely carpenter hath greet merveyle
Of Nicholas, or what thing mighte him eyle,
And seyde, 'I am adrad, by seint Thomas,
240   It stondeth nat aright with Nicholas.
God shilde that he deyde sodeynly!
This world is now ful tikel, sikerly;
I saugh to-day a cors y-born to chirche
That now, on Monday last, I saugh him wirche.

NO FEAR

Looks like you've got some competition there, Nicky! Well, one day while the carpenter was away in Osney again, Alison and Nicholas decided that they should play a little trick on her simpleton of a husband. And, if all went as planned, the two of them would even be able to sleep together at night, which was what both of them wanted to do very much. So, without any more fuss, Nicholas moved about a day or two's worth of food into his bedroom. He then told Alison to tell her husband that she hadn't seen Nicholas all day and that she guessed he was sick in bed in his room. Not even the maid's bustling around the house had woken him up. She was to say that his door had remained shut.

Nicholas did his part by staying shut up in his room all weekend. He ate there, slept there, and hung out there all day Saturday and Sunday.

The foolish carpenter was pretty surprised that Nicholas's door stayed closed all weekend, and he wondered what could have made him so sick. "By St. Thomas," he said, "I'm pretty worried about Nicholas. God, I hope he isn't dead in there! This world is full of uncertainty and doubt. Why, just today I passed a funeral procession for a guy I saw walking about town just last Monday."

Go up,' quod he unto his knave anoon,
'Clepe at his dore, or knokke with a stoon,
Loke how it is, and tel me boldely.'

This knave gooth him up ful sturdily,
And at the chambre-dore, whyl that he stood,
250 He cryde and knokked as that he were wood:—
'What! how! what do ye, maister Nicholay?
How may ye slepen al the longe day?'

But al for noght, he herde nat a word;
An hole he fond, ful lowe upon a bord,
Ther as the cat was wont in for to crepe;
And at that hole he looked in ful depe,
And at the laste he hadde of him a sighte.
This Nicholas sat gaping ever up-righte,
As he had kyked on the newe mone.
260 Adoun he gooth, and tolde his maister sone
In what array he saugh this ilke man.

This carpenter to blessen him bigan,
And seyde, 'help us, seinte Frideswyde!
A man woot litel what him shal bityde.
This man is falle, with his astromye,
In som woodnesse or in som agonye;
I thoghte ay wel how that it sholde be!
Men sholde nat knowe of Goddes privetee.
Ye, blessed be alwey a lewed man,
270 That noght but oonly his bileve can!
So ferde another clerk with astromye;
He walked in the feeldes for to prye
Upon the sterres, what ther sholde bifalle,
Til he was in a marle-pit y-falle;
He saugh nat that. But yet, by seint Thomas,
Me reweth sore of hende Nicholas.
He shal be rated of his studying,
If that I may, by Iesus, hevene king!

NO FEAR

245-247 He called his servant, Robin, and said to him, "Go upstairs to Nicholas's room and bang on his door with a rock until he opens it. Then come back down and tell me what's going on."

248-252 Robin did as he'd been told and knocked on Nicholas's door like crazy. "Master Nicholas? Master Nicholas! Are you okay in there? Are you asleep? You haven't been out all day!"

253-261 Try as he might, though, he got no answer. He looked around and spotted a small hole in the bottom of the door that the cat used for creeping through. He knelt down and peered through it to see if he could spot Nicholas inside. And there he saw him, just sitting there, staring up at the ceiling with his mouth wide open as if he'd spotted a new moon. The servant ran back downstairs and told the carpenter exactly what he'd seen.

262-278 The carpenter began praying and said, "Help us, St. Frideswide! Look what's happened all of a sudden! Nicholas has gone insane from all that astrology he does. I knew this would happen, I just knew it! People shouldn't mess around with divine power. Yes siree, blessed be the ignorant who stick to what they already know. Nicholas isn't the first astrologer to suffer the consequences. Why, once I heard about another astrologer who fell into a ditch while walking through the fields with his eyes fixed on the sky. All that knowledge, but he sure didn't see that coming! All the same, God knows I pity Nicholas. By God, I'll give him a good scolding for wasting all his time studying.

Get me a staf, that I may underspore,
280 Whyl that thou, Robin, hevest up the dore.
He shal out of his studying, as I gesse'—
And to the chambre-dore he gan him dresse.
His knave was a strong carl for the nones,
And by the haspe he haf it up atones;
In-to the floor the dore fil anon.
This Nicholas sat ay as stille as stoon,
And ever gaped upward in-to the eir.
This carpenter wende he were in despeir,
And hente him by the sholdres mightily,
290 And shook him harde, and cryde spitously,
'What! Nicholay! what, how! what! loke adoun!
Awake, and thenk on Cristes passioun;
I crouche thee from elves and fro wightes!'
Ther-with the night-spel seyde he anon-rightes
On foure halves of the hous aboute,
And on the threshfold of the dore with-oute:—
'Iesu Crist, and seynt Benedight,
Blesse this hous from every wikked wight,
For nightes verye, the white *pater-noster*!
300 Where wentestow, seynt Petres soster?'

And atte laste this hende Nicholas
Gan for to syke sore, and seyde, 'allas!
Shal al the world be lost eftsones now?'

This carpenter answerde, 'what seystow?
What! thenk on God, as we don, men that swinke.'

This Nicholas answerde, 'fecche me drinke;
And after wol I speke in privetee
Of certeyn thing that toucheth me and thee;
I wol telle it non other man, certeyn.'

310 This carpenter goth doun, and comth ageyn,
And broghte of mighty ale a large quart;
And whan that ech of hem had dronke his part,

NO FEAR

"Go grab me a crowbar, Robin, and I'll pry the door while you shove it open. That'll wake him up, I bet." And with that he worked on prying the door while Robin, who was a pretty strong guy, worked the knob with all his might until the door finally broke down. Nicholas kept sitting there through it all with his mouth agape as if he were oblivious. The carpenter thought Nicholas had gone insane, so he grabbed him by the shoulders and shook him hard, saying, "Hey! Nicholas! Look at me! Wake up and think of Christ's Passion." He then strode around the room muttering prayers to ward off elves and other spirits. He said things like,
"St. Benedict and Jesus Christ,
Save us from the poltergeist,
Let God above keep us from harm,
St. Peter's sister, hear this charm!"

301-303   At last Nicholas heaved a deep sigh and screamed, "It's the end of the world!"

304-305   Startled, the carpenter jumped back, and said, "Huh? What baloney! Keep your mind on God, boy, as we working men do."

306-309   Nicholas replied, "Get me something to drink. Then I want to talk with you in private about something that concerns just the two of us. This isn't for anyone else to hear—just you and me."

310-314   The carpenter went downstairs, then returned with a quart of ale for Nicholas and himself to share. When they'd finished drinking, Tricky Nicky latched the door shut and sat down beside the carpenter.

This Nicholas his dore faste shette,
And doun the carpenter by him he sette.

He seyde, 'Iohn, myn hoste lief and dere,
Thou shall upon thy trouthe swere me here,
That to no wight thou shalt this conseil wreye;
For it is Cristes conseil that I seye,
And if thou telle it man, thou are forlore;
320   For this vengaunce thou shalt han therfore,
That if thou wreye me, thou shalt be wood!'
'Nay, Crist forbede it, for his holy blood!'
Quod tho this sely man, 'I nam no labbe,
Ne, though I seye, I nam nat lief to gabbe.
Sey what thou wolt, I shal it never telle
To child ne wyf, by him that harwed helle!'

'Now John,' quod Nicholas, 'I wol nat lye;
I have y-founde in myn astrologye,
As I have loked in the mone bright,
330   That now, a Monday next, at quarter-night,
Shal falle a reyn and that so wilde and wood,
That half so greet was never Noës flood.
This world,' he seyde, 'in lasse than in an hour
Shal al be dreynt, so hidous is the shour;
Thus shal mankynde drenche and lese hir lyf.'

This carpenter answerde, 'allas, my wyf!
And shal she drenche? allas! myn Alisoun!'
For sorwe of this he fil almost adoun,
And seyde, 'is ther no remedie in this cas?'

340   'Why, yis, for gode,' quod hende Nicholas,
'If thou wolt werken after lore and reed;
Thou mayst nat werken after thyn owene heed.
For thus seith Salomon, that was ful trewe,
"Werk al by conseil, and thou shalt nat rewe."
And if thou werken wolt by good conseil,
I undertake, with-outen mast and seyl,

NO FEAR

315-326   "John, my host and my friend," he began. "You have to promise not to tell another living soul what I'm about to tell you because I'm going to let you in on one of God's little secrets. Tell this to anyone, and you'll go crazy and suffer God's wrath for betraying Him." "No," said the foolish carpenter, "I'm no blabbermouth. I swear by Christ not to tell, no matter what anyone says or does to me. My lips are sealed."

327-335   "Now John," said Nicholas. "I'm not lying to you when I say that I've learned through observation of the stars that there's going to be a torrential rainstorm on Monday night, which is going to be twice as bad as Noah's flood in the Bible. It's going to rain so hard that the whole world will be under water in less than an hour. Everyone on Earth is going to die.

336-339   The carpenter was shocked. "No! My wife!" he exclaimed. "Is she going to drown? No, no, not my Alison! Isn't there anything we can do?"

340-350   "Yes, in fact there is," answered Tricky Nicky. "You can get out of this alive if you follow some simple advice from those who are wise in these matters. No matter how strange it may sound, do as I say. As the wise King Solomon once said, 'Always seek advice, and you won't regret it.' I tell you that I know how to save you, your wife, and myself from drowning even though we don't have a ship. Haven't you heard the story about how Noah survived the flood because God warned him in advance?

Yet shal I saven hir and thee and me
Hastow nat herd how saved was Noë,
Whan that our Lord had warned him biforn
350　That al the world with water sholde be lorn?'

'Yis,' quod this carpenter, 'ful yore ago.'

'Hastow nat herd,' quod Nicholas, 'also
The sorwe of Noë with his felawshipe,
Er that he mighte gete his wyf to shipe?
Him had be lever, I dar wel undertake,
At thilke tyme, than alle hise wetheres blake,
That she hadde had a ship hir-self allone.
And ther-fore, wostou what is best to done?
This asketh haste, and of an hastif thing
360　Men may nat preche or maken tarying.

Anon go gete us faste in-to this in
A kneding-trogh, or elles a kimelin,
For ech of us, but loke that they be large,
In whiche we mowe swimme as in a barge,
And han ther-inne vitaille suffisant
But for a day; fy on the remenant!
The water shal aslake and goon away
Aboute pryme upon the nexte day.
But Robin may nat wite of this, thy knave,
370　Ne eek thy mayde Gille I may nat save;
Axe nat why, for though thou aske me,
I wol nat tellen Goddes privetee.
Suffiseth thee, but if thy wittes madde,
To han as greet a grace as Noë hadde.
Thy wyf shal I wel saven, out of doute,
Go now thy wey, and speed thee heer-aboute.

But whan thou hast, for hir and thee and me,
Y-geten us thise kneding-tubbes three,
Than shaltow hange hem in the roof ful hye,
380　That no man of our purveyaunce spye.

NO FEAR

351   "Yeah, of course," replied the carpenter. "In olden days."

352-360   "And haven't you heard how nervous Noah was before he'd got-
ten everyone on board the ark? His wife gave him so much trouble
In him getting on the ship that The he'd leave given up all his ani-
mals not to deal with her if he could. Point is, we've got to hurry if
we're going to make all the necessary arrangements to survive. We
don't have much time.

361-376   "Here's what you need to do: Go out and find three large troughs or
bathtubs for the three of us to use as boats to float in. Make sure you
put enough food in each tub to last a day. We won't need any more
that that because the flood will subside by nine o'clock the next
morning. Now, you can't tell Robin, your servant, or Jill, your maid,
any of this. Don't ask me why because I can't tell you all of God's
secrets. Just know that God has given you a special opportunity—
just as He gave Noah in the Bible—and I'll be able to save your wife
too. We've just got to hurry because we don't have a lot of time.

377-396   "Now, when you've gotten these three tubs, you should take some
rope and hang them from the rafters of the ceiling where no one will
be able to spot them. Do this and then put some food in them and
an axe so that we can cut ourselves free from the house and float

And whan thou thus hast doon as I have seyd,
And hast our vitaille faire in hem y-leyd,
And eek an ax, to smyte the corde atwo
When that the water comth, that we may go,
And broke an hole an heigh, upon the gable,
Unto the gardin-ward, over the stable,
That we may frely passen forth our way
Whan that the grete shour is goon away—
Than shaltow swimme as myrie, I undertake,
390   As doth the whyte doke after hir drake.
Than wol I clepe, "how! Alison! how! John!
Be myrie, for the flood wol passe anon."
And thou wolt seyn, "hayl, maister Nicholay!
Good morwe, I se thee wel, for it is day."
And than shul we be lordes al our lyf
Of al the world, as Noë and his wyf.

But of o thyng I warne thee ful right,
Be wel avysed, on that ilke night
That we ben entred in-to shippes bord,
400   That noon of us ne speke nat a word,
Ne clepe, ne crye, but been in his preyere;
For it is Goddes owne heste dere.

Thy wyf and thou mote hange fer a-twinne,
For that bitwixe yow shal be no sinne
No more in looking than ther shal in dede;
This ordinance is seyd, go, God thee spede!
Tomorwe at night, whan men ben alle aslepe,
In-to our kneding-tubbes wol we crepe,
And sitten ther, abyding Goddes grace.
410   Go now thy wey, I have no lenger space
To make of this no lenger sermoning.
Men seyn thus, "send the wyse, and sey no-thing;"
Thou art so wys, it nedeth thee nat teche;
Go, save our lyf, and that I thee biseche.'

away like swans. Do this and the next day we'll be able to say things such as, "How's it going, Alison? How're you doing, John? Don't worry, the flood will be over soon!" And you'll be able to reply, "Not bad! Look, it's morning and the flood is over!" And then we'll be lords of the world all our lives, just like Noah and his wife.

397-402 "Oh, but there's one other thing I forgot to mention: When we're in the boats and waiting for the flood, we can't talk to each other or make a sound, no matter what happens. We should be praying silently to ourselves because that's how God wants it.

403-414 "Oh, and you can't be too near your wife while you're in the tub hanging from the ceiling either. There's to be no hanky panky between you two. Don't even look at her, in fact. Okay, I think that's everything. Now go, go get everything ready, and tomorrow night, when everyone else is sleeping, we'll get into our bathtubs and wait out the rains and the flood. There really isn't any time for useless talking. You know what they say, 'Send the wise and say nothing.' Well, you're certainly pretty smart, John, so I don't need to say anything else. Our lives are in your hands."

This sely carpenter goth forth his wey.
Ful ofte he seith 'allas' and 'weylawey,'
And to his wyf he tolde his privetee;
And she was war, and knew it bet than he,
What al this queynte cast was for to seye.
420   But nathelees she ferde as she wolde deye,
And seyde, 'allas! go forth thy wey anon,
Help us to scape, or we ben lost echon;
I am thy trewe verray wedded wyf;
Go, dere spouse, and help to save our lyf.'

Lo! which a greet thyng is affeccioun!
Men may dye of imaginacioun,
So depe may impressioun be take.
This sely carpenter biginneth quake;
Him thinketh verraily that he may see
430   Noës flood come walwing as the see
To drenchen Alisoun, his hony dere.
He wepeth, weyleth, maketh sory chere,
He syketh with ful many a sory swogh.
He gooth and geteth him a kneding-trogh,
And after that a tubbe and a kimelin,
And prively he sente hem to his in,
And heng hem in the roof in privetee.
His owne hand he made laddres three,
To climben by the ronges and the stalkes
440   Unto the tubbes hanginge in the balkes,
And hem vitailled, bothe trogh and tubbe,
With breed and chese, and good ale in a lubbe,
Suffysinge right y-nogh as for a day.
But er that he had maad al this array,
He sente his knave, and eek his wenche also,
Upon his nede to London for to go.
And on the Monday, whan it drow to night,
He shette his dore with-oute candel-light,
And dressed al thing as it sholde be.
450   And shortly, up they clomben alle three;
They sitten stille wel a furlong-way.

NO FEAR

415-424   The stupid carpenter went off to get things done, muttering, "Oh no," and, "Oh my God," as he went. He told his wife what Nicholas had told him. She, of course, was in on Tricky Nicky's game, but she pretended to be scared. She said, "No! Go on, go or else we'll all die! I'm your faithful wife, so go, my husband, and save us."

425-451   This carpenter began shaking out of fear of the flood he thought was coming to kill him and his beloved wife. He cried and moaned and sighed and looked forelorn. Men can die of imaginary curses. He went out and bought three large tubs and secretly brought them to his home. Then he made three ladders himself so that they could climb into the tubs when they were hanging from the ceiling. He also put some bread and cheese and beer in each tub—enough to feed each of them for a day. Then he sent his servant and maid to London so that he could hang the tubs without them knowing. And finally, on Monday night he blew out the candles, and they all climbed up into their tubs and remained quiet for a long time.

'Now, Pater-noster, clom!' seyde Nicholay,
And 'clom,' quod John, and 'clom,' seyde Alisoun.
This carpenter seyde his devocioun,
And stille he sit, and biddeth his preyere,
Awaytinge on the reyn, if he it here.

The dede sleep, for wery bisinesse,
Fil on this carpenter right, as I gesse,
Aboute corfew-tyme, or litel more;
For travail of his goost he groneth sore,
And eft he routeth, for his heed mislay.
Doun of the laddre stalketh Nicholay,
And Alisoun, ful softe adoun she spedde;
With-outen wordes mo, they goon to bedde
Ther-as the carpenter is wont to lye.
Ther was the revel and the melodye;
And thus lyth Alison and Nicholas,
In bisinesse of mirthe and of solas,
Til that the belle of laudes gan to ringe,
And freres in the chauncel gonne singe.

This parish-clerk, this amorous Absolon,
That is for love alwey so wo bigon,
Upon the Monday was at Oseneye
With companye, him to disporte and pleye,
And axed upon cas a cloisterer
Ful prively after Iohn the carpenter;
And he drough him a-part out of the chirche,
And seyde, 'I noot, I saugh him here nat wirche
Sin Saterday; I trow that he be went
For timber, ther our abbot hath him sent;
For he is wont for timber for to go,
And dwellen at the grange a day or two;
Or elles he is at his hous, certeyn;
Wher that he be, I can nat sothly seyn.'

This Absolon ful Ioly was and light,
And thoghte, 'now is tyme wake al night;

460

470

480

452-456 "In God's name, quiet, quiet!" said Nicholas. "Sh!" said the carpenter and his wife. The carpenter said his devotions and sat quietly praying, while straining his ears to hear the rain he expected would come.

457-470 The carpenter was concentrating so hard on his prayers that by curfew time at dusk he'd fallen fast asleep. He moaned in his sleep from all his worries. As soon as he began snoring, Nicholas and Alison climbed out of their tubs, down the ladders, and into the carpenter's bed below. There they made love all night long until just before dawn when the monks began chanting and the church bells began ringing.

471-484 The lovesick parish clerk Absalom, meanwhile, spent Monday in Osney for a night on the town with some friends. At one point he casually tried to ask one of his friends about John the carpenter. His friend pulled him aside outside the church and said, "You know, I'm not sure. I haven't seen him since Saturday. I guess he went out of town to buy wood from the woodcutter. You know, the one our abbot recommended to him. He usually stays there for a couple days before coming back. He's either there or he's at home. I really don't know."

485-500 Absalom perked up when he heard that the carpenter was probably out of town. "Tonight's my chance to make my move on Alison," he

For sikirly I saugh him nat stiringe
Aboute his dore sin day bigan to springe.
So moot I thryve, I shal, at cokkes crowe,
490 Ful prively knokken at his windowe
That stant ful lowe upon his boures wal.
To Alison now wol I tellen al
My love-longing, for yet I shal nat misse
That at the leste wey I shal hir kisse.
Som maner confort shal I have, parfay,
My mouth hath icched al this longe day;
That is a signe of kissing atte leste.
Al night me mette eek, I was at a feste.
Therfor I wol gon slepe an houre or tweye,
500 And al the night than wol I wake and pleye.'

Whan that the firste cok hath crowe, anon
Up rist this Ioly lover Absolon,
And him arrayeth gay, at point-devys.
But first he cheweth greyn and lycorys,
To smellen swete, er he had kembd his heer.
Under his tonge a trewe love he beer,
For ther-by wende he to ben gracious.
He rometh to the carpenteres hous,
And stille he stant under the shot-windowe;
510 Unto his brest it raughte, it was so lowe;
And softe he cogheth with a semi-soun—
'What do ye, hony-comb, swete Alisoun?
My faire brid, my swete cinamome,
Awaketh, lemman myn, and speketh to me!
Wel litel thenken ye upon my wo,
That for your love I swete ther I go.
No wonder is thogh that I swelte and swete;
I moorne as doth a lamb after the tete.
Y-wis, lemman, I have swich love-longinge,
520 That lyk a turtel trewe is my moorninge;
I may nat ete na more than a mayde.'

thought to himself, "Since the carpenter doesn't seem to be around. In fact, tonight I'm going to knock quietly on Alison's bedroom window and tell her how much I love her. I'll be sure to get a kiss out of her at the very least, if not more! My mouth has been just itching to kiss her all day long. And last night I dreamt that I was at a feast, a good sign to be sure. So, I'll catch a few hours sleep, then stay up late and play all night, and visit her just before sunrise."

501-521 When the roosters began crowing just before dawn, Absalom woke up and carefully got ready. First, he chewed some licorice to make his breath smell sweet. Then he combed his hair and got dressed. Finally, he put a sprig of mint under his tongue so that his kisses would taste nice. When he finished he made his way over to the carpenter's house. He went up to Alison's bedroom window, which was so low it only came up to his chest. He cleared his throat, then rapped on the window, and said, "Hello? Sweet Alison? Honeycomb? My beautiful bird, my sweet cinnamon? Wake up, my darling, and speak to me. You don't know how much I want you, how much I need you. I break out in a cold sweat just thinking about you. I don't eat, and I melt when I see you. I'm like a lamb that craves its mother's milk. I'm so lovesick for you that I'm like a lost turtledove without its mate."

'Go fro the window, Iakke fool,' she sayde,
'As help me God, it wol nat be "com ba me,"
I love another, and elles I were to blame,
Wel bet than thee, by Iesu, Absolon!
Go forth thy wey, or I wol caste a ston,
And lat me slepe, a twenty devel wey!'

'Allas,' quod Absolon, 'and weylawey!
That trewe love was ever so yvel biset!
530   Than kisse me, sin it may be no bet,
For Iesus love and for the love of me.'

'Wiltow than go thy wey ther-with?' quod she.

'Ye, certes, lemman,' quod this Absolon.

'Thanne make thee redy,' quod she, 'I come anon;'
And unto Nicholas she seyde stille,
'Now hust, and thou shall laughen al thy fille.'

This Absolon doun sette him on his knees,
And seyde, 'I am a lord at alle degrees;
For after this I hope ther cometh more!
540   Lemman, thy grace, and swete brid, thyn ore!'

The window she undoth, and that in haste,
'Have do,' quod she, 'com of, and speed thee faste,
Lest that our neighebores thee espye.'

This Absolon gan wype his mouth ful drye;
Derk was the night as pich, or as the cole,
And at the window out she putte hir hole,
And Absolon, him fil no bet ne wers,
But with his mouth he kiste hir naked ers
Ful savourly, er he was war of this.

550   Abak he sterte, and thoghte it was amis,
For wel he wiste a womman hath no berd;

NO FEAR

522-527   "Get away from the window, you jack fool!" Alison called from inside the house. "So help me God, Absalom, I won't be coming to kiss you if I have to go over to that window. I don't love you. I love someone else much more. Now go away, damnit, and let me sleep or else I'll start throwing rocks at you!"

528-531   "No, no," Absalom replied. "Woe the day I ever fell in love with you! Well, since I have no chance with you, just give me a little kiss then ⸱⸱⸱⸱ ⸱⸱⸱ ⸱⸱ ⸱⸱⸱⸱ ⸱ ⸱⸱⸱ ⸱⸱⸱⸱ ⸱⸱⸱ ⸱⸱⸱⸱ "

532   "Will you go away if I give you a kiss?" she asked.

533   "Yes, of course, my darling," answered Absalom.

534-536   "Get ready then," she called out to him. "I'm coming." Then she turned to Nicholas lying in bed and whispered, "Be quiet and get a load of this!"

537-540   Absalom knelt down beneath the window ledge and said to himself, "Wow, I am *good*! I'm sure I'm going to get much more than a kiss tonight! Whatever you give, I'll take, my love!"

541-543   Alison quickly opened the window and said, "Come on now, hurry up. Let's get this over with before the neighbors see us."

544-549   Abasolm wiped his lips dry to prepare for the kiss. It was so pitch black outside that you couldn't see a thing, which meant that Absalom couldn't see that Alison had stuck her naked butt out of the window instead of her head. Absalom leaned in and kissed her deeply in the middle of her ass.

550-553   Abaslom sensed that something wasn't quite right, and he pulled back in surprise. He'd felt some long, rough hairs when he'd kissed her

He felte a thing al rough and long y-herd,
And seyde, 'fy! allas! what have I do?'

'Tehee!' quod she, and clapte the window to;
And Absolon goth forth a sory pas.

'A berd, a berd!' quod hende Nicholas,
'By Goddes corpus, this goth faire and weel!'

This sely Absolon herde every deel,
And on his lippe he gan for anger byte;
560 And to him-self he seyde, 'I shal thee quyte!'

Who rubbeth now, who froteth now his lippes
With dust, with sond, with straw, with clooth, with chippes,
But Absolon, that seith ful ofte, 'allas!
My soule bitake I unto Sathanas,
But me wer lever than al this toun,' quod he,
'Of this despyt awroken for to be!
Allas!' quod he, 'allas! I ne hadde y-bleynt!'
His hote love was cold and al y-queynt;
For fro that tyme that he had kiste hir ers,
570 Of paramours he sette nat a kers,
For he was heled of his maladye;
Ful ofte paramours he gan deffye,
And weep as dooth a child that is y-bete.
A softe paas he wente over the strete
Un-til a smith men cleped daun Gerveys,
That in his forge smithed plough-harneys;
He sharpeth shaar and culter bisily.
This Absolon knokketh al esily,
And seyde, 'undo, Gerveys, and that anon.'

580 'What, who artow?' 'It am I, Absolon.'
'What, Absolon! for Cristes swete tree,
Why ryse ye so rathe, ey, *benedicite*!
What eyleth yow? som gay gerl, God it woot,

even though he knew that she didn't have a beard. He quickly realized what had happened, and said, "Yuck! Yuck! What have I done?"

554-555 "Tee hee!" snickered Alison as she slammed the window shut and Abaslom stumbled backward.

556-557 Nicholas cracked up, "A beard! A beard! God, this is hilarious!"

558-560 Absalom heard Nicholas laughing inside, and he bit his lip in rage. "I'll get them back!" he swore to himself.

561-579 Well, you've never seen anyone rub his lips harder than Absalom. He used dirt, sand, straw, bark, and his arm sleeves to wipe his mouth as he kept saying, "Yuck!" over and over again. He said, "I'd trade my soul to Satan himself if he would punish them for me. Why didn't I turn my head at the last moment?" All his burning passion for Alison had disappeared the moment he'd kissed her ass, and he was completely cured of his lovesickness and now sick of women. He cried like a baby and swore he'd never love another girl again. He ran across the street to a blacksmith's shop, which was owned by a guy named Mr. Gervase, who happened to be working on some metal farming equipment. Absalom knocked on the shop door quietly and said, "Mr. Gervase? Please open up."

580-585 "Who's there?" called out Gervase. "It's me, Absalom," he replied. "Absalom! What the devil are you doing up so early?" asked the blacksmith. "What's the matter? You're after a taste of some girl, now aren't you? Yeah, you know what I mean!"

Hath broght yow thus upon the viritoot;
By sëynt Note, ye woot wel what I mene.'

This Absolon ne roghte nat a bene
Of al his pley, no word agayn he yaf;
He hadde more tow on his distaf
Than Gerveys knew, and seyde, 'freend so dere,
590   That hote culter in the chimenee here,
As lene it me, I have ther-with to done,
And I wol bringe it thee agayn ful sone.'

Gerveys answerde, 'certes, were it gold,
Or in a poke nobles alle untold,
Thou sholdest have, as I am trewe smith;
Ey, Cristes foo! what wol ye do ther-with?'

'Ther-of,' quod Absolon, 'be as be may;
I shal wel telle it thee to-morwe day'—
And caughte the culter by the colde stele.
600   Ful softe out at the dore he gan to stele,
And wente unto the carpenteres wal.
He cogheth first, and knokketh ther-with-al
Upon the windowe, right as he dide er.

This Alison answerde, 'Who is ther
That knokketh so? I warante it a theef.'

'Why, nay,' quod he, 'God woot, my swete leef,
I am thyn Absolon, my dereling!
Of gold,' quod he, 'I have thee broght a ring;
My moder yaf it me, so God me save,
610   Ful fyn it is, and ther-to wel y-grave;
This wol I yeve thee, if thou me kisse!'

This Nicholas was risen for to pisse,
And thoghte he wolde amenden al the Iape,
He sholde kisse his ers er that he scape.

Original Text

NO FEAR

586-592   Absalom didn't say anything but let the joke slide. Mr. Gervase was more right than he could've possibly known. Instead, he said, "My friend, would you lend me that red hot iron poker in the fireplace over there? There's something I need to use it for, but I'll bring it back to you right away."

593-596   "Go right ahead," Mr. Gervase answered. "I'd give you a bag full of money if you needed it, Absalom. I trust you. What in the world do you need a hot poker for, though?"

597-603   "I'd rather not go into it right now," Absalom said. "I'll tell you all about it tomorrow." And with that he took the iron poker by its cool handle, left the blacksmith's shop, and walked back across the street to the carpenter's house. He cleared his throat, then knocked on the bedroom window, just as he'd done earlier.

604-605   "Who's there knocking on the window?" Alison called. "It's not a thief, is it?"

606-611   "No, my darling, it's me, Absalom, sweet love. I've brought you a gold ring that my mother once gave me," he said. "It's very beautiful and even engraved. I'll give it to you if you'll give me another kiss!"

612-619   Nicholas, who'd gotten up to pee, heard Absalom outside and thought he'd make the night even funnier by making the priest kiss his ass too. He opened the window quickly and stuck out his butt as

And up the windowe dide he hastily,
And out his ers he putteth prively
Over the buttok, to the haunche-bon;
And ther-with spak this clerk, this Absolon,
'Spek, swete brid, I noot nat wher thou art.'

620   This Nicholas anon leet flee a fart,
As greet as it had been a thonder-dent,
That with the strook he was almost y-blent;
And he was redy with his iren hoot,
And Nicholas amidde the ers he smoot.

Of gooth the skin an hande-brede aboute,
The hole culter brende so his toute,
And for the smert he wende for to dye.
As he were wood, for wo he gan to crye—
Help! water! water! help, for Goddes herte!'

630   This carpenter out of his slomber sterte,
And herde oon cryen 'water' as he were wood,
And thoghte, 'Allas! now comth Nowelis flood!'
He sit him up with-outen wordes mo,
And with his ax he smoot the corde a-two,
And doun goth al; he fond neither to selle,
Ne breed ne ale, til he cam to the celle
Upon the floor; and ther aswowne he lay.

Up sterte hir Alison, and Nicholay,
And cryden 'out' and 'harrow' in the strete.
640   The neighebores, bothe smale and grete,
In ronnen, for to gauren on this man,
That yet aswowne he lay, bothe pale and wan;
For with the fal he brosten hadde his arm;
But stonde he moste unto his owne harm.
For whan he spak, he was anon bore doun
With hende Nicholas and Alisoun.
They tolden every man that he was wood,
He was agast so of 'Nowelis flood'

far as it would go, just at the moment Absalom said, "Say something, my sweet bird, so I know where you are."

620-624   Nicholas answered by ripping off an enormous fart as powerful as thunder that nearly blinded Absalom. He was ready with the hot poker, though, and rammed it right at Tricky Nicky's butt.

625-629   The poker burned Nicholas's butt so badly that the skin started peeling off. Nicholas thought he'd die from the pain, and he screamed like a madman, "Help! Water! Help! Water! For God's sake, water!"

630-637   Nicholas's screaming and cries for water woke up the carpenter, whose first thought was, "It's coming! Noah's flood is here!" He bolted upright in his bathtub, grabbed the axe, and cut the rope holding the tub up in the rafters. The tub crashed to the floor in less than a second, which knocked the carpenter out cold.

638-653   Alison and Nicholas jumped at the noise of the crash, and they dashed out into the street crying for help. The neighbors ran to the scene where they found the tub and the unconscious carpenter, who'd broken his arm in the fall. When he finally came to, he tried to explain to the neighbors what had happened, but Alison and Nicholas told everyone that John was crazy. They said that he'd imagined it all, and had tried to get them to help him hang three tubs to prepare for "Noel's flood," as he ignorantly called it. It was too bad for the carpenter, but he really couldn't blame anyone but himself for his own foolishness.

Thurgh fantasye, that of his vanitee
650   He hadde y-boght him kneding-tubbes three,
And hadde hem hanged in the roof above;
And that he preyed hem, for Goddes love,
To sitten in the roof, *par companye*.

The folk gan laughen at his fantasye;
In-to the roof they kyken and they gape,
And turned al his harm unto a Iape.
For what so that this carpenter answerde,
It was for noght, no man his reson herde;
With othes grete he was so sworn adoun,
660   That he was holden wood in al the toun;
For every clerk anon-right heeld with other.
They seyde, 'the man is wood, my leve brother;'
And every wight gan laughen of this stryf.

Thus swyved was the carpenteres wyf,
For al his keping and his Ialousye;
And Absolon hath kist hir nether yē;
And Nicholas is scalded in the toute.
This tale is doon, and God save al the route!

HERE ENDETH THE MILLERE HIS TALE.

NO FEAR

654-663 The neighbors laughed hysterically when they heard the carpenter's story. They poked their heads inside the house to look up at the other two tubs hanging from the ceiling and chuckled. Try as he might, though, the carpenter couldn't get anyone to believe what had really happened. From then on he was known throughout town as the crazy carpenter, and everyone swore at him, made fun of him, and spread rumors about him.

664-668 And that is how the carpenter's wife was screwed, for all the carpenter's watchfulness and paranoia; how Absolom kissed her nether eye; and how Nicholas got his ass burned. Thank you, and God bless every one of us!

THIS IS THE END OF THE MILLER'S TALE.

Prologue to the Wife of Bath's Tale

THE PROLOGE OF THE WYVES TALE OF BATHE.

'Experience, though noon auctoritee
Were in this world, were right y-nough to me
To speke of wo that is in mariage;
For, lordinges, sith I twelf yeer was of age,
Thonked be God that is eterne on lyve,
Housbondes at chirche-dore I have had fyve;
For I so ofte have y-wedded be;
And alle were worthy men in hir degree.
But me was told certeyn, nat longe agon is,
That sith that Crist ne wente never but onis
To wedding in the Cane of Galilee,
That by the same ensample taughte he me
That I ne sholde wedded be but ones.
Herke eek, lo! which a sharp word for the nones
Besyde a welle Iesus, God and man,
Spak in repreve of the Samaritan:
"Thou hast y-had fyve housbondes," quod he,
"And thilke man, the which that hath now thee,
Is noght thyn housbond;" thus seyde he certeyn;
What that he mente ther-by, I can nat seyn;
But that I axe, why that the fifthe man
Was noon housbond to the Samaritan?
How manye mighte she have in mariage?
Yet herde I never tellen in myn age
Upon this nombre diffinicioun;
Men may devyne and glosen up and doun.
But wel I woot expres, with-oute lye,
God bad us for to wexe and multiplye;
That gentil text can I wel understonde.
Eek wel I woot he seyde, myn housbonde
Sholde lete fader and moder, and take me;
But of no nombre mencioun made he,

10

20

30

Prologue to the Wife of Bath's Tale

PROLOGUE TO THE STORY TOLD BY THE WIFE FROM THE CITY OF BATH.

1-34   "My life experiences alone—even if there were no higher authority on the subject—qualify me to talk about the strife called marriage. You see, I've been married five times since I was twelve years old (thanks be to God), and all of my husbands had their good points. Someone told me not too long ago, though, that I should have only

John 2:1   gotten married once since Jesus himself only attended one wedding when he was alive—in Cana in Galilee. Or remember the sharp words that Jesus said to the Samaritan: 'You've had

John 4:17   five husbands,' He said. 'So the man you think you're married to now isn't your husband.' That's what He said, for sure, though what He meant exactly I'm not really sure. But I ask you this: Why wasn't the Samaritan's fifth mate her husband? How many men was she allowed to marry in her lifetime? I've never heard an exact number myself. People can read and reread the Bible over and over, but I know one thing for sure, and that's that God commanded

Genesis 1:28   us to increase and multiply. That nice little bit of scripture I can understand quite well. And I also know that He instructed my husbands to leave their mothers and fathers and take me as their wife. He never said, though, how many men I could marry over the course of my life, so why do people look down on marrying more than once—or eight times for that matter—as much as they do?

Of bigamye or of octogamye;
Why sholde men speke of it vileinye?

Lo, here the wyse king, dan Salomon;
I trowe he hadde wyves mo than oon;
As, wolde God, it leveful were to me
To be refresshed half so ofte as he!
Which yifte of God hadde he for alle his wyvis!
No man hath swich, that in this world alyve is.
God woot, this noble king, as to my wit,
The firste night had many a mery fit
With ech of hem, so wel was him on lyve!
Blessed be God that I have wedded fyve!
Welcome the sixte, whan that ever he shal.
For sothe, I wol nat kepe me chast in al;
Whan myn housbond is fro the world y-gon,
Som Cristen man shal wedde me anon;
For thanne thapostle seith, that I am free
To wedde, a Goddes half, wher it lyketh me.
He seith that to be wedded is no sinne;
Bet is to be wedded than to brinne.
What rekketh me, thogh folk seye vileinye
Of shrewed Lameth and his bigamye?
I woot wel Abraham was an holy man,
And Iacob eek, as ferforth as I can;
And ech of hem hadde wyves mo than two;
And many another holy man also.
Whan saugh ye ever, in any maner age,
That hye God defended mariage
By expres word? I pray you, telleth me;
Or wher comanded he virginitee?
I woot as wel as ye, it is no drede,
Thapostel, whan he speketh of maydenhede;
He seyde, that precept ther-of hadde he noon.
Men may conseille a womman to been oon,
But conseilling is no comandement;
He putte it in our owene Iugement.
For hadde God comanded maydenhede,

40

50

60

NO FEAR

35-76 "Just look at King Solomon—he had more than one wife. I wish to God I could get off as often as he must have! His many wives were certainly a very pleasurable gift from God. No one living today has received any gift like that. God knows Solomon probably had a few good rolls in the hay with each wife the first time he slept with her. Wow, he must have had a great life. Praise the Lord that I've been able to marry five men, and I'm looking forward to marrying the sixth whenever I meet him. I don't want to abstain from sex forever, you know. I hope it won't be long after my current husband dies before I'm able to marry my next husband. St Paul, the Apostle, said that I'll be free to marry again. He said that getting married is better than burning. So what, then, if people say bad things about marrying more than once? Lamech, Abraham, and Jacob were all holy men, as far as I can tell, and they all had more than a couple wives, as have many others like them. Has God ever expressly forbidden marriage before? Huh? Or has he ever commanded people to remain virgins all their lives? I know as well as you that St. Paul only recommended women to maintain their virginity—he never ordered it. Giving advice and making commands are two different things, and he left it up to us to decide how to live. Besides, if God preferred virgins, then He would pretty much be against marriage, now wouldn't He? And if people weren't having sex, well then how would we make more virgins? No, St. Paul would never order anything that God himself wouldn't want. Anyway, whoever wants to aspire to maintaining their virginity can do so, but we'll see who comes out on top in the end.

1 Corinthians 7:39

1 Corinthians 7:25

70   Thanne hadde he dampned wedding with the dede;
    And certes, if ther were no seed y-sowe,
    Virginitee, wher-of than sholde it growe?
    Poul dorste nat comanden atte leste
    A thing of which his maister yaf noon heste.
    The dart is set up for virginitee;
    Cacche who so may, who renneth best lat see.

    But this word is nat take of every wight,
    But ther as God list give it of his might.
    I woot wel, that thapostel was a mayde;
80   But natheless, thogh that he wroot and sayde,
    He wolde that every wight were swich as he,
    Al nis but conseil to virginitee;
    And for to been a wyf, he yaf me leve
    Of indulgence; so it is no repreve
    To wedde me, if that my make dye,
    With-oute excepcioun of bigamye.
    Al were it good no womman for to touche,
    He mente as in his bed or in his couche;
    For peril is bothe fyr and tow tassemble;
90   Ye knowe what this ensample may resemble.
    This is al and som, he heeld virginitee
    More parfit than wedding in freletee.
    Freeltee clepe I, but-if that he and she
    Wolde leden al hir lyf in chastitee.

    I graunte it wel, I have noon envye,
    Thogh maydenhede preferre bigamye;
    Hem lyketh to be clene, body and goost,
    Of myn estaat I nil nat make no boost.
    For wel ye knowe, a lord in his houshold,
100 He hath nat every vessel al of gold;
    Somme been of tree, and doon hir lord servyse.
    God clepeth folk to him in sondry wyse,
    And everich hath of God a propre yifte,
    Som this, som that,—as him lyketh shifte.

NO FEAR

77-94   "Of course, all this talk only applies to those whom God wants to
ᵣₑₘₐᵢₙ ᵥᵢᵣᵍᵢₙₛ. I know that St. Paul was a virgin, but I also know
→   that even though he wrote about virginity and talked a lot

1 Corinthians 7:7   about others remaining celibate like him, it all boiled down to
advice, nothing more. This means that there's nothing wrong
with me getting married and indulging in early pleasures, or even
getting married more than once—though he did probably mean
that I shouldn't be sleeping with my husbands. That must be the
long and the short of it now that I think about it: St. Paul believed
that virginity was better than marriage, unless the husband and wife
never sleep together.

95-114   "As for myself, though, I'm not upset that maidenhood is prefer-
able to getting married more than once. Some people prefer to be
clean in both body and soul, others not. I personally don't make any
claims about how purely I've lived my life. As you well know, not
→   everything in a person's house can be made of pure gold. Some

Timothy 2:20   things have to be made of wood so that people can actually use
them. God calls people to Him in a lot of different ways, and
→   every person brings different gifts to Him—some this, some

1 Corinthians 7:7   that, whatever he or she can.

Virginitee is greet perfeccioun,
And continence eek with devocioun.
But Crist, that of perfeccioun is welle,
Bad nat every wight he shold go selle
All that he hadde, and give it to the pore,
110   And in swich wyse folwe hime and his fore.
He spak to hem that wolde live parfitly;
And lordinges, by your leve, that am nat I.
I wol bistowe the flour of al myn age
In the actes and in fruit of mariage.

Telle me also, to what conclusioun
Were membres maad of generacioun,
And for what profit was a wight y-wroght?
Trusteth right wel, they wer nat maad for noght.
Glose who-so wole, and seye bothe up and doun,
120   That they were maked for purgacioun
Of urine, and our bothe thinges smale
Were eek to knowe a femele from a male,
And for noone other cause: sey ye no?
The experience woot wel it is noght so;
So that the clerkes be nat with me wrothe,
I sey this, that they maked been for bothe,
This is to seye, for office, and for ese
Of engendrure, ther we nat God displese.
Why sholde men elles in hir bokes sette,
130   That man shal yelde to his wyf hir dette?
Now wher-with sholde he make his payement,
If he ne used his sely instrument?
Than were they maad upon a creature,
To purge uryne, and eek for engendrure.

But I seye noght that every wight is holde,
That hath swich harneys as I to yow tolde,
To goon and usen hem in engendrure;
Than sholde men take of chastitee no cure.
Crist was a mayde, and shapen as a man,
140   And many a seint, sith that the world bigan,

"Virginity is a kind of perfection, as is devoted moderation. But Jesus—who is the epitome of perfection—never said we should be like him, sell everything we have, and give it to the poor. That message was intended for people who wanted to live perfect lives—and that, mind you, isn't me. I have chosen to invest everything I have in the acts and fruits of marriage.

115-134 "And another thing: Why were male and female genitals made so perfectly for each other if they weren't meant to be used? They weren't made for nothing, that's for sure! Some people will swear up and down until they're blue in the face that our privates were made for peeing and telling the difference between men and women and nothing else. What do you think of that? Experience, however, tells us this isn't so. But, for the sake of you nuns, priests, and friars riding with us, I'll just say that our private parts were made for both business and pleasure, so long as it's for having children so that we don't anger God. Why else do men write that husbands should

1 Corinthians 7:3 'pay their wives their debt,' i.e., give them sexual pleasure? Now, how can a guy go about 'paying his debt' to his wife unless he uses his masculine member? So you see, our privates were given to us for peeing and for having children.

135-162 "That doesn't mean, of course, that everyone who has genitals has to have as many kids as possible. If that were the case, then no one would care about things such as virginity and celibacy. Jesus, who had the body of a man, was a virgin, as were many of the holiest saints who lived before and after Him. I'm not jealous that they were virgins: Let some people be like white bread made of the purest wheat, and let us wives be more like coarser bread made of barley

Yet lived they ever in parfit chastitee.
I nil envye no virginitee;
Lat hem be breed of pured whete-seed,
And lat us wyves hoten barly-breed;
And yet with barly-breed, Mark telle can,
Our lord Iesu refresshed many a man.
In swich estaat as God hath cleped us
I wol persevere, I nam nat precious.
In wyfhode I wol use myn instrument
As frely as my maker hath it sent.
If I be daungerous, God yeve me sorwe!
Myn housbond shal it have bothe eve and morwe,
Whan that him list com forth and paye his dette.
An housbonde I wol have, I nil nat lette,
Which shal be bothe my dettour and my thral,
And have his tribulacioun with-al
Upon his flessh, whyl that I am his wyf.
I have the power duringe al my lyf
Upon his propre body, and noght he.
Right thus the apostel tolde it unto me;
And bad our housbondes for to love us weel.
Al this sentence me lyketh every-deel'—

Up sterte the Pardoner, and that anon,
'Now dame,' quod he, 'by God and by seint Iohn,
Ye been a noble prechour in this cas!
I was aboute to wedde a wyf; allas!
What sholde I bye it on my flesh so dere?
Yet hadde I lever wedde no wyf to-yere!'

'Abyde!' quod she, 'my tale is nat bigonne;
Nay, thou shalt drinken of another tonne
Er that I go, shal savoure wors than ale.
And whan that I have told thee forth my tale
Of tribulacioun in mariage,
Of which I am expert in al myn age,
This to seyn, my-self have been the whippe;—
Than maystow chese whether thou wolt sippe

like it says in Mark. Our Lord Jesus helped many people, but I don't mind if God has selected another path for me. I'll use my geni-

Mark 6:38 tals in my husband's bed as freely as God allows—and God punish me if I don't! My husband can get some morning and night, whenever he wants to 'pay his debt' to me! I'll make sex easy for him so that he can give me pleasure and orgasms as often as he likes. But, I'll have the final say when it comes to sex, and he'll have to make love to me really well, just as St. Paul said, which I

1 Corinthians 7:7 think is a great piece of scripture—"

163-168   "Oh my God," interrupted the Pardoner just then. "By God and Saint John, you sure do have a lot to say about marriage and sex! I thought about getting married soon, but I'm not so sure I want my wife to have control over my life and my body like that. Maybe I shouldn't get married at all!"

169-183   "Now hold on a second," the Wife from Bath replied. "I haven't even started telling my story yet. No, you'll change your mind on marriage once again by the time I finish my story. But don't make any rash decisions because I'm going to give you about a dozen examples of other married men. Men such as you should pay attention to stories about other men who didn't listen to the good advice given them. The Greek philosopher Ptolemy said this in his book the *Almagest*."

Of thilke tonne that I shal abroche.
Be war of it, er thou to ny approche;
For I shal telle ensamples mo than ten.
180 Who-so that nil be war by othere men,
By him shul othere men corrected be.
The same wordes wryteth Ptholomee;
Rede in his Almageste, and take it there.'

'Dame, I wolde praye yow, if your wil it were,'
Seyde this Pardoner, 'as ye bigan,
Telle forth your tale, spareth for no man,
And teche us yonge men of your praktike.'

'Gladly,' quod she, 'sith it may yow lyke.
But yet I praye to al this companye,
190 If that I speke after my fantasye,
As taketh not a-grief of that I seye;
For myn entente nis but for to pleye.

Now sires, now wol I telle forth my tale.—
As ever mote I drinken wyn or ale,
I shal seye sooth, tho housbondes that I hadde,
As three of hem were gode and two were badde.
The three men were gode, and riche, and olde;
Unnethe mighte they the statut holde
In which that they were bounden unto me.
200 Ye woot wel what I mene of this, pardee!
As help me God, I laughe whan I thinke
How pitously a-night I made hem swinke;
And by my fey, I tolde of it no stoor.
They had me yeven hir gold and hir tresoor;
Me neded nat do lenger diligence
To winne hir love, or doon hem reverence.
They loved me so wel, by God above,
That I ne tolde no deyntee of hir love!
A wys womman wol sette hir ever in oon
210 To gete hir love, ther as she hath noon.
But sith I hadde hem hoolly in myn hond,

NO FEAR

184-187   "My lady, please continue then, and don't let any one of us inter-rupt you anymore. I'm sure all of us young men can learn from your experience!" said the Pardoner in return.

188-192   "Thank you," the Wife from Bath said. "Just be careful, everyone, not to take what I'm going to say too seriously, since I'm really only try-ing to tell you a story that will make you laugh.

193-223   "Anyway, back to my story. Well, to tell you the truth, of the five husbands that I've had in my lifetime, three of them were good men, but two were pretty bad. The first three were the good ones. They were all rich but also very old. In fact, they were so old that they could barely get it up for me. I'm sure I don't need to go into detail! God help me, it makes me laugh remembering how much I made them work for sex each night! They had already given me their land and money and love, which meant I didn't have to put out to get any of it! They loved me so much that it was actually hard to love them back. A wise woman will focus on pleasuring the men who don't already love her, but since my husbands had already given me everything already, I didn't bother giving them sexual pleasure unless I was going to get pleasure out of it too. So I made them work hard every night to please me, which often made them sigh in frustration. I had each of them wrapped around my little finger so tightly that they were all too happy to buy me nice things and jump for joy whenever I said anything nice to them (because God knows I scolded them often!).

And sith they hadde me yeven all hir lond,
What sholde I taken hede hem for to plese,
But it were for my profit and myn ese?
I sette hem so a-werke, by my fey,
That many a night they songen "weilawey!"
The bacoun was nat fet for hem, I trowe,
That som men han in Essex at Dunmowe.
I governed hem so wel, after my lawe,
220 That ech of hem ful blisful was and fawe
To bringe me gaye thinges fro the fayre.
They were ful glad whan I spak to hem fayre;
For God it woot, I chidde hem spitously.

Now herkneth, how I bar me proprely,
Ye wyse wyves, that can understonde.

Thus shul ye speke and bere hem wrong on honde;
For half so boldely can ther no man
Swere and lyen as a womman can.
I sey nat this by wyves that ben wyse,
230 But-if it be whan they hem misavyse.
A wys wyf, if that she can hir good,
Shal beren him on hond the cow is wood,
And take witnesse of hir owene mayde
Of hir assent; but herkneth how I sayde.

'Sir olde kaynard, is this thyn array?
Why is my neighebores wyf so gay?
She is honoured over-al ther she goth;
I sitte at hoom, I have no thrifty cloth.
What dostow at my neighebores hous?
240 Is she so fair? artow so amorous?
What rowne ye with our mayde? *benedicite*!
Sir olde lechour, lat thy Iapes be!
And if I have a gossib or a freend,
With-outen gilt, thou chydest as a feend,
If that I walke or pleye unto his hous!
Thou comest hoom as dronken as a mous,

NO FEAR

"Now all you women listening to what I'm going to say, pay attention, and take note:

"You have to be really firm with your husbands and put them in their place. Women are better liars than men, and you have to know how to be as tough as a man so that you're the one in charge. A smart wife will be able to convince her husband of anything. Just listen, for example, to what I always said to my husbands:

"'Cheapskate, are these the only clothes you'll buy for me? Just look at the neighbor's wife. She looks so pretty and is admired all about town. I, however, have to stay at home because I don't have anything nice to wear. And why have you been spending so much time at the neighbor's house? Do you think the neighbor's wife is prettier than me? Are you in love with her? And why are you always flirting with the maid, for God's sake? You're a horny old man, that's what you are! If I visit a man I'm just friends with, you yell at me. But if you come home drunk off your rock, well that's your own fault then! You like to say that it's not fair when you have to marry a poor woman because she can't give you any money, but you also like to say that rich women are too proud and demanding. And if a woman is beau-

And prechest on thy bench, with yvel preef!
Thou seist to me, it is a greet meschief
To wedde a povre womman, for costage;
250   And if that she be riche, of heigh parage,
Than seistow that it is a tormentrye
To suffre hir pryde and hir malencolye.
And if that she be fair, thou verray knave,
Thou seyst that every holour wol hir have;
She may no whyle in chastitee abyde,
That is assailled upon ech a syde.

Thou seyst, som folk desyre us for richesse,
Somme for our shap, and somme for our fairnesse;
And som, for she can outher singe or daunce,
260   And som, for gentillesse and daliaunce;
Som, for hir handes and hir armes smale;
Thus goth al to the devel by thy tale.
Thou seyst, men may nat kepe a castel-wal;
It may so longe assailled been over-al.

And if that she be foul, thou seist that she
Coveiteth every man that she may se;
For as a spaynel she wol on him lepe,
Til that she finde som man hir to chepe;
Ne noon so grey goos goth ther in the lake,
270   As, seistow, that wol been with-oute make.
And seyst, it is an hard thing for to welde
A thing that no man wol, his thankes, helde.
Thus seistow, lorel, whan thow goost to bedde;
And that no wys man nedeth for to wedde,
Ne no man that entendeth unto hevene.
With wilde thonder-dint and firy levene
Mote thy welked nekke be to-broke!

Thow seyst that dropping houses, and eek smoke,
And chyding wyves, maken men to flee
280   Out of hir owene hous; a! *benedicite!*
What eyleth swich an old man for to chyde?

tiful, you men complain that she'll cheat on you some day because she won't be able to resist all the attention she gets from other men.

257-264 "'You tell us that some of these admirers like us for our money, others for our curvy figures, and some because we're too beautiful. Some men like a woman because she can sing and dance, while others like her because she comes from a good family or flirts a lot. Others like her small hands and arms. There's always some reason why she's going to fail you and cheat on you! As you men are fond of saying, "No castle wall can sustain constant attack."

265-277 "'But if a woman is ugly, then you claim that she wants to sleep with every man she lays eyes on and will hump any man who'll let her, just like a dog. There's someone for everyone out there no matter how ugly, you say. And you complain that it's hard to keep track of a wife who doesn't want to stay put and that you shouldn't have gotten married at all, even as you go to bed with her. May God strike you down and kill you!

278-284 "'You like to say that leaky roofs, fire, and nagging wives are the three things that will chase a man from his own house. But what in God's name did we ever do to you to deserve this kind of abuse? You say that we women have tricked you in marriage.

Thow seyst, we wyves wol our vyces hyde
Til we be fast, and than we wol hem shewe;
Wel may that be a proverbe of a shrewe!

Thou seist, that oxen, asses, hors, and houndes,
They been assayed at diverse stoundes;
Bacins, lavours, er that men hem bye,
Spones and stoles, and al swich housbondrye,
And so been pottes, clothes, and array;
But folk of wyves maken noon assay
Til they be wedded; olde dotard shrewe!
And than, seistow, we wol oure vices shewe.

Thou seist also, that it displeseth me
But-if that thou wolt preyse my beautee,
And but thou poure alwey upon my face,
And clepe me "faire dame" in every place;
And but thou make a feste on thilke day
That I was born, and make me fresh and gay,
And but thou do to my norice honour,
And to my chamberere with-inne my bour,
And to my fadres folk and his allyes;—
Thus seistow, olde barel ful of lyes!

And yet of our apprentice Ianekyn,
For his crisp heer, shyninge as gold so fyn,
And for he squiereth me bothe up and doun,
Yet hastow caught a fals suspicioun;
I wol hym noght, thogh thou were deed to-morwe.

But tel me this, why hydestow, with sorwe,
The keyes of thy cheste awey fro me?
It is my good as wel as thyn, pardee.
What wenestow make an idiot of our dame?
Now by that lord, that called is seint Iame,
Thou shalt nat bothe, thogh that thou were wood,
Be maister of my body and of my good;
That oon thou shalt forgo, maugree thyne yēn;

290

300

310

That's certainly a hypocritical thing for an abusive old scoundrel to say!

285-292   "'You like to point out that men examine their oxen, donkeys, horses, dogs, clothes, pots, and even the kitchen sink before buying them but then don't look at a woman thoroughly. A man can't try a woman out until he's married to her, and then it's too late to get rid of her once she's revealed all her faults.

293-302   "'You say that I'm not happy unless you tell me I'm pretty and fawn over me and call me "darling" and throw me parties on my birthday and buy me new clothes and say nice things to my servants and friends and family. Well, that's all a load of crap!

303-307   "'And worse, you think there's something going on between me and that kid Janken simply because he's handsome, has curly golden hair, and treats me kindly. Well, I wouldn't want to sleep with him even if you died tomorrow!

308-322   "'And tell me this: Why do you hide the keys to your safe from me, huh? The valuables inside belong to me just as much as they belong to you. You think you can fool me? By God and St. James you're not going to control both my body and everything I own. Even if it pisses you off more than anything else, you're not going to have both. So what will you gain by spying on me all the time? It's almost as if you want to put me in that safe of yours! I wish you'd say "Have fun, and go wherever you want—I trust you. I know you're loyal to

What nedeth thee of me to enquere or spyën?
I trowe, thou woldest loke me in thy chiste!
Thou sholdest seye, "wyf, go wher thee liste,
Tak your disport, I wol nat leve no talis;
320   I knowe yow for a trewe wyf, dame Alis."
We love no man that taketh kepe or charge
Wher that we goon, we wol ben at our large.

Of alle men y-blessed moot he be,
The wyse astrologien Dan Ptholome,
That seith this proverbe in his Almageste,
"Of alle men his wisdom is the hyeste,
That rekketh never who hath the world in honde."
By this proverbe thou shalt understonde,
Have thou y-nogh, what thar thee recche or care
330   How merily that othere folkes fare?
For certeyn, olde dotard, by your leve,
Ye shul have queynte right y-nough at eve.
He is to greet a nigard that wol werne
A man to lighte his candle at his lanterne;
He shal have never the lasse light, pardee;
Have thou y-nough, thee thar nat pleyne thee.

Thou seyst also, that if we make us gay
With clothing and with precious array,
That it is peril of our chastitee;
340   And yet, with sorwe, thou most enforce thee,
And seye thise wordes in the apostles name,
"In habit, maad with chastitee and shame,
Ye wommen shul apparaille yow," quod he,
"And noght in tressed heer and gay perree,
As perles, ne with gold, ne clothes riche;"
After thy text, ne after thy rubriche
I wol nat wirche as muchel as a gnat.
Thou seydest this, that I was lyk a cat;
For who-so wolde senge a cattes skin,
350   Thanne wolde the cat wel dwellen in his in;
And if the cattes skin be slyk and gay,

me, Lady Alison." We women don't want husbands that keep tabs on us all the time. We want some freedom too.

323-336 "'Ptolemy, who was the wisest philosopher who ever lived, says in his book the *Almagest* that 'The wisest man in the world is the one who doesn't care who's in charge." In other words, what does it matter what other people have if you yourself have all you want? Yes, yes, you'll get your fill of sex every night, but you're a miser if you forbid other men from lighting their candle at your lantern too. You'll get the same amount of light, so stop complaining if you're getting your fill!

This phrase is a metaphor for "having sex with your wife," just as "light" in the next line means "sex."

337-356 "'You also say that nice clothes and accessories will make women more likely to sleep around. You're so fond of quoting St. Paul: "You women should dress modestly and seriously instead of wearing curls, fancy jewelry, or pearls or gold or fancy clothes." Well I won't follow those rules at all! You once said that I was like a cat because if someone burns off a cat's fur, it'll stay at home in shame, unlike the beautiful cat who won't stay inside because she's showing off and meowing in heat. You think that if I have nice clothes, I'll never come home!

She wol nat dwelle in house half a day,
But forth she wole, er any day be dawed,
To shewe hir skin, and goon a-caterwawed;
This is to seye, if I be gay, sir shrewe,
I wol renne out, my borel for to shewe.

Sire olde fool, what eyleth thee to spyĕn?
Thogh thou preye Argus, with his hundred yĕn,
To be my warde-cors, as he can best,
In feith, he shal nat kepe me but me lest;
Yet coude I make his berd, so moot I thee.

Thou seydest eek, that ther ben thinges three,
The whiche thinges troublen al this erthe,
And that no wight ne may endure the ferthe;
O leve sir shrewe, Iesu shorte thy lyf!
Yet prechestow, and seyst, an hateful wyf
Y-rekened is for oon of thise meschances.
Been ther none othere maner resemblances
That ye may lykne your parables to,
But-if a sely wyf be oon of tho?

Thou lykenest wommanes love to helle,
To bareyne lond, ther water may not dwelle.
Thou lyknest it also to wilde fyr;
The more it brenneth, the more it hath desyr
To consume every thing that brent wol be.
Thou seyst, that right as wormes shende a tree,
Right so a wyf destroyeth hir housbonde;
This knowe they that been to wyves bonde.'

Lordinges, right thus, as ye have understonde,
Bar I stifly myne olde housbondes on honde,
That thus they seyden in hir dronkenesse;
And al was fals, but that I took witnesse
On Ianekin and on my nece also.
O lord, the peyne I dide hem and the wo,
Ful giltelees, by Goddes swete pyne!

360

370

380

357-361   "'Old fool! What do you think spying on me all the time will get you? Only Argus himself, bodyguard of the gods, with his hundred eyes could ever keep an eye on me, and I could even slip past him if I wanted to.

362-370   "'You say that there have been three things that have brought hardship to the world and that man can't endure a fourth. And still you go on and on about how women ruin the world. You old bastard, I hope Jesus takes you to heaven soon! Can't you find something else to complain about besides your wife?

371-378   "'You say that a woman's love is like a dry desert or even hell itself. You say a woman's love is like wildfire because the more it burns, the more it wants to burn down everything it can. You even say every married man knows that women are like a tree-killing fungus, and just like that a wife will destroy her husband.'

379-392   "So that's how I harassed my husbands. I told them they said these stupid things in their drunkenness. Nothing I said was actually true, but I had that guy Janken and my niece back me up by lying too. God, I harassed them so much, even though they hadn't done anything wrong! I bit and kicked like a horse, even though I was the guilty one and could have been caught in my lies dozens of times. The early bird gets the worm, as they say, so I made sure to always

For as an hors I coude byte and whyne.
I coude pleyne, thogh I were in the gilt,
Or elles often tyme hadde I ben spilt.
Who-so that first to mille comth, first grint;
I pleyned first, so was our werre y-stint.
They were ful glad to excusen hem ful blyve
Of thing of which they never agilte hir lyve.

Of wenches wolde I beren him on honde,
Whan that for syk unnethes mighte he stonde.
Yet tikled it his herte, for that he
Wende that I hadde of him so greet chiertee.
I swoor that al my walkinge out by nighte
Was for tespye wenches that he dighte;
Under that colour hadde I many a mirthe.
For al swich wit is yeven us in our birthe;
Deceite, weping, spinning God hath yive
To wommen kindely, whyl they may live.
And thus of o thing I avaunte me,
Atte ende I hadde the bettre in ech degree,
By sleighte, or force, or by som maner thing,
As by continuel murmur or grucching;
Namely a bedde hadden they meschaunce,
Ther wolde I chyde and do hem no plesaunce;
I wolde no lenger in the bed abyde,
If that I felte his arm over my syde,
Til he had maad his raunson unto me;
Than wolde I suffre him do his nycetee.
And ther-fore every man this tale I telle,
Winne who-so may, for al is for to selle.
With empty hand men may none haukes lure;
For winning wolde I al his lust endure,
And make me a feyned appetyt;
And yet in bacon hadde I never delyt;
That made me that ever I wolde hem chyde.
For thogh the pope had seten hem biside,
I wolde nat spare hem at hir owene bord.
For by my trouthe, I quitte hem word for word.

accuse him first in order to win our fights. They were always happy to just confess and apologize for things they hadn't even done.

393-430   "I'd accuse them of having affairs, even when they were sick and couldn't stand up straight, let alone do anything in bed. I think they secretly liked my accusations because they thought they reflected feelings of jealousy in me. I swore that I was out and about at night to find out who they were sleeping with when I was really out having fun. God made women naturally good at lying, crying, and spinning yarn. I can say that in the end I always got my way whether I lied, cheated, complained, or nagged my husbands. I particularly gave them a lot of trouble over sex, and I'd often make them go without getting any. If my husband was in the mood and started touching me at night, I'd refuse even to stay in bed with him unless he got me off first. Only then would I let him finish. The point is that everything has a price: Even though I wasn't attracted to my extremely old husbands, I pretended to be interested in them in order to get their money and the deeds to their land. That's why I harassed them all the time...because I couldn't actually stand them. Even if the pope himself were there, I'd still have lit into them. God help me, though, if I died right now I know that I'd have nothing to answer for regarding those marriages because I certainly paid my price in bed with them. They had to make some sacrifices for me because they sure struggled to get it up.

As help me verray God omnipotent,
Thogh I right now sholde make my testament,
I ne owe hem nat a word that it nis quit.
I broghte it so aboute by my wit,
That they moste yeve it up, as for the beste;
Or elles hadde we never been in reste.
For thogh he loked as a wood leoun,
430   Yet sholde he faille of his conclusioun.

Thanne wolde I seye, 'gode lief, tak keep
How mekely loketh Wilkin oure sheep;
Com neer, my spouse, lat me ba thy cheke!
Ye sholde been al pacient and meke,
And han a swete spyced conscience,
Sith ye so preche of Iobes pacience.
Suffreth alwey, sin ye so wel can preche;
And but ye do, certain we shal yow teche
That it is fair to have a wyf in pees.
440   Oon of us two moste bowen, doutelees;
And sith a man is more resonable
Than womman is, ye moste been suffrable.
What eyleth yow to grucche thus and grone?
Is it for ye wolde have my queynte allone?
Why taak it al, lo, have it every-deel;
Peter! I shrewe yow but ye love it weel!
For if I wolde selle my *bele chose*,
I coude walke as fresh as is a rose;
But I wol kepe it for your owene tooth.
450   Ye be to blame, by God, I sey yow sooth.'

Swiche maner wordes hadde we on honde.
Now wol I speken of my fourthe housbonde.

My fourthe housbonde was a revelour,
This is to seyn, he hadde a paramour;
And I was yong and ful of ragerye,
Stiborn and strong, and Ioly as a pye.
Wel coude I daunce to an harpe smale,

NO FEAR

"I'd say to them things like, 'Oh honey, Willy's looking pretty limp tonight. Come over here and let me kiss you! You're always talking about the virtues of patience, so just relax and give it some time. Be patient or else we won't be able to do anything. What's bothering you so much? Why are you groaning like that? Is it because you want to come inside me? Well, I'm waiting here for you—come on and hurry up! Lord, some stud you are—can't even get it up. You know, my vagina would be a lot happier if I were sleeping with another man. But that'd make me a bad wife, now wouldn't it? God knows this is all your fault.'

451-452 "We'd have so many conversations like this. Anyway, let's move on to my fourth husband.

453-468 "My fourth husband was a partier and a philanderer, and I was young and carefree and very headstrong. Give me a little wine, and I'd sing and dance all night long. You remember that old story about the ancient man named Metellius who beat his wife to death because she drank too much wine? Well, he sure wouldn't have stopped

And singe, y-wis, as any nightingale,
Whan I had dronke a draughte of swete wyn.
460 Metellius, the foule cherl, the swyn,
That with a staf birafte his wyf hir lyf,
For she drank wyn, thogh I hadde been his wyf,
He sholde nat han daunted me fro drinke;
And, after wyn, on Venus moste I thinke:
For al so siker as cold engendreth hayl,
A likerous mouth moste han a likerous tayl.
In womman vinolent is no defence,
This knowen lechours by experience.

But, lord Crist! whan that it remembreth me
470 Upon my yowthe, and on my Iolitee,
It tikleth me aboute myn herte rote.
Unto this day it dooth myn herte bote
That I have had my world as in my tyme.
But age, allas! that al wol envenyme,
Hath me biraft my beautee and my pith;
Lat go, fare-wel, the devel go therwith!
The flour is goon, ther is na-more to telle,
The bren, as I best can, now moste I selle;
But yet to be right mery wol I fonde.
480 Now wol I tellen of my fourthe housbonde.

I seye, I hadde in herte greet despyt
That he of any other had delyt.
But he was quit, by God and by seint Ioce!
I made him of the same wode a croce;
Nat of my body in no foul manere,
But certeinly, I made folk swich chere,
That in his owene grece I made him frye
For angre, and for verray Ialousye.
By God, in erthe I was his purgatorie,
490 For which I hope his soule be in glorie.
For God it woot, he sat ful ofte and song
Whan that his shoo ful bitterly him wrong.
Ther was no wight, save God and he, that wiste,

me from drinking! I always get horny when I'm drunk because sex and alcohol usually go hand-in-hand. And as any womanizer can tell you, women have a hard time fending off men's advances when they're drunk.

469-480 "Oh Lord in heaven! Remembering all those fun times I had when I was young tickles me to my core. It makes me glad knowing that I had those experiences in my youth. Too bad age has stolen my beauty and youthful energy. Oh well. I don't need them anyway! I'm not young any more, and that's just all there is to it. Now I just need to make do with what I have left and try to find some joy in that. Oh, anyway, back to my fourth husband.

481-502 "You know, it made me furious to think that he was sleeping around with other women. But by God, I got him in the end because two can play that game! I flirted with other men, which just cooked his goose. I put him through hell on earth, and I know he suffered because he was the kind of guy who'd whine about every little thing. Only he and God knew how much I tortured that man. He died shortly after I returned from my pilgrimage to Jerusalem. He's buried inside our church, though his grave isn't nearly as fancy as the tomb the architect Appelles built for Darius so long ago. Anything that nice would have been a waste on my fourth husband. Anyway, he's dead now, God rest his soul.

In many wyse, how sore I him twiste.
He deyde whan I cam fro Ierusalem,
And lyth y-grave under the rode-beem,
Al is his tombe noght so curious
As was the sepulcre of him, Darius,
Which that Appelles wroghte subtily;
It nis but wast to burie him preciously.
Lat him fare-wel, God yeve his soule reste,
He is now in the grave and in his cheste.

Now of my fifthe housbond wol I telle.
God lete his soule never come in helle!
And yet was he to me the moste shrewe;
That fele I on my ribbes al by rewe,
And ever shal, unto myn ending-day.
But in our bed he was so fresh and gay,
And ther-with-al so wel coude he me glose,
Whan that he wolde han my *bele chose*,
That thogh he hadde me bet on every boon,
He coude winne agayn my love anoon.
I trowe I loved him beste, for that he
Was of his love daungerous to me.
We wommen han, if that I shal nat lye,
In this matere a queynte fantasye;
Wayte what thing we may nat lightly have,
Ther-after wol we crye al-day and crave.
Forbede us thing, and that desyren we;
Prees on us faste, and thanne wol we flee.
With daunger oute we al our chaffare;
Greet prees at market maketh dere ware,
And to greet cheep is holde at litel prys;
This knoweth every womman that is wys.

My fifthe housbonde, God his soule blesse!
Which that I took for love and no richesse,
He som-tyme was a clerk of Oxenford,
And had left scole, and wente at hoom to bord
With my gossib, dwellinge in oure toun,

NO FEAR

"And then there was my fifth husband, Jankin, that young man I told you about before. May God save him from the pits of hell! He treated me so horribly that I can still feel the bruises he gave me all up and down my ribs and always will until the day I die. He was an animal in bed, though, and knew how to turn me on so much when he wanted my vagina that even if he beat every bone in my body, he could win my love again in no time at all. I believe I loved him the most of all my husbands because he'd hardly show his love or affection. There's this funny thing about women, you see, that we crave whatever we can't have. Tell us we can't have something, and we want it, but shove it in our faces, and then we run away. Be aloof, and we'll sell ourselves to you, but give it up too easily and we won't want you. Any woman worth her salt can tell you this.

"I actually married this last husband of mine—God bless his soul— for love, not money. He used to be a student at Oxford University, but he rented a room from a close friend of mine, who was also named Alison, when he left school and returned home. God bless her! My friend Alison knew everything about me and knew me

530 God have hir soule! hir name was Alisoun.
She knew myn herte and eek my privetee
Bet than our parisshe-preest, so moot I thee!
To hir biwreyed I my conseil al.
For had myn housbonde pissed on a wal,
Or doon a thing that sholde han cost his lyf,
To hir, and to another worthy wyf,
And to my nece, which that I loved weel,
I wolde han told his conseil every-deel.
And so I dide ful often, God it woot,
540 That made his face ful often reed and hoot
For verray shame, and blamed him-self for he
Had told to me so greet a privetee.

And so bifel that ones, in a Lente,
(So often tymes I to my gossib wente,
For ever yet I lovede to be gay,
And for to walke, in March, Averille, and May,
Fro hous to hous, to here sondry talis),
That Iankin clerk, and my gossib dame Alis,
And I my-self, in-to the feldes wente.
550 Myn housbond was at London al that Lente;
I hadde the bettre leyser for to pleye,
And for to see, and eek for to be seye
Of lusty folk; what wiste I wher my grace
Was shapen for to be, or in what place?
Therefore I made my visitaciouns,
To vigilies and to processiouns,
To preching eek and to thise pilgrimages,
To pleyes of miracles and mariages,
And wered upon my gaye scarlet gytes.
560 Thise wormes, ne thise motthes, ne thise mytes,
Upon my peril, frete hem never a deel;
And wostow why? for they were used weel.

Now wol I tellen forth what happed me.
I seye, that in the feeldes walked we,
Til trewely we hadde swich daliance,

even better that our local priest did. I confided all my secrets to her because, whether my husband pissed on a wall or did something truly illegal, I would have told her anything. In fact, I would tell her, another woman I was friends with, and my own niece, whom I'm very close with. God knows, I spilled Jankin's secrets to them all the time, which really embarrassed him and pissed him off for having trusted me in the first place.

543-562   "Well, one day during Lent (a time when I always enjoy visiting friends), Jankin and my good friend Alison and I went for a walk through the countryside, which I just love to do in March, April, and May. My fourth husband was in London at the time, which gave me all the more time to have fun, go out on the town, and hang out with attractive people. You just never know when your luck will change or where life will take you, you know. So I'd put on my red dress and go to all the big parties and banquets, to lectures and plays and weddings and on holy pilgrimages. Moths never had a chance to eat that red dress because I was always wearing it!

563-574   "Anyway, so here's what happened: We were walking through the fields, and Jankin and I were flirting with each other so much that I told him I'd marry him if my fourth husband ever died. I always

This clerk and I, that of my purveyance
I spak to him, and seyde him, how that he,
If I were widwe, sholde wedde me.
For certeinly, I sey for no bobance,
570   Yet was I never with-outen purveyance
Of mariage, nof othere thinges eek.
I holde a mouses herte nat worth a leek,
That hath but oon hole for to sterte to,
And if that faille, thanne is al y-do.

I bar him on honde, he hadde enchanted me;
My dame taughte me that soutiltee.
And eek I seyde, I mette of him al night;
He wolde han slayn me as I lay up-right,
And al my bed was ful of verray blood,
580   But yet I hope that he shal do me good;
For blood bitokeneth gold, as me was taught.
And al was fals, I dremed of it right naught,
But as I folwed ay my dames lore,
As wel of this as of other thinges more.

But now sir, lat me see, what I shal seyn?
A! ha! by God, I have my tale ageyn.

Whan that my fourthe housbond was on bere,
I weep algate, and made sory chere,
As wyves moten, for it is usage,
590   And with my coverchief covered my visage;
But for that I was purveyed of a make,
I weep but smal, and that I undertake.

To chirche was myn housbond born a-morwe
With neighebores, that for him maden sorwe;
And Iankin oure clerk was oon of tho.
As help me God, whan that I saugh him go
After the bere, me thoughte he hadde a paire
Of legges and of feet so clene and faire,
That al myn herte I yaf unto his hold.

have a backup plan in place when it comes to marriage and every-thing else I do because, as the saying goes, a mouse that has only one hole to hide in will always be stressed out, worrying what will happen if that hole gets covered.

575-584   "I made Jankin believe that I was utterly smitten with him, a little trick my mother taught me. I also told him that I'd dreamed he'd raped me as I was lying in bed and that I was covered in blood. This sounds pretty bad, but I said I knew this was a good dream because the blood symbolized gold. None of this was true, of course. I hadn't dreamed this at all. I was just following my mom's advice, as I do with most everything else.

585-586   "But wait a minute. Let me see . . . what was I talking about again? Oh, right! I remember now.

587-592   "When my fourth husband died, I cried, acted sad, wore a veil, and did everything a wife in mourning was supposed to do. But I didn't cry much, that's for sure, because I already had my next husband lined up.

593-626   "They brought the body of my dead husband to the church the next day, and all of our neighbors were there to mourn for him, includ-ing Jankin. So help me God, I swear I fell in love with him right then and there when I saw him walk into the church with his muscular legs and well-kept body. He was only twenty years old, I think, and I was forty, but I always did have a thing for younger men. I had a gap in my front teeth, which is the sign of Venus and lust. God, I was

600 He was, I trowe, a twenty winter old,
And I was fourty, if I shal seye sooth;
But yet I hadde alwey a coltes tooth.
Gat-tothed I was, and that bicam me weel;
I hadde the prente of sēynt Venus seel.
As help me God, I was a lusty oon,
And faire and riche, and yong, and wel bigoon;
And trewely, as myne housbondes tolde me,
I had the beste *quoniam* mighte be.
For certes, I am al Venerien
610 In felinge, and myn herte is Marcien.
Venus me yaf my lust, my likerousnesse,
And Mars yaf me my sturdy hardinesse.
Myn ascendent was Taur, and Mars ther-inne.
Allas! allas! that ever love was sinne!
I folwed ay myn inclinacioun
By vertu of my constellacioun;
That made me I coude noght withdrawe
My chambre of Venus from a good felawe.
Yet have I Martes mark upon my face,
620 And also in another privee place.
For, God so wis be my savacioun,
I ne loved never by no discrecioun,
But ever folwede myn appetyt,
Al were he short or long, or blak or whyt;
I took no kepe, so that he lyked me,
How pore he was, ne eek of what degree.

What sholde I seye, but, at the monthes ende,
This Ioly clerk Iankin, that was so hende,
Hath wedded me with greet solempnitee,
630 And to him yaf I al the lond and fee
That ever was me yeven ther-bifore;
But afterward repented me ful sore.
He nolde suffre nothing of my list.
By God, he smoot me ones on the list,
For that I rente out of his book a leef,
That of the strook myn ere wex al deef.

a horny one, young and beautiful and rich and, at least according to my husbands, the best piece of ass around. There's no doubt that everything I have comes from Venus and Mars: Venus gave me my lust and Mars my practicality. This is because Mars and Venus were in the sky when I was born. In fact, I still have the birthmark Mars gave me on my face—and on my private parts too. These traits control my body, which means I've never been able to keep hot guys out of my bed. It's too bad that sex is such a sin! I'm not too picky. I just go with whomever turns me on, whether he's short or tall, black or white, rich or poor. I don't care, as long as he can get me off

627-646　　"Well, there really isn't a whole lot more to say. Jankin and I got married about a month later, and I handed over all the money and property that all my previous husbands had left me, something I'd seriously regret doing later on. Jankin turned out to be so domineering that I wasn't allowed to do anything I wanted. In fact, one time he hit me so hard on the side of the head for tearing a page out of his most beloved book that I lost all the hearing in that ear permanently. Still, I was incredibly stubborn and wouldn't keep quiet. I continued to go out and visit my friends as I used to do, despite the fact that he ordered me to stay at home. For this reason he'd preach and

Stiborn I was as is a leonesse,
And of my tonge a verray Iangleresse,
And walke I wolde, as I had doon biforn,
640   From hous to hous, al-though he had it sworn.
For which he often tymes wolde preche,
And me of olde Romayn gestes teche,
How he, Simplicius Gallus, lefte his wyf,
And hir forsook for terme of al his lyf,
Noght but for open-heeded he hir say
Lokinge out at his dore upon a day.

Another Romayn tolde he me by name,
That, for his wyf was at a someres game
With-oute his witing, he forsook hir eke.
650   And than wolde he upon his Bible seke
That ilke proverbe of Ecclesiaste,
Wher he comandeth and forbedeth faste,
Man shal nat suffre his wyf go roule aboute;
Than wolde he seye right thus, with-outen doute,
"Who-so that buildeth his hous al of salwes,
And priketh his blinde hors over the falwes,
And suffreth his wyf to go seken halwes,
Is worthy to been hanged on the galwes!"
But al for noght, I sette noght an hawe
660   Of his proverbes nof his olde sawe,
Ne I wolde nat of him corrected be.
I hate him that my vices telleth me,
And so do mo, God woot! of us than I.
This made him with me wood al outrely;
I nolde noght forbere him in no cas.

Now wol I seye yow sooth, by seint Thomas,
Why that I rente out of his book a leef,
For which he smoot me so that I was deef.

He hadde a book that gladly, night and day,
670   For his desport he wolde rede alway.
He cleped it Valerie and Theofraste,

tell me stories of ancient Romans who controlled their wives, such as Simplicius Gallus, who divorced his wife simply because she had poked her head out the door one day without covering her head.

647-665   "He also told me of another Roman man who divorced his wife because she went to a sporting event without first asking for his permission. And then Jankin would break out his Bible to find that proverb in the book of Ecclesiasticus in the apocrypha that tells men not to let their wives go out and about. Then he'd always say, 'The guy who builds his house of straw and uses a blind horse to plow his fields and lets his wife go out by herself ought to be hanged!' As for men, though, I didn't give a rat's ass for his proverbs or his misogynistic crap, nor would I let him tell me what to do. I hate it when people point out my faults, and God knows, I'm not the only one either. My refusal to listen or obey really pissed him off, but I wouldn't ever back down.

666-668   "And now, by St. Thomas, I'll tell you why I tore a page out of that precious book of his, which made him hit me so hard that I went deaf.

669-710   "You see, Jankin had this book that he loved to read all the time, day and night. The name of the book was *Valerius and Theophrastus*, and it always made him laugh. This book actually consisted of

At whiche book he lough alwey ful faste.
And eek ther was som-tyme a clerk at Rome,
A cardinal, that highte Seint Ierome,
That made a book agayn Iovinian;
In whiche book eek ther was Tertulan,
Crisippus, Trotula, and Helowys,
That was abbesse nat fer fro Parys;
And eek the Parables of Salomon,
680 Ovydes Art, and bokes many on,
And alle thise wer bounden in o volume.
And every night and day was his custume,
Whan he had leyser and vacacioun,
From other worldly occupacioun,
To reden on this book of wikked wyves.
He knew of hem mo legendes and lyves
Than been of gode wyves in the Bible.
For trusteth wel, it is an impossible
That any clerk wol speke good of wyves,
690 But-if it be of holy seintes lyves,
Ne of noon other womman never the mo.
Who peyntede the leoun, tel me who?
By God, if wommen hadde writen stories,
As clerkes han with-inne hir oratories,
They wolde han writen of men more wikkednesse
Than all the mark of Adam may redresse.
The children of Mercurie and of Venus
Been in hir wirking ful contrarious;
Mercurie loveth wisdom and science,
700 And Venus loveth ryot and dispence.
And, for hir diverse disposicioun,
Ech falleth in otheres exaltacioun;
And thus, God woot! Mercurie is desolat
In Pisces, wher Venus is exaltat;
And Venus falleth ther Mercurie is reysed;
Therfore no womman of no clerk is preysed.
The clerk, whan he is old, and may noght do
Of Venus werkes worth his olde sho,

many books all bound up into a single volume and included the Roman cardinal St. Jerome's book against Jovinian as well as Ovid's *Art of Love*, the *Parables of Solomon*, and other misogynistic works by Tertulian, Chrysippus, Trotula, and Heloise, the nun from Paris. And whenever he had some free time, whether it be night or day, he'd sit down to read all about the evils of women in this book. In fact, he knew more about these women than he did about all the good women mentioned in the Bible. Trust me: No scholar will ever praise the virtues of a woman unless she happens to be a saint. But by God, if women had written those books instead of men, they'd be full of stories about men's wickedness, more evil than all of mankind could ever atone for. Men are from Mercury and women are from Venus, they say, and while Mercury loves learning, Venus loves having fun. And because they're polar opposites, each one loses power whenever the other one is in the sky, which means that no scholar would ever praise any daughter of Venus. And so, when scholarly men are old and grey and can't get it up anymore, they sit down and write awful things about women who cheat on their husbands!

Than sit he doun, and writ in his dotage
710 That wommen can nat kepe hir mariage!

But now to purpos, why I tolde thee
That I was beten for a book, pardee.
Upon a night Iankin, that was our syre,
Redde on his book, as he sat by the fyre,
Of Eva first, that, for hir wikkednesse,
Was al mankinde broght to wrecchednesse,
For which that Iesu Crist him-self was slayn,
That boghte us with his herte-blood agayn.
Lo, here expres of womman may ye finde,
720 That womman was the los of al mankinde.

Tho redde he me how Sampson loste his heres,
Slepinge, his lemman kitte hem with hir sheres;
Thurgh whiche tresoun loste he bothe his yën.

Tho redde he me, if that I shal nat lyen,
Of Hercules and of his Dianyre,
That caused him to sette himself a-fyre.

No-thing forgat he the penaunce and wo
That Socrates had with hise wyves two;
How Xantippa caste pisse upon his heed;
730 This sely man sat stille, as he were deed;
He wyped his heed, namore dorste he seyn
But "er that thonder stinte, comth a reyn."

Of Phasipha, that was the quene of Crete,
For shrewednesse, him thoughte the tale swete;
Fy! spek na-more—it is a grisly thing—
Of hir horrible lust and hir lyking.

Of Clitemistra, for hir lecherye,
That falsly made hir housbond for to dye,
He redde it with ful good devocioun.

711-720 "So anyway, Jankin beat me so hard because of that book. One night, you see, Jankin was sitting by the fire reading from this book about how Eve caused the fall of man, which is why Jesus had to be killed to save us all.

721-723 "Then he told me all about how Delilah cut off all of Samson's hair while he was sleeping, which ultimately led to the loss of his eyesight.

724-726 "Then he went on about Dejanira and how she caused Hercules to set himself on fire.

727-732 "And he talked about all the trouble the Greek philosopher Socrates had with his two wives and how he just sat there and said, 'When it rains, it pours,' when Xantippe threw piss on his head.

733-736 "And then he read the story of Pasiphaë, the queen of Crete, who slept with a bull and gave birth to the half-man, half-bull minotaur. Oh God, I can't talk about that anymore—it's too disgusting! Suffice it to say, he loved that story a lot.

737-746 "And then he brought up Clytemnestra, who cheated on her husband, which ultimately killed him. Jankin liked this story too.

740 He tolde me eek for what occasioun
Amphiorax at Thebes loste his lyf;
Myn housbond hadde a legende of his wyf,
Eriphilem, that for an ouche of gold
Hath prively unto the Grekes told
Wher that hir housbonde hidde him in a place,
For which he hadde at Thebes sory grace.

Of Lyma tolde he me, and of Lucye,
They bothe made hir housbondes for to dye;
That oon for love, that other was for hate;
750 Lyma hir housbond, on an even late,
Empoysoned hath, for that she was his fo.
Lucya, likerous, loved hir housbond so,
That, for he sholde alwey upon hir thinke,
She yaf him swich a maner love-drinke,
That he was deed, er it were by the morwe;
And thus algates housbondes han sorwe.

Than tolde he me, how oon Latumius
Compleyned to his felawe Arrius,
That in his gardin growed swich a tree,
760 On which, he seyde, how that his wyves three
Hanged hem-self for herte despitous.
"O leve brother," quod this Arrius,
"Yif me a plante of thilke blissed tree,
And in my gardin planted shal it be!"

Of latter date, of wyves hath he red,
That somme han slayn hir housbondes in hir bed,
And lete hir lechour dighte hir al the night
Whyl that the corps lay in the floor up-right.
And somme han drive nayles in hir brayn
770 Whyl that they slepte, and thus they han hem slayn.
Somme han hem yeve poysoun in hir drinke.
He spak more harm than herte may bithinke.
And ther-with-al, he knew of mo proverbes
Than in this world ther growen gras or herbes.

NO FEAR

"He told me the story about Eriphyle from the city of Thebes, who was married to Amphiarus and sold out her husband to the Greeks for a piece of gold jewelry.

747-756 "Then there was Livia and Lucilla, who murdered their husbands. Livia hated her husband, so she poisoned him one night. Lucilla, on the other hand, gave her husband a love potion so that he wouldn't think of other girls, but it ended up killing him in his sleep.

757-764 "Then Jankin told me about a guy named Latumisu who complained to his friend Arrius about how his three wives had hanged themselves from the branches of the peach tree in his garden out of spite. 'My dear friend,' Arrius had replied. 'That's great! Give me a seed from this tree so that I can plant it in my own garden!'

765-787 "My husband also read more recent stories of women who murdered their husbands while they slept, threw the dead bodies on the floor, and then screwed their lovers all night long. Or he'd tell me about women who had killed their husbands by driving nails into their heads as they slept. And then there'd be other stories of women who put poison in their husbands' drinks. Jankin knew more mysoginistic proverbs than there are blades of grass and more horrible stories about women than you could possibly imagine. He'd also say things such as, 'It's better to live with a lion or a ferocious dragon than with a woman who nags all the time.' And, 'It's better to be homeless than

"Bet is," quod he, "thyn habitacioun
Be with a leoun or a foul dragoun,
Than with a womman usinge for to chyde.
Bet is," quod he, "hye in the roof abyde
Than with an angry wyf doun in the hous;
780   They been so wikked and contrarious;
They haten that hir housbondes loveth ay."
He seyde, "a womman cast hir shame away,
Whan she cast of hir smok;" and forther-mo,
"A fair womman, but she be chaast also,
Is lyk a gold ring in a sowes nose."
Who wolde wenen, or who wolde suppose
The wo that in myn herte was, and pyne?

And whan I saugh he wolde never fyne
To reden on this cursed book al night,
790   Al sodeynly three leves have I plight
Out of his book, right as he radde, and eke,
I with my fist so took him on the cheke,
That in our fyr he fil bakward adoun.
And he up-stirte as dooth a wood leoun,
And with his fist he smoot me on the heed,
That in the floor I lay as I were deed.
And when he saugh how stille that I lay,
He was agast, and wolde han fled his way,
Til atte laste out of my swogh I breyde:
800   "O! hastow slayn me, false theef?" I seyde,
"And for my land thus hastow mordred me?
Er I be deed, yet wol I kisse thee."

And neer he cam, and kneled faire adoun,
And seyde, "dere suster Alisoun,
As help me God, I shal thee never smyte;
That I have doon, it is thy-self to wyte.
Foryeve it me, and that I thee biseke"—
And yet eft-sones I hitte him on the cheke,
And seyde, "theef, thus muchel am I wreke;
810   Now wol I dye, I may no lenger speke."

to live with a tyrannical wife, who is so wicked and contrary because she hates everything her husband loves.' Or, 'A beautiful woman is no better than a gold ring in a pig's nose unless she's also a virgin.' Can you imagine how awful and hurtful those words were?

788-802 "Well, when I realized that he was never going to stop saying such things, I got so angry that I ripped three pages out of the book, right there as he was reading it. I also punched him in the face with my fist so hard that he fell backward into the fire in the fireplace. He sprang up like a pouncing lion and punched me right back on the side of my head so hard that I fell down and didn't move, just as if I were dead. And when he saw what he had done and thought he'd killed me, he was so horrified that he would have run away had I not come to just then. 'Are you trying to kill me, you murderer? Are you going to kill me so that you can have all my money and land? Even so, let me kiss you one last time before I die.'

803-828 "He came over to me, knelt down, and said, 'What have I done? My dear wife, Alison, so help me God, I'll never hit you again. Please forgive me. I beg you.' As he said this, though, I punched him in the face once again and said, 'Take that, you bastard. I'm dying and can't talk anymore.' But, after much care and some more fighting, I finally recovered, and Jankin and I worked things out. He put me in charge of our household and over all our money and property, and he also promised that he wouldn't say such horrible things about women or

But atte laste, with muchel care and wo,
We fille acorded, by us selven two.
He yaf me al the brydel in myn hond
To han the governance of hous and lond,
And of his tonge and of his hond also,
And made him brenne his book anon right tho.
And whan that I hadde geten unto me,
By maistrie, al the soveraynetee,
And that he seyde, "myn owene trewe wyf,
820   Do as thee lust the terme of al thy lyf,
Keep thyn honour, and keep eek myn estaat"—
After that day we hadden never debaat.
God help me so, I was to him as kinde
As any wyf from Denmark unto Inde,
And also trewe, and so was he to me.
I prey to God that sit in magestee,
So blesse his soule, for his mercy dere!
Now wol I seye my tale, if ye wol here.'

BIHOLDE THE WORDES BITWEEN THE SOMONOUR AND
THE FRERE.

The Frere lough, whan he hadde herd al this,
830   'Now, dame,' quod he, 'so have I Ioye or blis,
This is a long preamble of a tale!'
And whan the Somnour herde the Frere gale,
'Lo!' quod the Somnour, 'Goddes armes two!
A frere wol entremette him ever-mo.
Lo, gode men, a flye and eek a frere
Wol falle in every dish and eek matere.
What spekestow of preambulacioun?
What! amble, or trotte, or pees, or go sit doun;
Thou lettest our disport in this manere.'

840   'Ye, woltow so, sir Somnour?' quod the Frere,
'Now, by my feith, I shal, er that I go,
Telle of a Somnour swich a tale or two,
That alle the folk shal laughen in this place.'

hit me again. And I made him burn that horrid book too. He told me, 'Alison, do whatever you want with your life, and I leave it to you to do what's best for the both of us.' And when I'd finally won complete freedom and control over my own affairs and destiny, we never had reason to fight again. In fact, I am now a better wife to him than any woman between Denmark and India has ever been. And he became an equally excellent husband. May God on high bless his soul! And on that note, I'm ready to begin my story."

HERE'S THE CONVERSATION BETWEEN THE SUMMONER AND THE FRIAR.

829-839   The Friar laughed when he heard all this and said, "Now ma'am, that was good, but it certainly was a long introduction to a story!" And when the Summoner heard the Friar say this, he exclaimed, "God! Friars are always butting in where they don't belong! I swear, a friar is no better than a fly because both like to buzz around your food and in other people's business. What do you mean she blabbed too much? You're blabbing too much yourself right now, so shut the hell up. You're ruining everyone else's good time!"

840-843   "That so, huh, Summoner?" shouted the Friar. "Well honest to God, when it's my turn, I'll tell you a story or two about summoners that'll make everyone laugh."

'Now elles, Frere, I bishrewe thy face,'
Quod this Somnour, 'and I bishrewe me,
But if I telle tales two or thre
Of freres er I come to Sidingborne,
That I shal make thyn herte for to morne;
For wel I wool thy patience is goon.'

850 Our hoste cryde 'pees! and that anoon!'
And seyde, 'lat the womman telle hir tale.
Ye fare as folk that dronken been of ale.
Do, dame, tel forth your tale, and that is best.'

'Al redy, sir,' quod she, 'right as yow lest,
If I have licence of this worthy Frere.'

'Yis, dame,' quod he, 'tel forth, and I wol here.'

HERE ENDETH THE WYF OF BATHE HIR PROLOGE.

844-849   "Damn you, Friar, and damn me if I don't tell everyone two or three tales about friars that'll make you cry before we reach the town of Sittingbourne. It's plain by the look of the things that you're getting pretty ornery."

850-853   "Stop it! Just stop!" said our Host. "Just let the woman tell her story. You two are acting like a couple of drunkards." Then he turned to the Wife from Bath and said, "Please, ma'am, continue with your story."

854-855   "Very well then," she said. "As long as I have your permission, Mr. Friar."

856   "Yes, ma'am," he answered. "Please continue, and I'll shut up."

THIS IS THE END OF THE PROLOGUE TO THE WIFE FROM BATH'S TALE.

The Wife of Bath's Tale

HERE BIGINNETH THE TALE OF THE WYF OF BATHE.

In tholde dayes of the king Arthour,
Of which that Britons speken greet honour,
All was this land fulfild of fayerye.
The elf-queen, with hir Ioly companye,
Daunced ful ofte in many a grene mede;
This was the olde opinion, as I rede,
I speke of manye hundred yeres ago;
But now can no man see none elves mo.
For now the grete charitee and prayeres
10   Of limitours and othere holy freres,
That serchen every lond and every streem,
As thikke as motes in the sonne-beem,
Blessinge halles, chambres, kichenes, boures,
Citees, burghes, castels, hye toures,
Thropes, bernes, shipnes, dayeryes,
This maketh that ther been no fayeryes.
For ther as wont to walken was an elf,
Ther walketh now the limitour him-self
In undermeles and in morweninges,
20   And seyth his matins and his holy thinges
As he goth in his limitacioun.
Wommen may go saufly up and doun,
In every bush, or under every tree;
Ther is noon other incubus but he,
And he ne wol doon hem but dishonour.

And so bifel it, that this king Arthour
Hadde in his hous a lusty bacheler,
That on a day cam rydinge fro river;
And happed that, allone as she was born,
30   He saugh a mayde walkinge him biforn,
Of whiche mayde anon, maugree hir heed,
By verray force he rafte hir maydenheed;
For which oppressioun was swich clamour

The Wife of Bath's Tale

HERE IS THE WIFE FROM THE CITY OF BATH'S TALE.

1-25 Back in the olden days, many hundreds of years ago when King Arthur ruled the land, England was still a country of magic. I read that they believed that there were elves and fairies and the like, and that the elf-queen herself could be seen dancing with other magical creatures in the forests. It's too bad you can't see any of these creatures any more. It's because they simply don't exist any longer. Now, instead of magical creatures, all you'll find in the forests are priests and friars. It sometimes seems as if these men are lurking around everywhere: in hallways, bedrooms, kitchens, cities, villages, castles, barns, dairies, high towers. It's because of them there aren't any fairies or elves any more. Now, women no longer have to worry about demons and imps hiding in the forest—only priests.

26-42 Well anyway, back in this time, one of King Arthur's young knights was riding through the forest one day. Pretty soon he came upon a young woman walking along the road, and he wanted her so badly that he violently raped her. The people were so angry that they went to King Arthur, who sentenced the knight to death—that was the punishment for rape back then, you know. This knight would have been beheaded for his crime were it not for the queen and other noblewomen who begged Arthur over and over again to have mercy

And swich pursute unto the king Arthour,
That dampned was this knight for to be deed
By cours of lawe, and sholde han lost his heed
Paraventure, swich was the statut tho;
But that the quene and othere ladies mo
So longe preyeden the king of grace,
40 Til he his lyf him graunted in the place,
And yaf him to the quene al at hir wille,
To chese, whether she wolde him save or spille.

The quene thanketh the king with al hir might,
And after this thus spak she to the knight,
Whan that she saugh hir tyme, upon a day:
'Thou standest yet,' quod she, 'in swich array,
That of thy lyf yet hastow no suretee.
I grante thee lyf, if thou canst tellen me
What thing is it that wommen most desyren?
50 Be war, and keep thy nekke-boon from yren.
And if thou canst nat tellen it anon,
Yet wol I yeve thee leve for to gon
A twelf-month and a day, to seche and lere
An answere suffisant in this matere.
And suretee wol I han, er that thou pace,
Thy body for to yelden in this place.'

Wo was this knight and sorwefully he syketh;
But what! he may nat do al as him lyketh.
And at the laste, he chees him for to wende,
60 And come agayn, right at the yeres ende,
With swich answere as God wolde him purveye;
And taketh his leve, and wendeth forth his weye.

He seketh every hous and every place,
Wher-as he hopeth for to finde grace,
To lerne, what thing wommen loven most;
But he ne coude arryven in no cost,
Wher-as he mighte finde in this matere
Two creatures accordinge in-fere.

on the knight. They pressured Arthur so much that he finally gave in, granted the knight clemency, and put his fate in the hands of the queen to do whatever she wanted with him.

43-56   The queen thanked Arthur from the bottom of her heart, then turned to the knight and said, "Now don't think this means you're not going to die. You're not in the clear just yet. I'll let you live if you can tell me what women want more than anything else in the world. Be careful, though, because your answer will determine whether you live or die. If you don't already know the answer, then you may go out and look for it and return in exactly a year and a day from now, which should be enough time to find the answer. You have to promise me, however, that you'll come back and turn yourself in on that day."

57-62   The sad knight heaved a deep sigh but had no answer for the queen. And so he decided to leave and search for whatever answer to the queen's question God found fit to give him.

63-72   The knight looked everywhere to find out what women want most. He looked in every house and in any place where people would talk with him. He couldn't find any place, though, where two people would give him the same answer.

70
Somme seyde, wommen loven best richesse,
Somme seyde, honour, somme seyde, Iolynesse;
Somme, riche array, somme seyden, lust abedde,
And ofte tyme to be widwe and wedde.

Somme seyde, that our hertes been most esed,
Whan that we been y-flatered and y-plesed.
He gooth ful ny the sothe, I wol nat lye;
A man shal winne us best with flaterye;
And with attendance, and with bisinesse,
Been we y-lymed, bothe more and lesse.

And somme seyn, how that we loven best
80
For to be free, and do right as us lest,
And that no man repreve us of our vyce,
But seye that we be wyse, and no-thing nyce.
For trewely, ther is noon of us alle,
If any wight wol clawe us on the galle,
That we nil kike, for he seith us sooth;
Assay, and he shal finde it that so dooth.
For be we never so vicious with-inne,
We wol been holden wyse, and clene of sinne.

And somme seyn, that greet delyt han we
90
For to ben holden stable and eek secree,
And in o purpos stedefastly to dwelle,
And nat biwreye thing that men us telle.
But that tale is nat worth a rake-stele;
Pardee, we wommen conne no-thing hele;
Witnesse on Myda; wol ye here the tale?

Ovyde, amonges othere thinges smale,
Seyde, Myda hadde, under his longe heres,
Growinge upon his heed two asses eres,
The which vyce he hidde, as he best mighte,
100
Ful subtilly from every mannes sighte,
That, save his wyf, ther wiste of it na-mo.

Some people told him that women love money the most. Others, honor. Some said happiness and laughter, and others claimed women like nice clothes and fine jewelry. Some said women want good sex, and others said women want to be able to marry multiple times.

73-78 Other people said that we women want to be flattered more than anything else, and—I'll confess—this is actually pretty close to the truth since we women can be won with nice words and constant attention.

79-88 Other people said that we women want freedom more than anything else, freedom to do whatever we want without having men around to scold and tell us how silly we are. No woman likes to hear this, even if it's the truth. Go ahead and try it, and see how your woman reacts!

89-95 Some people say that we women like people to think that we're good confidantes and secret-keepers and that we're the most loyal creatures on earth. This is just a bunch of crap, though, because everyone knows that women can't keep secrets. Just remember the story of King Midas!

96-104 The Roman poet Ovid tells the story of King Midas in his collection of tales. Midas had donkey ears growing out of his head, and he hid them with his long hair so well that no one except his wife knew they were there. He loved and trusted her very much and begged her not to tell anyone about his funny ears.

He loved hir most, and trusted hir also;
He preyede hir, that to no creature
She sholde tellen of his disfigure.

She swoor him 'nay, for al this world to winne,
She nolde do that vileinye or sinne,
To make hir housbond han so foul a name;
She nolde nat telle it for hir owene shame.'
But nathelees, hir thoughte that she dyde,
110   That she so longe sholde a conseil hyde;
Hir thoughte it swal so sore aboute hir herte,
That nedely som word hir moste asterte;
And sith she dorste telle it to no man,
Doun to a mareys faste by she ran;
Til she came there, hir herte was a-fyre,
And, as a bitore bombleth in the myre,
She leyde hir mouth unto the water doun:
'Biwreye me nat, thou water, with thy soun,'
Quod she, 'to thee I telle it, and namo;
120   Myn housbond hath longe asses eres two!
Now is myn herte all hool, now is it oute;
I mighte no lenger kepe it, out of doute,'
Heer may ye se, thogh we a tyme abyde,
Yet out it moot, we can no conseil hyde;
The remenant of the tale if ye wol here,
Redeth Ovyde, and ther ye may it lere.

This knight, of which my tale is specially,
Whan that he saugh he mighte nat come therby,
This is to seye, what wommen loven moost,
130   With-inne his brest ful sorweful was the goost;
But hoom he gooth, he mighte nat soiourne.
The day was come, that hoomward moste he tourne,
And in his wey it happed him to ryde,
In al this care, under a forest-syde,
Wher-as he saugh upon a daunce go
Of ladies foure and twenty, and yet mo;
Toward the whiche daunce he drow ful yerne,

NO FEAR

105-126 Midas's wife swore up and down that she'd never tell anyone about her husband's donkey ears. At the same time, though, she thought she'd die from having to keep such a juicy secret bottled up inside her forever. It seemed as if this secret was so strong it would burst out of her unless she could release it. But since she'd promised her husband she wouldn't tell anyone, she ran down to the lake, put her lips to the water, and said, 'Don't tell anyone what I'm about to tell you. You—and you—alone will hear my secret: My husband has the ears of a donkey! Okay, I've said it, and I feel much better because of it. I just couldn't stand it any longer.' You can read all about it in Ovid's *Metamorphoses* if you want to know the rest of the story. Still, this example shows that women can't keep secrets because it's only a matter of time before we let them slip out.

127-148 Well anyway, that knight that I was telling you about just couldn't find the answer to what women wanted most, which made him very depressed. Still, when it came time to report back to the queen, he went straight back as promised without dawdling. On his way home, however, he came upon more than two-dozen young ladies dancing on the edges of the forest. He rode toward them hoping that they might know what women want the most, but they vanished just before he reached them. In their place sat the ugliest old woman you could possibly imagine. She stood up as the knight approached and said, "Sir knight, there aren't any roads that go through this forest. But tell me what you're looking for. We old people know many things, and I might be able to help you."

Modern Translation   281

In hope that som wisdom sholde he lerne.
But certeinly, er he came fully there,
Vanisshed was this daunce, he niste where.
No creature saugh he that bar lyf,
Save on the grene he saugh sittinge a wyf;
A fouler wight ther may no man devyse.
Agayn the knight this olde wyf gan ryse,
And seyde, 'sir knight, heer-forth ne lyth no wey.
Tel me, what that ye seken, by your fey?
Paraventure it may the bettre be;
Thise olde folk can muchel thing,' quod she.

'My leve mooder,' quod this knight certeyn,
'I nam but deed, but-if that I can seyn
What thing it is that wommen most desyre;
Coude ye me wisse, I wolde wel quyte your hyre.'

'Plighte me thy trouthe, heer in myn hand,' quod she,
'The nexte thing that I requere thee,
Thou shalt it do, if it lye in thy might;
And I wol telle it yow er it be night.'
'Have heer my trouthe,' quod the knight, 'I grante.'

'Thanne,' quod she, 'I dar me wel avante,
Thy lyf is sauf, for I wol stonde therby,
Upon my lyf, the queen wol seye as I.
Lat see which is the proudeste of hem alle,
That wereth on a coverchief or a calle,
That dar seye nay, of that I shal thee teche;
Lat us go forth with-outen lenger speche.'
Tho rouned she a pistel in his ere,
And bad him to be glad, and have no fere.

Whan they be comen to the court, this knight
Seyde, 'he had holde his day, as he hadde hight,
And redy was his answere,' as he sayde.
Ful many a noble wyf, and many a mayde,
And many a widwe, for that they ben wyse,

NO FEAR

149-152   "Granny," the knight started, "I'm trying to find out what women want more than anything else in the world. I'm probably going to die very soon unless I can find the answer. If you know the answer, please tell me. It's worth a lot to me."

153-157   "Take my hand and promise me," the old woman replied, "that if I tell you the answer tonight, you'll do whatever I ask of you when I need it if it's in your power." "Yes, I swear," promised the knight.

158-166   "Then don't worry any more about being executed," she said, "Because I swear on my own life that the queen will agree with my answer! In fact, let's just see if even the proudest woman wearing scarves and headdresses will disagree with what I'm about to tell you." And with that, she whispered a few words in his ear and told him everything was going to be okay.

167-174   When the knight returned to court a year and a day later as promised, he told the queen that he was ready to give his answer. Many noblewomen, maidens, and old widows had assembled with the queen, who would judge the knight, to hear what he had to say. When everyone settled down, they called him in.

The quene hir-self sittinge as a Iustyse,
Assembled been, his answere for to here;
And afterward this knight was bode appere.

To every wight comanded was silence,
And that the knight sholde telle in audience,
What thing that worldly wommen loven best.
This knight ne stood nat stille as doth a best,
But to his questioun anon answerde
180   With manly voys, that al the court it herde:

'My lige lady, generally,' quod he,
'Wommen desyren to have sovereyntee
As wel over hir housbond as hir love,
And for to been in maistrie him above;
This is your moste desyr, thogh ye me kille,
Doth as yow list, I am heer at your wille.'

In al the court ne was ther wyf ne mayde,
Ne widwe, that contraried that he sayde,
But seyden, 'he was worthy han his lyf.'

190   And with that word up stirte the olde wyf,
Which that the knight saugh sittinge in the grene:
'Mercy,' quod she, 'my sovereyn lady quene!
Er that your court departe, do me right.
I taughte this answere unto the knight;
For which he plighte me his trouthe there,
The firste thing I wolde of him requere,
He wolde it do, if it lay in his might.
Bifore the court than preye I thee, sir knight,'
Quod she, 'that thou me take unto thy wyf;
200   For wel thou wost that I have kept thy lyf.
If I sey fals, sey nay, upon thy fey!'

NO FEAR

175-180 The queen ordered the crowd to be quiet, then turned to the knight and ordered him to tell everyone what women want most. The knight spoke up immediately in a clear voice so that everyone could hear him and said:

181-186 "My lady, generally speaking, women want to have power over their husbands and boyfriends and to have the final say in all matters. Even if you kill me, I know that this is what you women want most. I am at your mercy. Do with me what you will."

187-189 There wasn't a wife or widow or girl in the crowd who could disagree with this answer, and everyone believed that the knight had won the right to live.

190-201 When the knight finished talking, the ugly old woman stood up from where she'd been sitting in the crowd and said, "My lady, have mercy! Before you leave, please grant me a single request. I am the one who gave this knight the answer to your question, and he promised me in return that he'd do anything I asked. Well, in front of everyone gathered here today, I'd like to ask you, sir knight, to marry me. I saved your life, and you know you owe me."

This knight answerde, 'allas! and weylawey!
I woot right wel that swich was my biheste.
For Goddes love, as chees a newe requeste;
Tak al my good, and lat my body go.'

'Nay than,' quod she, 'I shrewe us bothe two!
For thogh that I be foul, and old, and pore,
I nolde for al the metal, ne for ore,
That under erthe is grave, or lyth above,
But-if thy wyf I were, and eek thy love.'

'My love?' quod he; 'nay, my dampnacioun!
Allas! that any of my nacioun
Sholde ever so foule disparaged be!'
But al for noght, the ende is this, that he
Constreyned was, he nedes moste hir wedde;
And taketh his olde wyf, and gooth to bedde.

Now wolden som men seye, paraventure,
That, for my necligence, I do no cure
To tellen yow the Ioye and al tharray
That at the feste was that ilke day.
To whiche thing shortly answere I shal;
I seye, ther nas no Ioye ne feste at al,
Ther nas but hevinesse and muche sorwe;
For prively he wedded hir on a morwe,
And al day after hidde him as an oule;
So wo was him, his wyf looked so foule.

Greet was the wo the knight hadde in his thoght,
Whan he was with his wyf a-bedde y-broght;
He walweth, and he turneth to and fro.
His olde wyf lay smylinge evermo,
And seyde, 'o dere housbond, *benedicite!*
Fareth every knight thus with his wyf as ye?
Is this the lawe of king Arthures hous?
Is every knight of his so dangerous?
I am your owene love and eek your wyf;

NO FEAR

202-205   "Oh my God, no!" cried the knight. "I know I promsed that I'd do anything you asked, but, for the love of God, please don't ask me to marry you. Take everything I own, but don't ask me this!"

206-210   "Damn us both straight to hell, then!" the old woman screamed. "Because even though I'm ugly and old and poor, I would still prefer to be your wife and your love than to have all the silver and gold in the world."

211-216   "You want my love?" the knight asked. "No, you want to ruin me! God, it would be so disgraceful for me, a handsome young knight, to have to marry this wretch!" Despite all his complaining, though, he knew he had no choice but to marry the old woman. After the wedding, he reluctantly took his new wife home, and they went to bed.

217-226   Now, some people might say that I'm skipping over all the happy parts of the story, and that I'm purposefully not telling you about the wedding feast and celebrations. Truth of the matter is, though, that there really wasn't anything fun or happy about their wedding. They got married in the morning, and then the knight hid himself like an owl all day, sad and miserable because his wife was so old and ugly.

227-241   The knight was so miserable and feeling so sorry for himself that when they went to bed that night he tossed and turned tirelessly. His old wife, meanwhile, just lay there smiling at him until she finally said, "My dear husband, please! Is this how all knights make love to their wives? Is this how it's done in King Arthur's court? Are you all so passionless? It's me—your wife and true love, the one who saved your life. I haven't done anything bad to you, so why are treating me like this on our first night together? You're acting like you've gone insane. Did I do something wrong? Tell me, and I'll try to make it better if I can."

I am she, which that saved hath your lyf;
And certes, yet dide I yow never unright;
Why fare ye thus with me this firste night?
Ye faren lyk a man had lost his wit;
240   What is my gilt? for Goddes love, tel me it,
And it shal been amended, if I may.'

'Amended?' quod this knight, 'allas! nay, nay!
It wol nat been amended never mo!
Thou art so loothly, and so old also,
And ther-to comen of so lowe a kinde,
That litel wonder is, thogh I walwe and winde.
So wolde God myn herte wolde breste!'

'Is this,' quod she, 'the cause of your unreste?'

'Ye, certainly,' quod he, 'no wonder is.'

250   'Now, sire,' quod she, 'I coude amende al this,
If that me liste, er it were dayes three,
So wel ye mighte here yow unto me.

But for ye speken of swich gentillesse
As is descended out of old richesse,
That therfore sholden ye be gentil men,
Swich arrogance is nat worth an hen.
Loke who that is most vertuous alway,
Privee and apert, and most entendeth ay
To do the gentil dedes that he can,
260   And tak him for the grettest gentil man.
Crist wol, we clayme of him our gentillesse,
Nat of our eldres for hir old richesse.
For thogh they yeve us al hir heritage,
For which we clayme to been of heigh parage,
Yet may they nat biquethe, for no-thing,
To noon of us hir vertuous living,
That made hem gentil men y-called be;
And bad us folwen hem in swich degree.

NO FEAR

242-247 "Make it better? Make it better?" asked the knight incredulously. "No, no, of course you can't make it better! You're so old and disgusting! And you're also poor and low class and a nobody. It's no wonder that I'm tossing and turning. God, I wish I were dead!"

248 "Is that what's bothering you?" she asked.

249 "What do you think? Of course it is!" snapped the knight.

250-252 "Well then," she said, "That isn't a problem. I could fix all of this for you if I wanted to in just three days' time if you'd just treat me a little better.

253-268 "As for the belief that ancient titles and land and heredity make people noble—well that's just stupid. The noblest men on earth are the ones who are virtuous both inside and outside the home and who work hard and do good deeds. Christ wants our virtue to come from our faith, not from old family riches. Even though our ancestors can give us a family lineage, they can't pass along virtue, which is the strength of a true nobleman.

Wel can the wyse poete of Florence,
270   That highte Dant, speken in this sentence;
Lo in swich maner rym is Dantes tale:
"Ful selde up ryseth by his branches smale
Prowesse of man, for God, of his goodnesse,
Wol that of him we clayme our gentillesse;"
For of our eldres may we no-thing clayme
But temporel thing, that man may hurte and mayme.

Eek every wight wot this as wel as I,
If gentillesse were planted naturelly
Unto a certeyn linage, doun the lyne,
280   Privee ne apert, than wolde they never fyne
To doon of gentillesse the faire offyce;
They mighte do no vileinye or vyce.

Tak fyr, and ber it in the derkeste hous
Bitwix this and the mount of Caucasus,
And lat men shette the dores and go thenne;
Yet wol the fyr as faire lye and brenne,
As twenty thousand men mighte it biholde;
His office naturel ay wol it holde,
Up peril of my lyf, til that it dye.

290   Heer may ye see wel, how that genterye
Is nat annexed to possessioun,
Sith folk ne doon hir operacioun
Alwey, as dooth the fyr, lo! in his kinde.
For, God it woot, men may wel often finde
A lordes sone do shame and vileinye;
And he that wol han prys of his gentrye
For he was boren of a gentil hous,
And hadde hise eldres noble and vertuous,
And nil him-selven do no gentil dedis,
300   Ne folwe his gentil auncestre that deed is,
He nis nat gentil, be he duk or erl;
For vileyns sinful dedes make a cherl.
For gentillesse nis but renomee

NO FEAR

269-276   "The great poet Dante from Florence, Italy, knows all about this, and he wrote about it in *The Divine Comedy*. 'A person's strength comes not from the branches of a family tree,' he said, 'but from the grace of God.' Our ancestors can only give us our bodies, which are feeble and weak and will one day die.

277-282   And everyone knows as well as I do that if nobility were handed down through the family line, then every generation would be just as noble as the one before, incapable of doing anything bad.

283-289   "If you light a fire in a dark room anywhere between here and the Caucasus Mountains in Russia and then leave the room and shut the door, the fire will burn the same just as if 20,0 people were staring at it. It'll never change until it dies out, of that I'm sure.

290-308   "Virtue and nobility are just like fire because they aren't tied to earthly things. God knows that people aren't like fire, though: They do things differently from one generation to the next. We all know examples of noblemen's sons who break the law and do awful things. Anyone born into a noble household who does evil things isn't really noble at all, even if he is a duke or an earl. Evil deeds make him a villain nonetheless. True nobility only comes from God and has nothing to do with how rich or poor one's family is.

Of thyne auncestres, for hir heigh bountee,
Which is a strange thing to thy persone.
Thy gentillesse cometh fro God allone;
Than comth our verray gentillesse of grace,
It was no-thing biquethe us with our place.

Thenketh how noble, as seith Valerius,
310   Was thilke Tullius Hostilius,
That out of povert roos to heigh noblesse.
Redeth Senek, and redeth eek Boëce,
Ther shul ye seen expres that it no drede is,
That he is gentil that doth gentil dedis;
And therfore, leve housbond, I thus conclude,
Al were it that myne auncestres were rude,
Yet may the hye God, and so hope I,
Grante me grace to liven vertuously.
Thanne am I gentil, whan that I biginne
320   To liven vertuously and weyve sinne.

And ther-as ye of povert me repreve,
The hye God, on whom that we bileve,
In wilful povert chees to live his lyf.
And certes every man, mayden, or wyf,
May understonde that Iesus, hevene king,
Ne wolde nat chese a vicious living.
Glad povert is an honest thing, certeyn;
This wol Senek and othere clerkes seyn.
Who-so that halt him payd of his poverte,
330   I holde him riche, al hadde he nat a sherte.
He that coveyteth is a povre wight,
For he wolde han that is nat in his might.
But he that noght hath, ne coveyteth have,
Is riche, al-though ye holde him but a knave.

Verray povert, it singeth proprely;
Iuvenal seith of povert merily:
"The povre man, whan he goth by the weye,
Bifore the theves he may singe and pleye."

NO FEAR

309-320　"Remember the story the writer Valerius tells us of Tullius Hostilius, who was born to a poor family but eventually became the ruler of Rome. Or read the Roman philosophers Seneca and Boethius, who clearly say that nobility comes from doing good deeds. Therefore, my dear husband, even though I too come from a poor family, God knows that I was noble from the moment I chose to live virtuously.

321-334　"And if you're upset because I'm so poor, well then just remember that Jesus also chose to live in poverty. And every man, woman, and child knows that Jesus, king of heaven, would never choose to sin. There's nothing wrong with living happily in poverty. Seneca and other philosophers have said so themselves. I think that whoever can live happily in poverty is actually very wealthy, even if she doesn't have a dime to her name. The person who is greedy is actually the poor one because he wants more and more and can never do anything about it. But the person who doesn't have anything and doesn't want anything is truly wealthy, even if everyone else pities her because she doesn't own any worldy things.

335-350　"The Roman poet Juvenal tells us of the virtues of being poor. 'The poor man can sing and play happily whenever thieves pass by because he has nothing to lose.' Poverty is one of those good things that no one wants, and, I guess, it's one of those things that

Povert is hateful good, and, as I gesse,
340   A ful greet bringer out of bisinesse;
A greet amender eek of sapience
To him that taketh it in pacience.
Povert is this, al-though it seme elenge:
Possessioun, that no wight wol chalenge.
Povert ful ofte, whan a man is lowe,
Maketh his God and eek him-self to knowe.
Povert a spectacle is, as thinketh me,
Thurgh which he may his verray frendes see.
And therfore, sire, sin that I noght yow greve,
350   Of my povert na-more ye me repreve.

Now, sire, of elde ye repreve me;
And certes, sire, thogh noon auctoritee
Were in no book, ye gentils of honour
Seyn that men sholde an old wight doon favour,
And clepe him fader, for your gentillesse;
And auctours shal I finden, as I gesse.

Now ther ye seye, that I am foul and old,
Than drede you noght to been a cokewold;
For filthe and elde, also moot I thee,
360   Been grete wardeyns upon chastitee.
But nathelees, sin I knowe your delyt,
I shal fulfille your worldly appetyt.

Chese now,' quod she, 'oon of thise thinges tweye,
To han me foul and old til that I deye,
And be to yow a trewe humble wyf,
And never yow displese in al my lyf,
Or elles ye wol han me yong and fair,
And take your aventure of the repair
That shal be to your hous, by-cause of me,
370   Or in som other place, may wel be.
Now chese your-selven, whether that yow lyketh.'

can give you less to worry about and make you that much smarter. Being poor may seem bad, but it actually means you have something that no one can take away from you. Poverty helps make people know God and themselves better and lets them know who their real friends are. So don't give me a hard time about being poor since it doesn't hurt you anyway.

351-356 "You also criticize the fact that I am old, but aren't you knights always saying that old people should be respected and honored for their wisdom? I'm sure I can find those kinds of sayings in lots of other books too.

357-362 "You also say that I'm ugly and disgusting. Well then, you don't have to worry about me cheating on you, now do you? Ugliness and age, I think, keep people faithful. But, since I know what turns you on, I'll make your wish come true.

363-371 "I'll give you a choice," she said, "between one of two things. I can be old and disgusting until the day I die but be humble and faithful to you and never upset you, or you can have me be young and beautiful and take the risk that I'll cheat on you with the many men who'll try to seduce me. Now, make your decision, whichever you prefer."

This knight avyseth him and sore syketh,
But atte laste he seyde in this manere,
'My lady and my love, and wyf so dere,
I put me in your wyse governance;
Cheseth your-self, which may be most plesance,
And most honour to yow and me also.
I do no fors the whether of the two;
For as yow lyketh, it suffiseth me.'

380 'Thanne have I gete of yow maistrye,' quod she,
'Sin I may chese, and governe as me lest?'

'Ye, certes, wyf,' quod he, 'I holde it best.'

'Kis me,' quod she, 'we be no lenger wrothe;
For, by my trouthe, I wol be to yow bothe,
This is to seyn, ye, bothe fair and good.
I prey to God that I mot sterven wood,
But I to yow be al-so good and trewe
As ever was wyf, sin that the world was newe.
And, but I be to-morn as fair to sene
390 As any lady, emperyce, or quene,
That is bitwixe the est and eke the west,
Doth with my lyf and deeth right as yow lest.
Cast up the curtin, loke how that it is.'

And whan the knight saugh verraily al this,
That she so fair was, and so yong ther-to,
For Ioye he hente hir in his armes two,
His herte bathed in a bath of blisse;
A thousand tyme a-rewe he gan hir kisse.
And she obeyed him in every thing
400 That mighte doon him plesance or lyking.

And thus they live, unto hir lyves ende,
In parfit Ioye; and Iesu Crist us sende
Housbondes meke, yonge, and fresshe a-bedde,
And grace toverbyde hem that we wedde.

NO FEAR

372-379 The knight thought a moment, sighed, and then finally said, "My lady, my love, my wife. I put myself in your good hands. You decide which of these options will be better for yourself and for me. I don't care which of the two you decide. I'll be happy with whichever you choose."

380-381 "Then do I have control over your life and destiny because I get to the make the decisions?" she asked.

382 "Yes. Yes, you do. Because I think it's best that way," he replied.

383-393 "Then kiss me, and let's stop fighting," she said. "Because I promise that I'll be both beautiful and faithful to you. I pray to God that I go insane if I'm ever bad or unfaithful to you and not the best wife the world has ever seen. And if you wake up in the morning and don't find that I've become beautiful enough to be a queen or an empress, then you can kill me if you like. Pull back the curtains in the morning to see for yourself."

394-400 And the next morning when the knight saw that what she'd said was true—that she'd become a beautiful young woman—he grabbed her in his arm and showered her with a thousand kisses. And she obeyed him in everything that he asked of her.

401-408 And that's how they lived, in perfect happiness, for the rest of their lives. Jesus Christ, let us women marry husbands who are humble and young and good in bed. And let us women be fortunate enough to outlive our husbands too. And Jesus, please shorten the lives of

And eek I preye Iesu shorte hir lyves
That wol nat be governed by hir wyves;
And olde and angry nigardes of dispence,
God sende hem sone verray pestilence.

HERE ENDETH THE WYVES TALE OF BATHE.

the husbands who won't take direction from their wives. And may God send a plague on all those old, abusive, cheapskate husbands out there!

THIS IS THE END OF THE WIFE FROM BATH'S TALE.

Prologue to the Pardoner's Tale

HERE FOLWETH THE PROLOGE OF THE PARDONERS TALE.

'Lordings,' quod he, 'in chirches whan I preche,
I peyne me to han an hauteyn speche,
And ringe it out as round as gooth a belle,
For I can al by rote that I telle.
My theme is alwey oon, and ever was—
"*Radix malorum est Cupiditas.*"

First I pronounce whennes that I come,
And than my bulles shewe I, alle and somme.
Our lige lordes seel on my patente,
10   That shewe I first, my body to warente,
That no man be so bold, ne preest ne clerk,
Me to destourbe of Cristes holy werk;
And after that than telle I forth my tales,
Bulles of popes and of cardinales,
Of patriarkes, and bishoppes I shewe;
And in Latyn I speke a wordes fewe,
To saffron with my predicacioun,
And for to stire men to devocioun.
Than shewe I forth my longe cristal stones,
20   Y-crammed ful of cloutes and of bones;
Reliks been they, as wenen they echoon.
Than have I in latoun a sholder-boon
Which that was of an holy Iewes shepe.
"Good men," seye I, "tak of my wordes kepe;
If that this boon be wasshe in any welle,
If cow, or calf, or sheep, or oxe swelle
That any worm hath ete, or worm y-stonge,
Tak water of that welle, and wash his tonge,
And it is hool anon; and forthermore,
30   Of pokkes and of scabbe, and every sore
Shal every sheep be hool, that of this welle
Drinketh a draughte; tak kepe eek what I telle.
If that the good-man, that the bestes oweth,

Prologue to the Pardoner's Tale

HERE IS THE PROLOGUE TO THE PARDONER'S TALE.

1-6 "Ladies and gentlemen," the Pardoner began, "whenever I give a sermon in church, I try really hard to speak out in a loud voice that resonates like a bell. I know all my sermons by heart and they're all centered on the same theme: *Radix malorum est cupiditas*—the love of money is the root of all evil.

7-43 "The first thing I do when I preach is I tell people where I come from, and then I show all my letters authorizing me to preach and issue church pardons. These are letters that the pope himself has signed. I always start by showing the pope's official seal that's on my passport in order to protect myself from priests and government official who want to arrest me or stop me from doing Christ's holy work. After that, I tell my stories. I show all my letters signed by the pope, cardinals, and various bishops, and I sprinkle a few Latin sayings in here and there to spice up my sermons and make them sound holy. Then I pull out all my boxes crammed full of old cloth and bones, which everyone assumes to be holy relics. I've also got a piece of bone from the shoulder of a Jew's sheep that I keep in a brass box. 'Ladies and gentlemen,' I say, 'Listen carefully. Put this bone in a well so that when your cow or calf or sheep or ox gets worms or is bitten by a snake, you can wash its tongue with the special well water and heal it. Furthermore, any sheep that has the pox or scabies that drinks from this well will be cured. And if an honest farmer drinks some of this well water before dawn, before breakfast, just as this Jew taught our ancestors, then all his farm animals will multiply. This water will also get rid of jealousy. If you make soup from it, you'll never doubt your wife's faithfulness again, even if you have reason to suspect she's cheating on you or if she's had an affair with two or three priests.

Wol every wike, er that the cok him croweth,
Fastinge, drinken of this welle a draughte,
As thilke holy Iewe our eldres taughte,
His bestes and his stoor shal multiplye.
And, sirs, also it heleth Ialousye;
For, though a man be falle in Ialous rage,
Let maken with this water his potage,
And never shal he more his wyf mistriste,
Though he the sooth of hir defaute wiste;
Al had she taken preestes two or three.

Heer is a miteyn eek, that ye may see.
He that his hond wol putte in this miteyn,
He shal have multiplying of his greyn,
Whan he hath sowen, be it whete or otes,
So that he offre pens, or elles grotes.

Good men and wommen, o thing warne I yow,
If any wight be in this chirche now,
That hath doon sinne horrible, that he
Dar nat, for shame, of it y-shriven be,
Or any womman, be she yong or old,
That hath y-maad hir housbond cokewold,
Swich folk shul have no power ne no grace
To offren to my reliks in this place.
And who-so findeth him out of swich blame,
He wol com up and offre in Goddes name,
And I assoille him by the auctoritee
Which that by bulle y-graunted was to me."

By this gaude have I wonne, yeer by yeer,
An hundred mark sith I was Pardoner.
I stonde lyk a clerk in my pulpet,
And whan the lewed peple is doun y-set,
I preche, so as ye han herd bifore,
And telle an hundred false Iapes more.
Than peyne I me to strecche forth the nekke,
And est and west upon the peple I bekke,

NO FEAR

44-48   "'I also have this mitten that will increase your grain harvest, whether it's wheat or oats, if you wear it—and offer a small fee, of course.

49-60   "'Ladies and gentlemen, I warn you though, that my relics won't help any man who's committed a horrible sin or any woman, whether she's young or old, who's cheated on her husband. For those of you who remain seated and decline to come up and make an offering, well, we'll all know that you must fall into this category. But, all of you who've only committed little sins here and there should come up and see me. Make an offering in God's name, and I'll use my power that the pope has given me to pardon you so that you'll be absolved of your sins.'

61-94   "With this trick, I've earned myself a salary of about a hundred gold coins a year. I stand up there in front of the people like I'm a priest or something and preach and tell a hundred lies like the kind I just mentioned. All the stupid people sit in front of me and soak up every word I say. I make a good show of it, straining my neck to look at all the people to the right and left of me, just like a bird in a barn. I gesticulate with my hands and speak quickly, which makes my speeches dramatic and fun to watch. I always preach about greed

As doth a dowve sitting on a berne.
70   Myn hondes and my tonge goon so yerne,
That it is Ioye to see my bisinesse.
Of avaryce and of swich cursednesse
Is al my preching, for to make hem free
To yeve her pens, and namely unto me.
For my entente is nat but for to winne,
And no-thing for correccioun of sinne.
I rekke never, whan that they ben beried,
Though that her soules goon a-blakeberied!
For certes, many a predicacioun
80   Comth ofte tyme of yvel entencioun;
Som for plesaunce of folk and flaterye,
To been avaunced by ipocrisye,
And som for veyne glorie, and som for hate.
For, whan I dar non other weyes debate,
Than wol I stinge him with my tonge smerte
In preching, so that he shal nat asterte
To been defamed falsly, if that he
Hath trespased to my brethren or to me.
For, though I telle noght his propre name,
90   Men shal wel knowe that it is the same
By signes and by othere circumstances.
Thus quyte I folk that doon us displesances;
Thus spitte I out my venim under hewe
Of holynesse, to seme holy and trewe.

But shortly myn entente I wol devyse;
I preche of no-thing but for coveityse.
Therfor my theme is yet, and ever was—
"*Radix malorum est cupiditas.*"
Thus can I preche agayn that same vyce
100 Which that I use, and that is avaryce.
But, though my-self be gilty in that sinne,
Yet can I maken other folk to twinne
From avaryce, and sore to repente.
But that is nat my principal entente.

and the other deadly sins, which makes them happy to give away their money—namely, to me. I'm only in this for the money you know, not for cleansing immortal souls. Why, I don't give a damn if their souls are as rotten as garbage when they die! Of course, I'm not the first person who's preached with an ulterior motive either. Some priests give sermons to make people feel good about themselves so that they'll get promoted to bishop. Others preach for love of fame or to fan the fires of hate. I only preach to make money and sometimes to get back at people who've said nasty things about me or my fellow pardoners. I can rail against a person in the audience to ruin his reputation, for example, and, even if I don't mention his name, everyone will know whom I'm talking about. That's how I get back at my enemies, by spitting out my venom under the guise of being holy and virtuous.

95-106 "Let me put it another way: I preach out of sheer greed. That's why I usually only give sermons about how the love of money is the root of all evil. That way I can preach about the same sin that I myself indulge in. But even if I'm guilty of the sin of greed, that doesn't mean I can't help others not to be greedy, now does it? But who am I kidding? I said I'm not preaching to save their souls. I preach only because I want to make money, and that, my friends, is that.

I preche no-thing but for coveityse;
Of this matere it oughte y-nogh suffyse.

Than telle I hem ensamples many oon
Of olde stories, longe tyme agoon:
For lewed peple loven tales olde;
110   Swich thinges can they wel reporte and holde.
What? trowe ye, the whyles I may preche,
And winne gold and silver for I teche,
That I wol live in povert wilfully?
Nay, nay, I thoghte it never trewely!
For I wol preche and begge in sondry londes;
I wol not do no labour with myn hondes,
Ne make baskettes, and live therby,
Because I wol nat beggen ydelly.
I wol non of the apostles counterfete;
120   I wol have money, wolle, chese, and whete,
Al were it yeven of the povrest page,
Or of the povrest widwe in a village,
Al sholde hir children sterve for famyne.
Nay! I wol drinke licour of the vyne,
And have a Ioly wenche in every toun.
But herkneth, lordings, in conclusioun;
Your lyking is that I shal telle a tale.
Now, have I dronke a draughte of corny ale,
By God, I hope I shal yow telle a thing
130   That shal, by resoun, been at your lyking.
For, though myself be a ful vicious man,
A moral tale yet I yow telle can,
Which I am wont to preche, for to winne.
Now holde your pees, my tale I wol beginne.

107-134   "Anyway, then I tell the people all the old familiar tales that they just love to hear over and over again. Stupid people like to hear those old stories, you know, because they're easy to remember. And do you think that since I help cure the people of their greed by taking all their gold and silver that means I would ever live in poverty? Hell no! I refuse to live like a simpleton, working with my hands, making baskets. Being a traveling preacher is much more lucrative. I'm not trying to be an apostle who lives in holiness. No, I want money, nice clothes, and expensive food, even if I receive it from the poorest workingman or the poorest widow who can't even feed her own starving children. No! I want wine and a woman in every town. But listen, listen. Now that I've drunk a beer or two, I'm going to tell you a story that I hope you'll like because, even though I'm a pretty awful guy, I can still tell you a moral tale, one of the ones I usually tell people only for money. So sit back, relax, and I'll tell you my story."

The Pardoner's Tale

THE PARDONERS TALE.

In Flaundres whylom was a companye
Of yonge folk, that haunteden folye,
As ryot, hasard, stewes, and tavernes,
Wher-as, with harpes, lutes, and giternes,
They daunce and pleye at dees bothe day and night,
And ete also and drinken over hir might,
Thurgh which they doon the devel sacrifyse
With-in that develes temple, in cursed wyse,
By superfluitee abhominable;
10 Hir othes been so grete and so dampnable,
That it is grisly for to here hem swere;
Our blissed lordes body they to-tere;
Hem thoughte Iewes rente him noght y-nough;
And ech of hem at otheres sinne lough.
And right anon than comen tombesteres
Fetys and smale, and yonge fruytesteres,
Singers with harpes, baudes, wafereres,
Whiche been the verray develes officeres
To kindle and blowe the fyr of lecherye,
20 That is annexed unto glotonye;
The holy writ take I to my witnesse,
That luxurie is in wyn and dronkenesse.

Lo, how that dronken Loth, unkindely,
Lay by his doghtres two, unwitingly;
So dronke he was, he niste what he wroghte.

Herodes, (who-so wel the stories soghte),
Whan he of wyn was replet at his feste,
Right at his owene table he yaf his heste
To sleen the Baptist Iohn ful giltelees.

30 Senek seith eek a good word doutelees;
He seith, he can no difference finde

The Pardoner's Tale

THE PARDONER'S TALE.

1-22 Once upon a time there were three young men who lived in Belgium who liked to live on the wild side. They partied, gambled, visited brothels, and went to bars where they stuffed themselves with food and wine and danced all night and day to the music of harps and lutes and guitars. They lived gluttonous lives of sin, worshipping the ways of the devil. They cursed and swore like sailors and would tear the blessed Lord's body to pieces with their foul language and by using His name in vain, (as if the Jews hadn't already done enough damage when they'd had him killed). They encouraged each other to sin and would sit around and laugh at all the horrible things they did. And then the thin and shapely dancing girls and the young girls selling fruit and the singers with their harps and the whores and women selling sweets would come over to them to seduce them and encourage them to sin—which is so easy for gluttons to do anyway. Just look in the Bible for all those instances when wine and drunkenness led to sin.

23-25 Recall, for example, how Lot unknowingly had sex with his two daughters. He was in a drunken stupor and didn't know what he was doing.

Genesis 19:30

26-29 Or remember the story of Herod, the man who, when he was drunk and full from feasting, ordered John the Baptist's execution, even though John hadn't done anything wrong.

Luke 3 and Matthew 14

30-42 Seneca also talks about drunkenness. He says that drunkenness and insanity are one and the same, with the exception that insanity is a defect and lasts longer than drunkenness.

Seneca: A Roman philosopher.

Bitwix a man that is out of his minde
And a man which that is dronkelewe,
But that woodnesse, y-fallen in a shrewe,
Persevereth lenger than doth dronkenesse.
O glotonye, ful of cursednesse,
O cause first of our confusioun,
O original of our dampnacioun,
Til Crist had boght us with his blood agayn!
40 Lo, how dere, shortly for to sayn,
Aboght was thilke cursed vileinye;
Corrupt was al this world for glotonye!

Adam our fader, and his wyf also,
Fro Paradys to labour and to wo
Were driven for that vyce, it is no drede;
For whyl that Adam fasted, as I rede,
He was in Paradys; and whan that he
Eet of the fruyt defended on the tree,
Anon he was out-cast to wo and peyne.
50 O glotonye, on thee wel oghte us pleyne!
O, wiste a man how many maladyes
Folwen of excesse and of glotonyes,
He wolde been the more mesurable
Of his diete, sittinge at his table.
Allas! the shorte throte, the tendre mouth,
Maketh that, Est and West, and North and South,
In erthe, in eir, in water men to-swinke
To gete a glotoun deyntee mete and drinke!
Of this matere, o Paul, wel canstow trete,
60 'Mete unto wombe, and wombe eek unto mete,
Shal God destroyen bothe,' as Paulus seith.
Allas! a foul thing is it, by my feith,
To seye this word, and fouler is the dede,
Whan man so drinketh of the whyte and rede,
That of his throte he maketh his privee,
Thurgh thilke cursed superfluitee.

NO FEAR

Oh, gluttony is such an awful sin! It brought the downfall of mankind and doomed us until Christ saved us by sacrificing himself. Gluttony has caused so much trouble and corrupted the world so much.

43-66 You see, God banished Adam and Eve from Paradise to live lives of misery and toil because they were gluttons. Everything was fine in the Garden of Eden as long as Adam didn't eat anything, but they got kicked out when he ate the forbidden fruit on the tree. Oh gluttony, we have every right to hate you! If people only knew how much sickness and disease overeating causes, they'd eat more moderately, that's for sure. God! The wealthy glutton's taste for fine food and wine makes the working folk everywhere—in the East and West and North and South, on land and at sea—work to death. St. Paul knew this, which is why he wrote, "Meats for the belly, and the

1 Corinthians 6:13 belly for meats, but God shall destroy both it and them" Ugh, it's awful, I swear, to talk about gluttony, and it's far worse to actually be a glutton and turn your mouth into a toilet from drinking so much red and white wine.

The apostel weping seith ful pitously,
'Ther walken many of whiche yow told have I,
I seye it now weping with pitous voys,
That they been enemys of Cristes croys,
Of whiche the ende is deeth, wombe is her God.'
O wombe! O bely! O stinking cod,
Fulfild of donge and of corrupcioun!
At either ende of thee foul is the soun.
How greet labour and cost is thee to finde!
Thise cokes, how they stampe, and streyne, and grinde,
And turnen substaunce in-to accident,
To fulfille al thy likerous talent!
Out of the harde bones knokke they
The mary, for they caste noght a-wey
That may go thurgh the golet softe and swote;
Of spicerye, of leef, and bark, and rote
Shal been his sauce y-maked by delyt,
To make him yet a newer appetyt.
But certes, he that haunteth swich delyces
Is deed, whyl that he liveth in tho vyces.

A lecherous thing is wyn, and dronkenesse
Is ful of stryving and of wrecchednesse.
O dronke man, disfigured is thy face,
Sour is thy breeth, foul artow to embrace,
And thurgh thy dronke nose semeth the soun
As though thou seydest ay 'Sampsoun, Sampsoun';
And yet, God wot, Sampsoun drank never no wyn.
Thou fallest, as it were a stiked swyn;
Thy tonge is lost, and al thyn honest cure;
For dronkenesse is verray sepulture
Of mannes wit and his discrecioun.
In whom that drinke hath dominacioun,
He can no conseil kepe, it is no drede.
Now kepe yow fro the whyte and fro the rede,
And namely fro the whyte wyn of Lepe,
That is to selle in Fish-strete or in Chepe.
This wyn of Spayne crepeth subtilly

Line numbers in margin: 70, 80, 90, 100

NO FEAR

67-86 St. Paul, the apostle, wept when he said, "There are many men ⬅————————
out there who will tell you that they don't care about Christ Philippians 3:18
and say that their stomachs are their only gods. It makes me
weep to just think about it." Stupid stomach! You are filled with cor-
ruption and dung. Both ends make awful sounds when burping or
farting. It costs so much and requires so much effort to feed you!
Just look at all the cooks who knead and grind and strain to make
food for you to keep you satisfied! They mix spices and herbs and
roots and bark to make tasty sauces for you. They even work extra
hard to extract the marrow out of the animals' bones to give you
something sweet to eat. Everyone who lives for these vices, though,
is surely already dead for having sinned so much.

87-110 Wine only leads to lecherousness, and drunkenness leads to fight-
ing and misery. Let me tell each of you drunkards out there that
your face is disgusting and fleshy, your breath reeks, and no one
wants to touch you. You're clumsy, you never know what you're say-
ing, and you have no sense of decency because the wine has ruined
your intellect and ability to speak. You can't even keep secrets when
you're drunk, and you make an awful wheezing sound through your
nose that sounds like you're saying, "Samson, Samson," even though,
God knows, Samson in the Bible never had a drop to drink. You
should stay away from both white and red wine, particularly from
those cheap wines from Lepe in Spain that are sold on Fishstreet and
Cheapside. Drink that stuff and in no time you'll be saying "Samson,
Samson" for sure.

In othere wynes, growing faste by,
Of which ther ryseth swich fumositee,
That whan a man hath dronken draughtes three,
And weneth that he be at hoom in Chepe,
He is in Spayne, right at the toune of Lepe,
Nat at the Rochel, ne at Burdeux toun;
And thanne wol he seye, 'Sampsoun, Sampsoun.'

But herkneth, lordings, o word, I yow preye,
That alle the sovereyn actes, dar I seye,
Of victories in the olde testament,
Thurgh verray God, that is omnipotent,
Were doon in abstinence and in preyere;
Loketh the Bible, and ther ye may it lere.

Loke, Attila, the grete conquerour,
Deyde in his sleep, with shame and dishonour,
Bledinge ay at his nose in dronkenesse;
A capitayn shoulde live in sobrenesse.
And over al this, avyseth yow right wel
What was comaunded unto Lamuel—
Nat Samuel, but Lamuel, seye I—
Redeth the Bible, and finde it expresly
Of wyn-yeving to hem that han Iustyse.
Na-more of this, for it may wel suffyse.

And now that I have spoke of glotonye,
Now wol I yow defenden hasardrye.
Hasard is verray moder of lesinges,
And of deceite, and cursed forsweringes,
Blaspheme of Crist, manslaughtre, and wast also
Of catel and of tyme; and forthermo,
It is repreve and contrarie of honour
For to ben holde a commune hasardour.
And ever the hyér he is of estaat,
The more is he holden desolaat.
If that a prince useth hasardrye,
In alle governaunce and policye

NO FEAR

111-116   Let me put it this way: All of the greatest deeds and triumphs you read about in the Old Testament that were done in the name of God, the omnipotent, were all done through prayer and without liquor. Just look in the Bible and you'll see what I'm talking about.

117-126   Or look at how the great warrior Atilla the Hun died in his sleep from a nosebleed he got from drunkenness. He died with nothing but shame and dishonor. Too bad. Leaders should always be sober.

Proverbs 31:4 Or just remember the warning Lemuel—not Samuel, mind, you, but Lemuel—received about how judges who decide legal cases shouldn't drink wine. I could go on and on, but you get the idea.

127-140   Gluttony isn't the only horrible vice, though. Gambling is just as bad. Gambling rolls so many other vices into one, including lying and cheating. It goes against God and is the biggest waste of time and money. That's why being called a gambler is such a great shame. And the richer you are, the more shameful it is if you gamble. No one likes a king who is a gambler, for example, because who knows if he'll also take such risks with the policies concerning his country and his people.

He is, as by commune opinoun,
140 Y-holde the lasse in reputacioun.

Stilbon, that was a wys embassadour,
Was sent to Corinthe, in ful greet honour,
Fro Lacidomie, to make hir alliaunce.
And whan he cam, him happede, par chaunce,
That alle the grettest that were of that lond,
Pleyinge atte hasard he hem fond.
For which, as sone as it mighte be,
He stal him hoom agayn to his contree,
And seyde, 'ther wol I nat lese my name;
150 Ne I wol nat take on me so greet defame,
Yow for to allye unto none hasardours.
Sendeth othere wyse embassadours;
For, by my trouthe, me were lever dye,
Than I yow sholde to hasardours allye.
For ye that been so glorious in honours
Shul nat allyen yow with hasardours
As by my wil, ne as by my tretee.'
This wyse philosophre thus seyde he.

Loke eek that, to the king Demetrius
160 The king of Parthes, as the book seith us,
Sente him a paire of dees of gold in scorn,
For he hadde used hasard ther-biforn;
For which he heeld his glorie or his renoun
At no value or reputacioun.
Lordes may finden other maner pley
Honeste y-nough to dryve the day awey.

Now wol I speke of othes false and grete
A word or two, as olde bokes trete.
Gret swering is a thing abhominable,
170 And false swering is yet more reprevable.
The heighe God forbad swering at al,
Witnesse on Mathew; but in special
Of swering seith the holy Ieremye,

NO FEAR

141-158　　The Greek writer named Stilbon, who was a wise ambassador, was once sent from Sparta on a diplomatic mission to Corinth to strike an alliance between the two powers. But when he arrived, he happened to find all the Corinthian leaders participating in a great gambling tournament. That's why he turned around and immediately went straight back to Corinth, where he told the Corinthians, "I don't want to lose my good name, and I won't do you the dishonor of allying Sparta with gamblers. Send another ambassador to make the deal if you want, but I'd rather die than ally you with gamblers." That's what the wise philosopher said.

159-166　　Then there's the example you can find in the writings of John Salisbury of the king of Parthia in Persia, who sent a pair of golden dice to King Demetrius, a gambler. This was a true sign that the king of Parthia looked down on Demetrius because of his bad habit. There are certainly lots of more important things a king can do all day besides gambling!

167-198　　Oh, and then there's swearing, another evil that old books talk a lot about. Strong language is abominable, and swearing for no good reason is even worse. God on high forbade swearing altogether you know. It says so in Matthew and Jeremiah. Jeremiah says,

Matthew 5:34 and
Jeremiah 4:2　　"Swear only to make a promise—not when you're lying—and then only in righteousness." Casual swearing for no real purpose is a sin. I mean, it's so bad that it's even one of the Ten Commandments:

'Thou shalt seye sooth thyn othes, and nat lye,
And swere in dome, and eek in rightwisnesse;'
But ydel swering is a cursednesse.
Bihold and see, that in the firste table
Of heighe Goddes hestes honurable,
How that the seconde heste of him is this—
'Tak nat my name in ydel or amis.'
Lo, rather he forbedeth swich swering
Than homicyde or many a cursed thing;
I seye that, as by ordre, thus it stondeth;
This knowen, that his hestes understondeth,
How that the second heste of God is that.
And forther over, I wol thee telle al plat,
That vengeance shal nat parten from his hous,
That of his othes is to outrageous.
'By Goddes precious herte, and by his nayles,
And by the blode of Crist, that it is in Hayles,
Seven is my chaunce, and thyn is cink and treye;
By Goddes armes, if thou falsly pleye,
This dagger shal thurgh-out thyn herte go'—
This fruyt cometh of the bicched bones two,
Forswering, ire, falsnesse, homicyde.
Now, for the love of Crist that for us dyde,
Leveth your othes, bothe grete and smale;
But, sirs, now wol I telle forth my tale.

Thise ryotoures three, of whiche I telle,
Longe erst er pryme rong of any belle,
Were set hem in a taverne for to drinke;
And as they satte, they herde a belle clinke
Biforn a cors, was caried to his grave;
That oon of hem gan callen to his knave,
'Go bet,' quod he, 'and axe redily,
What cors is this that passeth heer forby;
And look that thou reporte his name wel.'

'Sir,' quod this boy, 'it nedeth never-a-del.
It was me told, er ye cam heer, two houres;

180

190

200

NO FEAR

"Thou shalt not use the Lord's name in vain." God thinks cursing is so bad that this commandment even comes before those against murder and other heinous crimes. God will have his revenge on anyone who swears too much, that's for sure! Saying things such as, "By God's own heart!" and "The blood of Christ!" or "Seven's my lucky number and yours is three and five!" and "By God, if you cheat me, I'll kill you with this dagger!" will all get you into trouble. And it all stems from gambling. So for the love of Christ who died for our sins, don't curse, even if it's just a small swear. Okay, okay . . . now I'll tell you my story.

199-207   Well one morning before the churchbells had even rung for morning mass, the three rogues I was telling you about a minute ago were drinking in a bar. While they were sitting there, they saw a man ringing a bell as he led a cart with a dead body on it through the streets on the way to the graveyard. When the rogues saw this, one of them called the waiter over and said, "Go out right now and find out whose body that is."

208-222   "Mister, I don't need to go out there and ask," the boy replied. "Someone told me about a couple hours before you came in here

210   He was, pardee, an old felawe of youres;
And sodeynly he was y-slayn to-night,
For-dronke, as he sat on his bench upright;
Ther cam a privee theef, men clepeth Deeth,
That in this contree al the peple sleeth,
And with his spere he smoot his herte a-two,
And wente his wey with-outen wordes mo.
He hath a thousand slayn this pestilence:
And, maister, er ye come in his presence,
Me thinketh that it were necessarie
220   For to be war of swich an adversarie:
Beth redy for to mete him evermore.
Thus taughte me my dame, I sey na-more.'

'By seinte Marie,' seyde this taverner,
'The child seith sooth, for he hath slayn this yeer,
Henne over a myle, with-in a greet village,
Both man and womman, child and hyne, and page.
I trowe his habitacioun be there;
To been avysed greet wisdom it were,
Er that he dide a man a dishonour.'

230   'Ye, Goddes armes,' quod this ryotour,
'Is it swich peril with him for to mete?
I shal him seke by wey and eek by strete,
I make avow to Goddes digne bones!
Herkneth, felawes, we three been al ones;
Lat ech of us holde up his hond til other,
And ech of us bicomen otheres brother,
And we wol sleen this false traytour Deeth;
He shal be slayn, which that so many sleeth,
By Goddes dignitee, er it be night.'

240   Togidres han thise three her trouthes plight,
To live and dyen ech of hem for other,
As though he were his owene y-boren brother.
And up they sterte al dronken, in this rage,
And forth they goon towardes that village,

that it's an old friend of yours who was slain as he was sitting drunk in a chair last night. The shadowy thief that people call Death, who kills everyone in this land, drove his scythe into the man's heart and sliced it in two before silently moving on again. He has killed a thousand people during this outbreak of the plague. Sir, I should warn you, though, in case you ever meet him that you should be careful around him and always be prepared to meet him unexpectedly. That's what my mother always told me, anyway.

223-229 "By St. Mary," interrupted the bartender, "the kid is right. This year alone, Death has killed men, women, children, laborers, and wealthier folk alike in a large village just about a mile from here. I reckon Death probably lives there, and we'd be wise to be on guard in case we happen to meet him."

230-239 "By God's arms!" said one of the rogues. "Is he really that deadly? Then I swear to God that I'll search all the streets and hunt him down! My friends, are you thinking what I'm thinking? Let's all grab hands and take an oath so that the three of us become brothers. We'll vow to kill this villain Death who has killed so many people. We'll find him and cut him down before nightfall!"

240-248 Together the three delinquents swore to live and die for the others just as if they'd been blood brothers from birth. Then they stood up, furious and very drunk, and set out for that village the bartender had told them about. On their way, they swore like sailors to kill Death, and they tore Christ's body apart with their foul language.

Of which the taverner had spoke biforn,
And many a grisly ooth than han they sworn,
And Cristes blessed body they to-rente—
'Deeth shal be deed, if that they may him hente.'

Whan they han goon nat fully half a myle,
250 Right as they wolde han troden over a style,
An old man and a povre with hem mette.
This olde man ful mekely hem grette,
And seyde thus, 'now, lordes, God yow see!'

The proudest of thise ryotoures three
Answerde agayn, 'what? carl, with sory grace,
Why artow al forwrapped save thy face?
Why livestow so longe in so greet age?'

This olde man gan loke in his visage,
And seyde thus, 'for I ne can nat finde
260 A man, though that I walked in-to Inde,
Neither in citee nor in no village,
That wolde chaunge his youthe for myn age;
And therfore moot I han myn age stille,
As longe time as it is Goddes wille.

Ne deeth, allas! ne wol nat han my lyf;
Thus walke I, lyk a restelees caityf,
And on the ground, which is my modres gate,
I knokke with my staf, bothe erly and late,
And seye, "leve moder, leet me in!
270 Lo, how I vanish, flesh, and blood, and skin!
Allas! whan shul my bones been at reste?
Moder, with yow wolde I chaunge my cheste,
That in my chambre longe tyme hath be,
Ye! for an heyre clout to wrappe me!"
But yet to me she wol nat do that grace,
For which ful pale and welked is my face.

NO FEAR

249-253　When they'd gone only about half a mile, though, they came upon a poor old man, just as they were about to hop over a fence. The old man greeted them politely and said, "Gentlemen, may God bless you and keep you well!"

254-257　"What the hell do you want, old man?" the most arrogant of the ruffians asked. "Why are you all wrapped up except for your face? And how have you lived to be so frickin old? Shouldn't you be dead by now?

258-264　The old man just looked him in the eyes awhile before finally saying, "Even if I walked all the way to India, I'd never find anyone who'd want to trade me their youth for my age, so I have no choice but to be as old as I am until God changes His mind.

265-287　"Unfortunately, Death doesn't want me either, which is why I'm as old and disgusting as I am. All I can do is wander around like a restless soul, knocking my walking stick on the ground morning and night hoping Mother Earth will take me back. 'Mother Earth, let me in!' I say. 'Just look at how wretched I am. My flesh and blood and skin are all drying up. When will my tired bones be laid to rest? Mother, I wish I could trade that beautiful chest in my bedroom for a burial shroud to put myself in!' But so far, she hasn't helped me at all, which is why I'm so pale and rickety.

But, sirs, to yow it is no curteisye
To speken to an old man vileinye,
But he trespasse in worde, or elles in dede.
280 In holy writ ye may your-self wel rede,
"Agayns an old man, hoor upon his heed,
Ye sholde aryse;" wherfor I yeve yow reed,
Ne dooth unto an old man noon harm now,
Na-more than ye wolde men dide to yow
In age, if that ye so longe abyde;
And God be with yow, wher ye go or ryde.
I moot go thider as I have to go.'

'Nay, olde cherl, by God, thou shall nat so,'
Seyde this other hasardour anon;
290 'Thou partest nat so lightly, by seint Iohn!
Thou spak right now of thilke traitour Deeth,
That in this contree alle our frendes sleeth.
Have heer my trouthe, as thou art his aspye,
Tel wher he is, or thou shalt it abye,
By God, and by the holy sacrament!
For soothly thou art oon of his assent,
To sleen us yonge folk, thou false theef!'

'Now, sirs,' quod he, 'if that yow be so leef
To finde Deeth, turne up this croked wey,
300 For in that grove I lafte him, by my fey,
Under a tree, and ther he wol abyde;
Nat for your boost he wol him no-thing hyde.
See ye that ook? right ther ye shul him finde.
God save yow, that boghte agayn mankinde,
And yow amende!'—thus seyde this olde man.

And everich of thise ryotoures ran,
Til he cam to that tree, and ther they founde
Of florins fyne of golde y-coyned rounde
Wel ny an eighte busshels, as hem thoughte.
310 No lenger thanne after Deeth they soughte,
But ech of hem so glad was of that sighte,

NO FEAR

"Still, it isn't very nice of you to speak to an old man the way you did, unless he's done something really bad to you. Remember that it says 'Thou shalt rise up before the hoary head!'. In other words, respect your elders. Don't do or say things to an old man that you wouldn't want done or said to you. And may God go with you, wherever you go. As for me, I should continue on now."

Leviticus 19:32

288-297   "Not so fast, gramps," one of the other hooligans said. "You're not going anywhere, old man. We're not going to let you get away that easily! You seem to know a lot about this bastard Death who's been killing our friends around here. I'm thinking that you're in cahoots with him, that you're his spy, and that you're trying to kill all the young people! By God and the Bible, you better tell me where Death is or you'll regret it!

298-305   "Well, gentlemen," the old man replied, "if you really want to find Death, then all you have to do is walk up this crooked path because I just left him over there in that grove of trees. See that oak tree? He's right under that one. He isn't going anywhere, and he's certainly not going to run away from you. May God who saved mankind save you!"

306-314   The three scoundrels ran off in that direction until they came to the oak tree. Instead of finding Death, though, they discovered about eight bushels of gold florins. They were so awestruck by the shiny gold coins that they completely forgot about hunting and killing Death. They sat down next to the bags of gold for a while, until the worst of the three finally said:

For that the florins been so faire and brighte,
That doun they sette hem by this precious hord.
The worste of hem he spake the firste word.

'Brethren,' quod he, 'tak kepe what I seye;
My wit is greet, though that I bourde and pleye.
This tresor hath fortune unto us yiven,
In mirthe and Iolitee our lyf to liven,
And lightly as it comth, so wol we spende.
320   Ey! Goddes precious dignitee! who wende
To-day, that we sholde han so fair a grace?
But mighte this gold be caried fro this place
Hoom to myn hous, or elles unto youres—
For wel ye woot that al this gold is oures—
Than were we in heigh felicitee.
But trewely, by daye it may nat be;
Men wolde seyn that we were theves stronge,
And for our owene tresor doon us honge.
This tresor moste y-caried be by nighte
330   As wysly and as slyly as it mighte.
Wherfore I rede that cut among us alle
Be drawe, and lat se wher the cut wol falle;
And he that hath the cut with herte blythe
Shal renne to the toune, and that ful swythe,
And bringe us breed and wyn ful prively.
And two of us shul kepen subtilly
This tresor wel; and, if he wol nat tarie,
Whan it is night, we wol this tresor carie

By oon assent, wher-as us thinketh best.'
340   That oon of hem the cut broughte in his fest,
And bad hem drawe, and loke wher it wol falle;
And it fil on the yongeste of hem alle;
And forth toward the toun he wente anon.
And al-so sone as that he was gon,
That oon of hem spak thus unto that other,
'Thou knowest wel thou art my sworne brother,
Thy profit wol I telle thee anon.

NO FEAR

315-338 "My brothers, listen up. I've got an idea. I may goof off a lot, but I'm pretty sharp. Fortune has given us this treasure so that we can always live our lives in comfort and revelry. I'm sure we can find ways to spend all this! Who in God's name would have thought that today would be so lucky for us? I say this gold is ours because we found it. And if we could carry all this money to my house—or one of your houses—we'd never have to worry about money again. We can't move this money in broad daylight, though, because people would accuse us of stealing it and hang us for moving our own money. No, we'll have to transport it at night and do it as carefully as possible so that no one will see. Now, two of us should stay here and guard the money, while the third goes to town and gets some bread and wine for us to eat until we can safely move the gold tonight. I think we should draw straws to see who should be the one to run to town and get the food.

339-353 He then put three straws in his fist and had each of the other two take one to see who'd be the runner. The youngest of the three picked the shortest straw, so he set off immediately for the town below. As soon as he was gone, one of the remaining two rogues turned to the other one and said, "You know, we swore an oath to be brothers, which is why I want to tell you something that I think will interest you. We have all this money here to divide among the three of us. But wouldn't it be great if we could figure out some way so that we'd only have to divide it between the two of us? Wouldn't you like that?"

Modern Translation   327

Thou woost wel that our felawe is agon;
And heer is gold, and that ful greet plentee,
350　That shal departed been among us three.
But natheles, if I can shape it so
That it departed were among us two,
Hadde I nat doon a freendes torn to thee?'

That other answerde, 'I noot how that may be;
He woot how that the gold is with us tweye,
What shal we doon, what shal we to him seye?'

'Shal it be conseil?' seyde the firste shrewe,
'And I shal tellen thee, in wordes fewe,
What we shal doon, and bringe it wel aboute.'

360　'I graunte,' quod that other, 'out of doute,
That, by my trouthe, I wol thee nat biwreye.'

'Now,' quod the firste, 'thou woost wel we be tweye,
And two of us shul strenger be than oon.
Look whan that he is set, and right anoon
Arys, as though thou woldest with him pleye;
And I shal ryve him thurgh the sydes tweye
Whyl that thou strogelest with him as in game,
And with thy dagger look thou do the same;
And than shal al this gold departed be,
370　My dere freend, bitwixen me and thee;
Than may we bothe our lustes al fulfille,
And pleye at dees right at our owene wille.'
And thus acorded been thise shrewes tweye
To sleen the thridde, as ye han herd me seye.

This yongest, which that wente unto the toun,
Ful ofte in herte he rolleth up and doun
The beautee of thise florins newe and brighte.
'O lord!' quod he, 'if so were that I mighte
Have al this tresor to my-self allone,
380　Ther is no man that liveth under the trone

<table>
<tr><td>354-356</td><td>"Yeah, that'd be great," the other one answered. "But I don't know how you're planning on doing that, considering our younger friend knows about the gold. What would we say to him? What are you thinking?"</td></tr>
<tr><td>357-359</td><td>"I have a plan that I think will work," the first rogue replied. "Can you keep a secret?"</td></tr>
<tr><td>360-361</td><td>"I swear I won't tell anyone anything," said the other guy. "I give you my word that I won't betray you."</td></tr>
<tr><td>362-374</td><td>"Well," the first one began, "there are two of us and only one of him, which means that we can take him. When he comes back, wait for him to sit down, and then jump up and grab him as if you wanted to horse around. Then, while the two of you are wrestling, I'll sneak up behind him and stab him with my dagger. Then you can pull out your dagger and do the same. Then we'll have all this money to ourselves and will only have to divide it two ways instead of three. That'll give each of us more money to play around and gamble with and do whatever we want." The other ruffian liked this idea, so the two of them agreed to this plan to kill their friend.</td></tr>
<tr><td>375-396</td><td>The youngest of the three, meanwhile, couldn't stop thinking about those bright new gold florins as he headed into town. "Lord!" he exclaimed to himself. "If only there were some way I could have all that money to myself. There wouldn't be any man alive who'd live as happily as me." He thought about it and thought about it until finally the devil himself, enemy of all mankind, put it in his thoughts</td></tr>
</table>

Of God, that sholde live so mery as I!'
And atte laste the feend, our enemy,
Putte in his thought that he shold poyson beye,
With which he mighte sleen his felawes tweye;
For-why the feend fond him in swich lyvinge,
That he had leve him to sorwe bringe,
For this was outrely his fulle entente
To sleen hem bothe, and never to repente.
And forth he gooth, no lenger wolde he tarie,
390 Into the toun, unto a pothecarie,
And preyed him, that he him wolde selle
Som poyson, that he mighte his rattes quelle;
And eek ther was a polcat in his hawe,
That, as he seyde, his capouns hadde y-slawe,
And fayn he wolde wreke him, if he mighte,
On vermin, that destroyed him by nighte.

The pothecarie answerde, 'and thou shalt have
A thing that, al-so God my soule save,
In al this world ther nis no creature,
400 That ete or dronke hath of this confiture
Noght but the mountance of a corn of whete,
That he ne shal his lyf anon forlete;
Ye, sterve he shal, and that in lasse whyle
Than thou wolt goon a paas nat but a myle;
This poyson is so strong and violent.'

This cursed man hath in his hond y-hent
This poyson in a box, and sith he ran
In-to the nexte strete, unto a man,
And borwed [of] him large botels three;
410 And in the two his poyson poured he;
The thridde he kepte clene for his drinke.
For al the night he shoop him for to swinke
In caryinge of the gold out of that place.
And whan this ryotour, with sory grace,
Had filled with wyn his grete botels three,
To his felawes agayn repaireth he.

that he should poison his two friends so that he could have all the money to himself. He headed straight for the town drugstore, where he asked the clerk if he could buy some poison to kill the rats in his house and the skunk that had been eating his chickens at night.

397-405 "Sure, I can sell you some strong poison," the clerk said. "This stuff is so strong that no living creature in the world will be able to survive if it eats or drinks this. It's fast-acting too, and will take effect in less time than it'd take you to walk a mile.

406-426 The young rogue bought the poison and then went to see a guy on the next street over to borrow three large empty bottles. He put poison in two of them, but he kept the third bottle clean for his own drink, which he knew he'd need later that night because he planned to move all the gold by himself. And after he'd filled the big bottles with wine, he headed back to where his two friends were waiting for him at the oak tree.

What nedeth it to sermone of it more?
For right as they had cast his deeth bifore,
Right so they han him slayn, and that anon.
420　And whan that this was doon, thus spak that oon,
'Now lat us sitte and drinke, and make us merie,
And afterward we wol his body berie.'
And with that word it happed him, par cas,
To take the botel ther the poyson was,
And drank, and yaf his felawe drinke also,
For which anon they storven bothe two.

But, certes, I suppose that Avicen
Wroot never in no canon, ne in no fen,
Mo wonder signes of empoisoning
430　Than hadde thise wrecches two, er hir ending.
Thus ended been thise homicydes two,
And eek the false empoysoner also.

O cursed sinne, ful of cursednesse!
O traytours homicyde, o wikkednesse!
O glotonye, luxurie, and hasardrye!
Thou blasphemour of Crist with vileinye
And othes grete, of usage and of pryde!
Allas! mankinde, how may it bityde,
That to thy creatour which that thee wroghte,
440　And with his precious herte-blood thee boghte,
Thou art so fals and so unkinde, allas!

Now, goode men, God forgeve yow your trespas,
And ware yow fro the sinne of avaryce.
Myn holy pardoun may yow alle waryce,
So that ye offre nobles or sterlinges,
Or elles silver broches, spones, ringes.
Boweth your heed under this holy bulle!
Cometh up, ye wyves, offreth of your wolle!
Your name I entre heer in my rolle anon;
450　In-to the blisse of hevene shul ye gon;
I yow assoile, by myn heigh power,

Well, there really isn't a whole lot more to say. The two older friends killed the youngest right after he'd returned with the food and wine, just as they'd planned. And when they'd finished, the first rogue said, "Now let's sit and relax for a bit before burying the body." As luck would have it, he grabbed and drank from one of the bottles with poison in it and gave the other poisoned bottle to his friend. And in no time at all, they were both dead.

427-432 These two scoundrels suffered horribly as they died. I doubt even Avicenna himself, the great Arab writer on medical herbs and poisons, had ever encountered such awful effects. Anyway, that's how these two hooligans died shortly after they'd killed their own poisoner.

433-441 You see what gluttony, lechery, and gambling gets you! Evil! Sin! Wickedness! Murder! All you arrogant, addicted villains with your swearing on Christ's body! How is it that you can treat your creator so horribly when he has saved you with his own precious blood?

442-456 Now, ladies and gentlemen, may God forgive you for your sins and keep you safe from the sin of greed. A holy pardon from me can save you—for a modest fee of a few silver coins. I also accept jewelry, silverware, and rings, mind you. I mean, this is a great opportunity here for you! This is in your own interest. I'm not trying to trick you here. Come on, ladies, trade in some of your extra clothing for a pardon. I'll write your name down in my official notebook so that you'll have no trouble going straight to heaven when you die. I will absolve you—those of you who make an offering, that is—of any past wrongdoing to make you as clean and holy as the day you were

Yow that wol offre, as clene and eek as cleer
As ye were born; and, lo, sirs, thus I preche.
And Iesu Crist, that is our soules leche,
So graunte yow his pardon to receyve;
For that is best; I wol yow nat deceyve.

But sirs, o word forgat I in my tale,
I have relikes and pardon in my male,
As faire as any man in Engelond,
460 Whiche were me yeven by the popes hond.
If any of yow wol, of devocioun,
Offren, and han myn absolucioun,
Cometh forth anon, and kneleth heer adoun,
And mekely receyveth my pardoun:
Or elles, taketh pardon as ye wende,
Al newe and fresh, at every tounes ende,
So that ye offren alwey newe and newe
Nobles and pens, which that be gode and trewe.
It is an honour to everich that is heer,
470 That ye mowe have a suffisant pardoneer
Tassoille yow, in contree as ye ryde,
For aventures which that may bityde.
Peraventure ther may falle oon or two
Doun of his hors, and breke his nekke atwo.
Look which a seuretee is it to yow alle
That I am in your felaweship y-falle,
That may assoille yow, bothe more and lasse,
Whan that the soule shal fro the body passe,
I rede that our hoste heer shal biginne,
480 For he is most envoluped in sinne.
Com forth, sir hoste, and offre first anon,
And thou shalt kisse the reliks everichon,
Ye, for a grote! unbokel anon thy purs.'

'Nay, nay,' quod he, 'than have I Cristes curs!
Lat be,' quod he, 'it shal nat be, so theech!
Thou woldest make me kisse thyn old breech,
And swere it were a relik of a seint,

born. That's what I do, and may Jesus Christ, caretaker of our souls, receive my pardon.

457-483 Oh! But I forgot to add one thing. I have right here in my bag some holy relics that are as good as any other relics in England. The pope himself gave them to me, actually. If any of you feels compelled by your faith to make an offering and see the relics, well then you can come right over here, kneel down, and humbly receive absolution from me. Or you're more than welcome to offer up your shiny new coins to receive a pardon every so often along the way so that you'll know you'll be free of sin and guilt by the time we reach Canterbury. You should all be glad that you have me, an excellent pardoner, riding with you in case you need to be forgiven. I mean, maybe you'll fall off your horse and break your neck or something and need to be pardoned before you die. Aren't you just lucky that I'm here so that your soul won't have any problem finding its way to heaven? I think that our Host here should be pardoned first because he runs a tavern, which is a veritable breeding ground for sin. Come here, sir Host, and be the first to make an offering. I'll even let you kiss all of my relics. That's right, it'll only cost you one silver coin. Take out your wallet, step up, and make an offering.

484-493 "Oh no," said the Host. "Christ send me to hell first! I'll never give you anything as long as I live. You'd call your own pants a relic and make me kiss them even though they're soiled with crap! By the true cross that St. Helena found, I wish I could have your balls in

Thogh it were with thy fundement depeint!
But by the croys which that seint Eleyne fond,
490   I wolde I hadde thy coillons in myn hond
In stede of relikes or of seintuarie;
Lat cutte hem of, I wol thee helpe hem carie;
Thay shul be shryned in an hogges tord.'

This pardoner answerde nat a word;
So wrooth he was, no word ne wolde he seye.

'Now,' quod our host, 'I wol no lenger pleye
With thee, ne with noon other angry man.'
But right anon the worthy knight bigan,
Whan that he saugh that al the peple lough,
500   'Na-more of this, for it is right y-nough;
Sir pardoner, be glad and mery of chere;
And ye, sir host, that been to me so dere,
I prey yow that ye kisse the pardoner.
And pardoner, I prey thee, drawe thee neer,
And, as we diden, lat us laughe and pleye.'
Anon they kiste, and riden forth hir weye.

HERE IS ENDED THE PARDONERS TALE.

my hands instead of your so-called relics so that I could cut them off and have them smashed into pig turd!"

494-495   The Pardoner didn't say anything. He just stared at the Host because he was too angry to speak.

496-506   "Okay," said the Host. "No more fooling around, with you or anyone else." By this point, though, everyone was already laughing hysterically, which prompted the Knight to say, "All right, all right, that's enough. Mr. Host, I like you a lot, so please just give the Pardoner a kiss and make up. And Mr. Pardoner, calm down and go over to our Host. Let's put this behind us so that we can laugh and relax like we were doing earlier." And with that, the Pardoner and the Host kissed and put the matter behind them, and we all continued on our way to Canterbury.

THIS IS THE END OF THE PARDONER'S TALE.

Prologue to Sir Thopas

PROLOGUE TO SIR THOPAS.

BIHOLD THE MURYE WORDES OF THE HOST TO CHAUCER.

Whan seyd was al this miracle, every man
As sobre was, that wonder was to se,
Til that our hoste Iapen tho bigan,
And than at erst he loked upon me,
And seyde thus, 'what man artow?' quod he;
'Thou lokest as thou woldest finde an hare,
For ever upon the ground I see thee stare.

Approche neer, and loke up merily.
Now war yow, sirs, and lat this man have place;
10   He in the waast is shape as wel as I;
This were a popet in an arm tenbrace
For any womman, smal and fair of face.
He semeth elvish by his contenaunce,
For unto no wight dooth he daliaunce.

Sey now somwhat, sin other folk han sayd;
Tel us a tale of mirthe, and that anoon;'—
'Hoste,' quod I, 'ne beth nat yvel apayd,
For other tale certes can I noon,
But of a ryme I lerned longe agoon.'
20   'Ye, that is good,' quod he; 'now shul we here
Som deyntee thing, me thinketh by his chere.'

Prologue to Sir Thopas

PROLOGUE TO CHAUCER'S OWN TALE ABOUT SIR THOPAS.

LISTEN TO WHAT THE HOST SAID TO CHAUCER:

1-7　When the Prioress finished her story, everyone was in a pretty serious and somber mood. It was actually quite interesting to see everyone so quiet. But pretty soon the Host was back to telling his jokes, until he suddenly turned to me and said, "Everything okay? You're staring so much at the ground—you look like you're studying it intently!

8-14　"Come on now, chin up! Be happy! Make room, everyone, for this guy here. He and I are of about the same build—any woman would love to hold him in her arms. There's something funny about this guy—he only speaks when he absolutely has to.

15-21　"Come on, speak up now, and tell us a story like the others have. And make it a happy story too. Let's hear it!" "You'll have to forgive me," I answered him. "I'm pretty bad at telling stories. I really only know this short one I once learned long ago." "Yeah, yeah, that's fine," the Host replied, "But get on with it. I can tell this is going to be good just by the look on your face!"

The Tale of Sir Thopas

HERE BIGINNETH CHAUCERS TALE OF THOPAS.

Listeth, lordes, in good entent,
And I wol telle verrayment
    Of mirthe and of solas;
Al of a knyght was fair and gent
In bataille and in tourneyment,
    His name was sir Thopas.

Y-born he was in fer contree,
In Flaundres, al biyonde the see,
    At Popering, in the place;
10 His fader was a man ful free,
And lord he was of that contree,
    As it was Goddes grace.

Sir Thopas wex a doghty swayn,
Whyt was his face as payndemayn,
    His lippes rede as rose;
His rode is lyk scarlet in grayn,
And I yow telle in good certayn,
    He hadde a semely nose.

His heer, his berd was lyk saffroun,
20 That to his girdel raughte adoun;
    His shoon of Cordewane.
Of Brugges were his hosen broun,
His robe was of ciclatoun,
    That coste many a Iane.

He coude hunte at wilde deer,
And ryde an hauking for riveer,
    With grey goshauk on honde;
Ther-to he was a good archeer,

NO FEAR

The Tale of Sir Thopas

HERE'S CHAUCER'S OWN TALE ABOUT A KNIGHT NAMED
SIR THOPAS.

1-6   Listen, lords, with good intent,
      And I'll tell you a true event,
          Of bliss and happiness;
      About a knight who was a gent,
      In battle and in tournament.
          His name was Sir Thopas.

7-12 He was born in a far country,
      In Belgium, way beyond the sea,
          In the town of Poperinghe, where
      His father was wealthy and free,
      And was the king of that country,
          Where he ruled in God's care.

13-18 Sir Thopas grew so strong and couth,
      With pale skin as white as a tooth,
          And lips as red as a rose,
      With skin the reddish color of youth
      And—now I'll tell you the truth—
          A very handsome nose.

19-24 His hair fell to his waist from his head;
      That and his beard were firey red.
          His leather shoes were from Spain;
      His brown socks from Belgium instead;
      His robe made of very fine thread
          Which was anything but mundane.

25-30 He hunted deer in all weather,
      And liked to hawk by the river,
          With his bird on his hand;
      He was a very good archer

Of wrastling was ther noon his peer,
30   Ther any ram shal stonde.

Ful many a mayde, bright in bour,
They moorne for him, paramour,
     Whan hem were bet to slepe;
But he was chast and no lechour,
And sweet as is the bremble-flour
     That bereth the rede hepe.

And so bifel upon a day,
For sothe, as I yow telle may,
     Sir Thopas wolde out ryde;
40   He worth upon his stede gray,
And in his honde a launcegay,
     A long swerd by his syde.

He priketh thurgh a fair forest,
Ther-inne is many a wilde best,
     Ye, bothe bukke and hare;
And, as he priketh north and est,
I telle it yow, him hadde almest
     Bitid a sory care.

Ther springen herbes grete and smale,
50   The lycorys and cetewale,
     And many a clowe-gilofre;
And notemuge to putte in ale,
Whether it be moyste or stale,
     Or for to leye in cofre.

The briddes singe, it is no nay,
The sparhauk and the papeiay,
     That Ioye it was to here;
The thrustelcok made eek his lay,
The wodedowve upon the spray
60   She sang ful loude and clere.

And at wrestling no one was better
He was the best in the land.

31-36   Young maidens, at night tucked in bed
Would yearn for him, they all said,
    To make love at all hours.
But he wouldn't have sex while unwed;
He was so sweet, like the fruit that is shed
    By the bramble flowers.

37-42   Now, I'm not lying when I say,
That it so happened one day,
    Thopas went on a ride;
His war horse was the color gray,
And he brought his lance with him that day,
    While his sword hung at his side.

43-48   He rode through ten forests at least,
Filled with a hundred kinds of beast,
    Including rabbits and deer.
And as he rode far north and east,
His troubles never once ceased,
    And his hardship was severe.

49-54   The spring flowers great and small,
The licorice and ginger, and all
    Of the large fields of cloves,
And nutmeg to put in alcohol—
Whether in beer or wine for the fall—
    Were all blooming in droves.

55-60   The birds were singing so gay,
Including the sparrow and popinjay,
    That it was joyous to hear.
The missel thrush had eggs to lay,
And birds in the trees that lined the way
    Sang so loud and clear.

Sir Thopas fil in love-longinge
Al whan he herde the thrustel singe,
　　And priked as he were wood:
His faire stede in his prikinge
So swatte that men mighte him wringe,
　　His sydes were al blood.

Sir Thopas eek so wery was
For prikinge on the softe gras,
　　So fiers was his corage,
That doun he leyde him in that plas
To make his stede som solas,
　　And yaf him good forage.

'O seinte Marie, *benedicite*!
What eyleth this love at me
　　To binde me so sore?
Me dremed al this night, pardee,
An elf-queen shal my lemman be,
　　And slepe under my gore.

An elf-queen wol I love, y-wis,
For in this world no womman is
　　Worthy to be my make
　　　　In toune;
Alle othere wommen I forsake,
And to an elf-queen I me take
　　By dale and eek by doune!'

In-to his sadel he clamb anoon,
And priketh over style and stoon
　　An elf-queen for tespye,
Til he so longe had riden and goon
That he fond, in a privee woon,
　　The contree of Fairye
　　　　So wilde;
For in that contree was ther noon

70

80

90

NO FEAR

The thrush's song that did emerge,
Gave Thopas a crazy sex urge.
   He kicked and gave a yowl,
Which made the horse bolt with a surge.
On its flanks the sweat did converge;
   You could've wrung him like a wet towel.

67-72 Well Sir Thopas grew so tired,
From all that energy required,
   To race through the deep wood.
So he stopped his horse and retired,
Lay down in the grass and perspired,
   While the horse ate what it could.

73-78 He cried, "Saint Mary, please help me!
Love has made me all squirmy
   It has made me unclean!
Last night as I slept so dreamy
I pictured something so steamy:
   Me having sex with an elf-queen!

79-85 "I'll sleep with an elf-queen, you'll see!
No other is good enough for me,
   The elf-queen's without compare
     it seems.
I refuse to have an affair
With any other women out there,
   Except the one in my dreams!"

86-95 And so he climbed back on his horse,
And without an ounce of remorse,
   Searched for an elf-queen.
He rode far off the beaten course,
And finally came to the source,
   Of all that is pristine,
     And pure;
Because there he had recourse,

That to him dorste ryde or goon,
   Neither wyf ne childe.

Til that ther cam a greet geaunt,
His name was sir Olifaunt,
   A perilous man of dede;
He seyde, 'child, by Termagaunt,
But-if thou prike out of myn haunt,
Anon I slee thy stede
       With mace.
Heer is the queen of Fayërye,
With harpe and pype and simphonye
Dwelling in this place.'

The child seyde, 'al-so mote I thee,
Tomorwe wol I mete thee
   Whan I have myn armoure;
And yet I hope, *par ma fay*,
That thou shalt with this launcegay
   Abyen it ful soure;
       Thy mawe
Shal I percen, if I may,
Er it be fully pryme of day,
   For heer thou shalt be slawe.'

Sir Thopas drow abak ful faste;
This geaunt at him stones caste
   Out of a fel staf-slinge;
But faire escapeth child Thopas,
And al it was thurgh Goddes gras,
   And thurgh his fair beringe.

Yet listeth, lordes, to my tale
Merier than the nightingale,
   For now I wol yow roune
How sir Thopas with sydes smale,
Priking over hil and dale,
   Is come agayn to toune.

100

110

120

NO FEAR

To fairies and sprites, of course,
And other magical things, I'm sure.

96-105 But suddenly, there came a giant,
A huge man named Sir Elephant,
Who was dangerous indeed.
He said, "Bug off, you little pissant!
If you don't I'll knock your eyes aslant
And kill your beautiful steed
With my spoon.
The elf-queen lives on this ground
Where magical creatures abound,
So get the hell outta here!"

106-115 Sir Thopas only gave a nod,
Drew up, and said, "I swear to God,"
I'll return tomorrow.
Dressed in armor and with my lance,
I'll slay you through your underpants,
And end your sorrow,
With your guts bestrewn.
Now I'm not bragging when I say,
Live fully and enjoy this day—
You'll die before tomorrow noon!"

116-121 Then Sir Thopas turned and rode away,
Dodging rocks the giant threw his way,
With his enormous sling.   ·
It was only by God's good grace,
That Sir Elephant was not an ace—
He missed Sir Thopas by a shoestring.

122-127 But keep listening, everyone,
My story is not quite yet done—
It ends on a happy note.
Know that Sir Thopas rode back to town,
And prepared for the final showdown,
In that meadow so remote.

His merie men comanded he
To make him bothe game and glee,
　　For nedes moste he fighte
With a geaunt with hevedes three,
For paramour and Iolitee
Of oon that shoon ful brighte.

'Do come,' he seyde, 'my minstrales,
And gestours, for to tellen tales
　　Anon in myn arminge;
Of romances that been royales,
Of popes and of cardinales,
　　And eek of love-lykinge.'

They fette him first the swete wyn,
And mede eek in a maselyn,
　　And royal spicerye;
Of gingebreed that was ful fyn,
And lycorys, and eek comyn,
With sugre that is so trye.

He dide next his whyte lere
Of clooth of lake fyn and clere
　　A breech and eek a sherte;
And next his sherte an aketoun,
And over that an habergeoun
　　For percinge of his herte;

And over that a fyn hauberk,
Was al y-wroght of Iewes werk,
　　Ful strong it was of plate;
And over that his cote-armour
As whyt as is a lily-flour,
　　In which he wol debate.

His sheeld was al of gold so reed,
And ther-in was a bores heed,
　　A charbocle bisyde;

NO FEAR

128-133
He gathered an enormous crowd,
Which gave him cheers so very loud,
 To prepare him for the fight.
"I'll kill a giant with three heads!" he vowed,
"For love and honor—to make you proud!"
 They rallied all through the night.

134-139
He called for his faithful pages,
To tell him stories from the ages,
 While he put his armor on.
Of love and romance that engages,
Popes and kings and other sages,
 And tales woebegone.

140-145
His servants brought him mead and wine,
In wooden goblets made of pine,
 And royal spices to bake
The gingerbread that was so fine
Licorice, cumin, with such refine
 And sugar of truest make.

146-151
Then he put on some pants so white,
And then a shirt that shone like light,
 So that he looked suave and smart.
And just in case he lost the fight,
He wore chain mail so very tight,
 To protect his beating heart.

152-157
This mail was made of the best steel,
Strong enough for the coming ordeal,
 A great test of strength and will.
He also wore a coat that did reveal,
His family colors and great seal,
 To advertise his noble skill.

158-163
His shield burned metallic red,
Emblazoned with a big boar's head,
 For all to see and fear.

And there he swoor, on ale and breed,
How that 'the geaunt shal be deed,
   Bityde what bityde!'

His Iambeux were of quirboilly,
His swerdes shethe of yvory,
   His helm of laton bright;
His sadel was of rewel-boon,
His brydel as the sonne shoon,
   Or as the mone light.

170   His spere was of fyn ciprees,
That bodeth werre, and no-thing pees,
   The heed ful sharpe y-grounde;
His stede was al dappel-gray,
It gooth an ambel in the way
   Ful softely and rounde
      In londe.
Lo, lordes myne, heer is a fit!
If ye wol any more of it,
   To telle it wol I fonde.

180   Now hold your mouth, *par charitee*,
Bothe knight and lady free,
   And herkneth to my spelle;
Of bataille and of chivalry,
And of ladyes love-drury
   Anon I wol yow telle.

Men speke of romances of prys,
Of Horn child and of Ypotys,
   Of Bevis and sir Gy,
Of sir Libeux and Pleyn-damour;
190   But sir Thopas, he bereth the flour
   Of royal chivalry.

His gode stede al he bistrood,
And forth upon his wey he glood

NO FEAR

Then he swore, looked up, and said,
That he would kill the giant dead,
   With his trusty spear.

164-169   His legs were covered in tough deer hide;
An ivory-hilt sword hung at his side;
   His helmet was shiny brass;
His armor shone in the sun outside;
And on a whale bone saddle he did ride;
   All other knights he did outclass.

170-179   His spear was made of cypress wood,
And he grinded it as best he could,
   To prepare it for the kill.
His horse was prepped and made for war,
Readied in full for what's in store—
   A battle and a test of will,
     You know.
And this, my friends, ends part one,
Of this story—but I'm not done,
   Part two will quickly follow.

180-185   Okay now, everyone, shush up!
Stop your chatting and gossip.
   And listen to my tale.
I know you'd rather I speed up,
But I want to let suspense build up,
   Of the drama and travail.

186-191   You have heard other men recite,
Stories of Arthur and his knight-
   Table that was round.
Those stories I will not rewrite,
But none quite give the same delight,
   As my story, I have found.

192-197   Well, Sir Thopas mounted and rode away,
Ran through the woods all night and day,

As sparkle out of the bronde;
Upon his crest he bar a tour,
And ther-in stiked a lily-flour,
    God shilde his cors fro shonde!

And for he was a knight auntrous,
He nolde slepen in non hous,
    But liggen in his hode;
His brighte helm was his wonger,
And by him baiteth his dextrer
Of herbes fyne and gode.

Him-self drank water of the wel,
As did the knight sir Percivel,
    So worthy under wede,
Til on a day——

Until it grew dim.
He put a flower on display,
In his lapel as if to say,
That God and luck were with him.

198-203   On the way he lived like a tramp,
Stopping each night to set up camp,
Instead of sleeping in a bed.
The ground gave him quite a cramp,
Did he complain? No, he was a champ
As long as he was well fed.

204-207   He would drink water from a well,
As knights do in the tales they tell,
About Sir Percival.
It just so happened—

The Host Interrupts Chaucer

HERE THE HOST STINTETH CHAUCER OF HIS TALE
OF THOPAS.

'No more of this, for Goddes dignitee,'
Quod oure hoste, 'for thou makest me
So wery of thy verray lewednesse
That, also wisly God my soule blesse,
Myn eres aken of thy drasty speche;
Now swiche a rym the devel I biteche!
This may wel be rym dogerel,' quod he.

'Why so?' quod I, 'why wiltow lette me
More of my tale than another man,
Sin that it is the beste rym I can?'

'By God,' quod he, 'for pleynly, at a word,
Thy drasty ryming is nat worth a tord;
Thou doost nought elles but despendest tyme,
Sir, at o word, thou shall no lenger ryme.
Lat see wher thou canst tellen aught in geste,
Or telle in prose somwhat at the leste
In which ther be som mirthe or som doctryne.'

The Host Interrupts Chaucer

1-7   "Oh my God, stop, stop, stop! I can't take any more of this horrible story!" the Host cried. "It's perverse, not to mention just plain stupid, and your poetry sucks!

8-10   "But why won't you let me finish my story when everyone else so far has been allowed to finish theirs?" I asked. "It's really the best story I know."

11-17   "Good God," the Host answered. "Your disgusting little rhyme isn't worth a turd. You're wasting everyone's time, so I'm putting a stop to it here and now and putting the kibosh on any more of your damned poetry! Now, how about a nicer story, one that's uplifting or at least funny. Just don't put it in rhyme!"

Prologue to the Nun's Priest's Tale

THE PROLOGUE OF THE NONNE PREESTES TALE.

'Ho!' quod the knight, 'good sir, na-more of this,
That ye han seyd is right y-nough, y-wis,
And mochel more; for litel hevinesse
Is right y-nough to mochel folk, I gesse.
I seye for me, it is a greet disese
Wher-as men han ben in greet welthe and ese,
To heren of hir sodeyn fal, allas!
And the contrarie is Ioie and greet solas,
As whan a man hath been in povre estaat,
10 And clymbeth up, and wexeth fortunat,
And ther abydeth in prosperitee,
Swich thing is gladsom, as it thinketh me,
And of swich thing were goodly for to telle.'
'Ye,' quod our hoste, 'by seint Poules belle,
Ye seye right sooth; this monk, he clappeth loude,
He spak how "fortune covered with a cloude"
I noot never what, and als of a "Tragedie"
Right now ye herde, and parde! no remedie
It is for to biwaille, ne compleyne
20 That that is doon, and als it is a peyne,
As ye han seyd, to here of hevinesse.

Sir monk, na-more of this, so God yow blesse!
Your tale anoyeth al this companye;
Swich talking is nat worth a boterflye;
For ther-in is ther no desport ne game.
Wherfor, sir Monk, or dan Piers by your name,
I preye yow hertely, telle us somwhat elles,
For sikerly, nere clinking of your belles,
That on your brydel hange on every syde,
30 By heven king, that for us alle dyde,
I sholde er this han fallen doun for slepe,
Although the slough had never been so depe;
Than had your tale al be told in vayn.

Prologue to the Nun's Priest's Tale

THIS IS THE PROLOGUE TO THE TALE TOLD BY THE PRIEST
WHO WAS TRAVELING WITH THE PRIORESS.

1-21   "Wait," said the Knight. "I can't take any more of this, sir.
I'm sure what you're saying is true enough, but I think we've
heard enough depressing stories to last us for a while. I cer-
tainly know it's hard for me to hear about wealthy people
who live the good life suddenly losing everything they have!
Now, it's nice to hear stories about poor people who hit a run
of good luck and become more prosperous. That kind of story is
much better to hear and tell." "Yes!" said our Host. "By Saint Paul's
bell, you're absolutely right! This Monk is going on and on about
other people's bad luck and how life is a great tragedy. There's noth-
ing we can do about it, he says—whatever will be, will be. It's a pain
in the butt to hear about all this misery.

The monk has just narrated 17 edifying vignettes about noble figures who tragically "fall" to disgrace.

22-36   "Mr. Monk, God bless you, but I can't take any more of this! Your
story is killing us. Hearing it is a waste of time because there's noth-
ing to be gained by it. So Brother Peter—that's your name, right?—
I'm begging you, please tell us a different story. God only knows
that last story of yours was so boring that I would've fallen asleep
and fallen right off my horse into the gutter if it weren't for the jan-
gling of those bells on your horse's bridle. Then everything you said
would've been for nothing because I wouldn't have been around to
hear it! It's just like the old saying, 'If no one's listening, it ain't worth
talking.'

For certeinly, as that thise clerkes seyn,
"Wher-as a man may have noon audience,
Noght helpeth it to tellen his sentence."

And wel I woot the substance is in me,
If any thing shal wel reported be.
Sir, sey somwhat of hunting, I yow preye.'

40　'Nay,' quod this monk, 'I have no lust to pleye;
Now let another telle, as I have told.'
Than spak our host, with rude speche and bold,
And seyde unto the Nonnes Preest anon,
'Com neer, thou preest, com hider, thou sir Iohn,
Tel us swich thing as may our hertes glade,
Be blythe, though thou ryde upon a Iade.
What though thyn hors be bothe foule and lene,
If he wol serve thee, rekke nat a bene;
Look that thyn herte be mery evermo.'
50　'Yis, sir,' quod he, 'yis, host, so mote I go,
But I be mery, y-wis, I wol be blamed:'—
And right anon his tale he hath attamed,
And thus he seyde unto us everichon,
This swete preest, this goodly man, sir Iohn.

NO FEAR

"Now, I know a good story when I hear one—and that wasn't one. I know, why don't you tell us another one, maybe one about hunting? Yeah, that'd be good."

"Uh . . . no, I'm not really in the mood to tell a happy story," the Monk replied. "Why doesn't someone else take a turn?" So our Host turned to one of the two priests traveling with the Prioress, a man named John, and said in his usual rude voice, "Hey pal, get over here. I know you ain't got much—just look at that pathetic horse you're riding!—but maybe you can pretend like you're better off and tell us a happier story." "Sure thing," Brother John answered. "I'll try and be a little happier for you." And this is what that priest, Brother John, told us:

The Nun's Priest's Tale

HERE BIGINNETH THE NONNE PREESTES TALE OF THE COK
AND HEN, CHAUNTECLEER AND PERTELOTE.

A povre widwe, somdel stope in age,
Was whylom dwelling in a narwe cotage,
Bisyde a grove, stonding in a dale.
This widwe, of which I telle yow my tale,
Sin thilke day that she was last a wyf,
In pacience ladde a ful simple lyf,
For litel was hir catel and hir rente;
By housbondrye, of such as God hir sente,
She fond hir-self, and eek hir doghtren two.
₁₀ Three large sowes hadde she, and namo,
Three kyn, and eek a sheep that highte Malle.
Ful sooty was hir bour, and eek hir halle,
In which she eet ful many a sclendre meel.
Of poynaunt sauce hir neded never a deel.
No deyntee morsel passed thurgh hir throte;
Hir dyete was accordant to hir cote.
Repleccioun ne made hir never syk;
Attempree dyete was al hir phisyk,
And exercyse, and hertes suffisaunce.
₂₀ The goute lette hir no-thing for to daunce,
Napoplexye shente nat hir heed;
No wyn ne drank she, neither whyt ne reed;
Hir bord was served most with whyt and blak,
Milk and broun breed, in which she fond no lak,
Seynd bacoun, and somtyme an ey or tweye,
For she was as it were a maner deye.

A yerd she hadde, enclosed al aboute
With stikkes, and a drye dich with-oute,
In which she hadde a cok, hight Chauntecleer,
₃₀ In al the land of crowing nas his peer.
His vois was merier than the mery orgon
On messe-dayes that in the chirche gon;

The Nun's Priest's Tale

THIS IS THE NUN'S PRIEST'S STORY ABOUT A ROOSTER NAMED
CHANTICLEER AND A HEN NAMED PERTELOTE.

1-26   There once was a poor old widow who lived in a little cottage in a
valley on the edge of a forest. She lived a simple life since her hus-
band died, and she didn't have much. Still, she managed to support
her two daughters with what she did have, which included three
pigs and a sheep named Moll. Her house was pretty dirty, and she
and her daughters ate peasant food of mostly milk and bread, some-
times with a bit of bacon or an egg or two on the side, because she
was a dairywoman. She didn't have any use for gourmet tidbits or
spicy sauces, or even red or white wine. She didn't have gout, so
she could dance all she wanted, and she never really lost her tem-
per. No, a modest diet, exercise, and a positive attitude were all the
medicine she needed to stay healthy and strong.

27-44   This old woman had fenced-in her front yard and surrounded it
with a dry ditch. In the yard she kept a rooster named Chanticleer.
Chanticleer's comb was redder than the reddest coral and stuck up
high into the air like a castle wall. He had a beak as black as obsid-
ian, blue feet and toes, white claws, and feathers that burned with
the color of gold. This rooster was better at crowing than any other

Wel sikerer was his crowing in his logge,
Than is a clokke, or an abbey orlogge.
By nature knew he ech ascencioun
Of equinoxial in thilke toun;
For whan degrees fiftene were ascended,
Thanne crew he, that it mighte nat ben amended.
His comb was redder than the fyn coral,
40   And batailed, as it were a castel-wal.
His bile was blak, and as the Ieet it shoon;
Lyk asur were his legges, and his toon;
His nayles whytter than the lilie flour,
And lyk the burned gold was his colour.

This gentil cok hadde in his governaunce
Sevene hennes, for to doon al his plesaunce,
Whiche were his sustres and his paramours,
And wonder lyk to him, as of colours.
Of whiche the faireste hewed on hir throte
50   Was cleped faire damoysele Pertelote.
Curteys she was, discreet, and debonaire,
And compaignable, and bar hir-self so faire,
Sin thilke day that she was seven night old,
That trewely she hath the herte in hold
Of Chauntecleer loken in every lith;
He loved hir so, that wel was him therwith.
But such a Ioye was it to here hem singe,
Whan that the brighte sonne gan to springe,
In swete accord, 'my lief is faren in londe.'
60   For thilke tyme, as I have understonde,
Bestes and briddes coude speke and singe.

And so bifel, that in a daweninge,
As Chauntecleer among his wyves alle
Sat on his perche, that was in the halle,
And next him sat this faire Pertelote,
This Chauntecleer gan gronen in his throte,
As man that in his dreem is drecched sore.
And whan that Pertelote thus herde him rore,

rooster around. He had a clear, strong crow that was just as beautiful as the sound of a pipe organ playing in church at mass. He was also more dependable than any clock, even the clocks in the church abbeys. Instinct told him about the daily movements of the sun and the moon and the stars, and he'd keep in time with all of them, even if they moved only slightly.

45-61 Now, this cock had a harem of seven hens for his pleasure. These hens were both his sisters and his lovers and looked very much like him. The most beautiful of them all was the fair damsel Pertelote. Pertelote was modest, polite, and easy to get along with, and she was so charming that Chanticleer had been completely smitten with her since she was only a week old. He loved her through and through, and it was a pleasure to hear them singing "My love has gone away" together in harmony every morning when the sun came up—for back then, birds and animals could talk and sing, you know.

62-71 Well one morning at dawn, as Chanticleer was sitting on his perch in his hall with Pertelote and his other wives perched next to him, Chanticleer began groaning as if he were having a nightmare. Worried, Pertelote asked, "What's wrong, my dear? Why are you groaning like that? You're usually such a sound sleeper!"

She was agast, and seyde, 'O herte dere,
70　What eyleth yow, to grone in this manere?
Ye been a verray sleper, fy for shame!'

And he answerde and seyde thus, 'madame,
I pray yow, that ye take it nat a-grief:
By God, me mette I was in swich meschief
Right now, that yet myn herte is sore afright.
Now God,' quod he, 'my swevene recche aright,
And keep my body out of foul prisoun!
Me mette, how that I romed up and doun
Withinne our yerde, wher-as I saugh a beste,
80　Was lyk an hound, and wolde han maad areste
Upon my body, and wolde han had me deed.
His colour was bitwixe yelwe and reed;
And tipped was his tail, and bothe his eres,
With blak, unlyk the remenant of his heres;
His snowte smal, with glowinge eyen tweye.
Yet of his look for fere almost I deye;
This caused me my groning, doutelees.'

'Avoy!' quod she, 'fy on yow, hertelees!
Allas!' quod she, 'for, by that God above,
90　Now han ye lost myn herte and al my love;
I can nat love a coward, by my feith.
For certes, what so any womman seith,
We alle desyren, if it mighte be,
To han housbondes hardy, wyse, and free,
And secree, and no nigard, ne no fool,
Ne him that is agast of every tool,
Ne noon avauntour, by that God above!
How dorste ye seyn for shame unto your love,
That any thing mighte make yow aferd?
100　Have ye no mannes herte, and han a berd?
Allas! and conne ye been agast of swevenis?
No-thing, God wot, but vanitee, in sweven is.
Swevenes engendren of replecciouns,
And ofte of fume, and of complecciouns,

NO FEAR

"Nothing, nothing's wrong." Chanticleer answered. "I just had a horrible nightmare. It was so awful that my heart's still racing with fear. God, help me figure out what this dream means, and keep me safe from getting locked up! I dreamt that I was walking around in the yard when I saw an enormous doglike beast that wanted to catch me and kill me. This beast was a reddish-yellow color, but black on the tips of its tale and ears. It had a small nose and two glowing eyes. It's still scaring me to death just thinking about it, which is probably what caused my groaning."

"Ugh, go away!" Pertelote cried. "Shame on you, you coward! God knows you've lost my heart and all my love. I can't love a coward. No matter what women may say, deep down they all want husbands who are strong and brave and kind and know how to keep a secret, not someone who's stupid and foolish, nor someone who's scared of the sword! Shame on you for telling me that something scares you. Be a man! And, God, this wasn't even real—it was a dream! Dreams are nothing but silliness caused by gas and indigestion from overeating. The fluids in your body must just be out of whack. This nightmare you had probably just means you had too much red bile in your stomach, which leads to bad dreams of fire and beasts that want to eat you, just as too much black bile in your stomach makes people dream about black bears and bulls and devils. Nightmares can come from other bodily fluids being out of whack too. I could go on, but you get the idea.

Whan humours been to habundant in a wight.
Certes this dreem, which ye han met to-night,
Cometh of the grete superfluitee
Of youre rede *colera*, pardee,
Which causeth folk to dreden in here dremes
110 Of arwes, and of fyr with rede lemes,
Of grete bestes, that they wol hem byte,
Of contek, and of whelpes grete and lyte;
Right as the humour of malencolye
Causeth ful many a man, in sleep, to crye,
For fere of blake beres, or boles blake,
Or elles, blake develes wole hem take.
Of othere humours coude I telle also,
That werken many a man in sleep ful wo;
But I wol passe as lightly as I can.

120 Lo Catoun, which that was so wys a man,
Seyde he nat thus, ne do no fors of dremes?
Now, sire,' quod she, 'whan we flee fro the bemes,
For Goddes love, as tak som laxatyf;
Up peril of my soule, and of my lyf,
I counseille yow the beste, I wol nat lye,
That bothe of colere and of malencolye
Ye purge yow; and for ye shul nat tarie,
Though in this toun is noon apotecarie,
I shal my-self to herbes techen yow,
130 That shul ben for your hele, and for your prow;
And in our yerd tho herbes shal I finde,
The whiche han of hir propretee, by kinde,
To purgen yow binethe, and eek above.
Forget not this, for Goddes owene love!
Ye been ful colerik of compleccioun.
Ware the sonne in his ascencioun
Ne fynde yow nat repleet of humours hote;
And if it do, I dar wel leye a grote,
That ye shul have a fevere terciane,
140 Or an agu, that may be youre bane.
A day or two ye shul have digestyves

NO FEAR

120-149 "Wasn't it the great Roman writer Cato who said, 'Pay no attention to your dreams?' Now, when we fly down from the rafters this morning, take a laxative, for the love of God, and purge your body of whatever it is that gave you those nightmares. I swear to God I'm only trying to help you. And since there isn't a pharmacy in this town, I'll show you the herbs that are growing in our yard that you should take to purge your system. Don't forget that you have a finicky stomach, and you wouldn't want to be caught sick when the sun rises and it's time to crow. If you are still sick when the sun comes up, I'll bet you a shilling that you've got malaria or some other kind of serious sickness. If so, you might have to take some kind of strange medicine or something to help you get rid of it. Now, buck up, husband, and do your father proud. Don't worry about your dreams. They're just foolishness."

Of wormes, er ye take your laxatyves,
Of lauriol, centaure, and fumetere,
Or elles of ellebor, that groweth there,
Of catapuce, or of gaytres beryis,
Of erbe yve, growing in our yerd, that mery is;
Pekke hem up right as they growe, and ete hem in.
Be mery, housbond, for your fader kin!
Dredeth no dreem; I can say yow na-more.'

150   'Madame,' quod he, '*graunt mercy* of your lore.
But nathelees, as touching daun Catoun,
That hath of wisdom such a greet renoun,
Though that he bad no dremes for to drede,
By God, men may in olde bokes rede
Of many a man, more of auctoritee
Than ever Catoun was, so mote I thee,
Than al the revers seyn of his sentence,
And han wel founden by experience,
That dremes ben significaciouns,
160   As wel of Ioye as tribulaciouns
That folk enduren in this lyf present.
Ther nedeth make of this noon argument;
The verray preve sheweth it in dede.

Oon of the gretteste auctours that men rede
Seith thus, that whylom two felawes wente
On pilgrimage, in a ful good entente;
And happed so, thay come into a toun,
Wher-as ther was swich congregacioun
Of peple, and eek so streit of herbergage,
170   That they ne founde as muche as o cotage,
In which they bothe mighte y-logged be.
Wherfor thay mosten, of necessitee,
As for that night, departen compaignye;
And ech of hem goth to his hostelrye,
And took his logging as it wolde falle.
That oon of hem was logged in a stalle,
Fer in a yerd, with oxen of the plough;

NO FEAR

"Thank you for your advice, Madame," responded Chanticleer. "Cato certainly was known for his wisdom. But even though he said not to worry about dreams, there were plenty of other writers who were even older and wiser than Cato who said just the opposite. They seem to say from their own experience that dreams are signs of the happiness or tragedy that is to come. Let me tell you about some examples:

"One of the greatest authors people read once told a story about two friends who set out on a holy pilgrimage. On their journey they came to a town that was so crowded with people that they couldn't find so much as a cottage where they could both stay for the night. So they decided to split up, and each went his own way to find somewhere to sleep. One of them found a place in an oxen barn. Fortune—who controls all our fates—smiled on the other man, who found a much better place to stay in an inn.

That other man was logged wel y-nough,
As was his aventure, or his fortune,
180   That us governeth alle as in commune.

And so bifel, that, longe er it were day,
This man mette in his bed, ther-as he lay,
How that his felawe gan upon him calle,
And seyde, 'allas! for in an oxes stalle
This night I shal be mordred ther I lye.
Now help me, dere brother, er I dye;
In alle haste com to me,' he sayde.
This man out of his sleep for fere abrayde;
But whan that he was wakned of his sleep,
190   He turned him, and took of this no keep;
Him thoughte his dreem nas but a vanitee.
Thus twyës in his sleping dremed he.
And atte thridde tyme yet his felawe
Cam, as him thoughte, and seide, 'I am now slawe;
Bihold my blody woundes, depe and wyde!
Arys up erly in the morwe-tyde,
And at the west gate of the toun,' quod he,
'A carte ful of donge ther shaltow see,
In which my body is hid ful prively;
200   Do thilke carte aresten boldely.
My gold caused my mordre, sooth to sayn;'
And tolde him every poynt how he was slayn,
With a ful pitous face, pale of hewe.
And truste wel, his dreem he fond ful trewe;
For on the morwe, as sone as it was day,
To his felawes in he took the way;
And whan that he cam to this oxes stalle,
After his felawe he bigan to calle.

The hostiler answered him anon,
210   And seyde, 'sire, your felawe is agon,
As sone as day he wente out of the toun.'
This man gan fallen in suspecioun,
Remembring on his dremes that he mette,

NO FEAR

181-208   "Now, it just so happened that the second man had a dream about his companion in the middle of the night. His friend called to him in the dream and said, 'I'm going to be murdered tonight while I'm sleeping in the barn. Hurry up and help me, dear brother, and save my life!' The second man jolted awake from the nightmare, but he quickly rolled over and fell back asleep because he thought the dream was nothing but nonsense. He had this same dream again, woke with a start, and went back to sleep again. On the third time, however, his friend appeared to him and said, 'I have been killed. Just look at the bloody wounds and gashes on my body! I was murdered for my money. Get up early tomorrow morning and go to the west gate of the town. There you'll find a cart full of dung in which my body has been secretly hidden.' And with a pale and pitiful face he told his friend all about how he was robbed and murdered. And wouldn't you know, everything in the dream turned out to be true. When the second man woke up in the morning, he set out for the oxen barn where his friend had stayed. When he got there, he began looking for his friend and calling out his name.

209-229   "The owner of the barn soon appeared and said, 'Sir, your friend has already left. He woke up early this morning and split.' Remembering his dreams from last night, the pilgrim was suspicious and ran to the west gate of the town. There, he found a cart of dung intended to be used as fertilizer, just as his friend had described in the dream.

And forth he goth, no lenger wolde he lette,
Unto the west gate of the toun, and fond
A dong-carte, as it were to donge lond,
That was arrayed in the same wyse
As ye han herd the dede man devyse;
And with an hardy herte he gan to crye
220 Vengeaunce and Iustice of this felonye:
'My felawe mordred is this same night,
And in this carte he lyth gapinge upright.
I crye out on the ministres,' quod he,
'That sholden kepe and reulen this citee;
Harrow! allas! her lyth my felawe slayn!'
What sholde I more unto this tale sayn?
The peple out-sterte, and caste the cart to grounde,
And in the middel of the dong they founde
The dede man, that mordred was al newe.

230 O blisful God, that art so Iust and trewe!
Lo, how that thou biwreyest mordre alway!
Mordre wol out, that see we day by day.
Mordre is so wlatsom and abhominable
To God, that is so Iust and resonable,
That he ne wol nat suffre it heled be;
Though it abyde a yeer, or two, or three,
Mordre wol out, this my conclusioun.
And right anoon, ministres of that toun
Han hent the carter, and so sore him pyned,
240 And eek the hostiler so sore engyned,
That thay biknewe hir wikkednesse anoon,
And were an-hanged by the nekke-boon.

Here may men seen that dremes been to drede.
And certes, in the same book I rede,
Right in the nexte chapitre after this,
(I gabbe nat, so have I Ioye or blis,)
Two men that wolde han passed over see,
For certeyn cause, in-to a fer contree,
If that the wind ne hadde been contrarie,

372   Original Text

Outraged, he cried out at the top of his lungs for vengeance and justice. 'Police! Help! My friend was murdered last night, and his body lies in this cartload of dung. Police!' The townspeople rushed out, tipped over the cart, and found the man's body buried beneath a ton of dung.

230-242　"The police immediately arrested and tortured the man who owned the cart as well as the man who owned the oxen barn, who was stretched out on the rack. Both men eventually confessed their crime and were hanged by their necks. Oh bless the Lord, who is so just and true! He always reveals murder. Murder is unholy and abominable to God, who is so just and reasonable, that he won't allow it to remain hidden away. Even if it takes a year or two or three, I know that God will always make it be known.

243-265　"There is proof, Pertelote, that we should fear our dreams. I also read in the next chapter of that same book—and I'm not making this up—that a man dreamed about his own death right before he set out on a voyage to cross the sea. He and another man had some business or other in another country across the sea, but they had to wait a while at port until the winds were favorable. And finally, when the winds did change, the two men agreed to set out the next

250 That made hem in a citee for to tarie,
That stood ful mery upon an haven-syde.
But on a day, agayn the even-tyde,
The wind gan chaunge, and blew right as hem leste.
Iolif and glad they wente unto hir reste,
And casten hem ful erly for to saille;
But to that oo man fil a greet mervaille.
That oon of hem, in sleping as he lay,
Him mette a wonder dreem, agayn the day;
Him thoughte a man stood by his beddes syde,
260 And him comaunded, that he sholde abyde,
And seyde him thus, 'if thou to-morwe wende,
Thou shalt be dreynt; my tale is at an ende.'
He wook, and tolde his felawe what he mette,
And preyde him his viage for to lette;
As for that day, he preyde him to abyde.

His felawe, that lay by his beddes syde,
Gan for to laughe, and scorned him ful faste.
'No dreem,' quod he, 'may so myn herte agaste,
That I wol lette for to do my thinges.
270 I sette not a straw by thy dreminges,
For swevenes been but vanitees and Iapes.
Men dreme al-day of owles or of apes,
And eke of many a mase therwithal;
Men dreme of thing that nevere was ne shal.
But sith I see that thou wolt heer abyde,
And thus for-sleuthen wilfully thy tyde,
God wot it reweth me; and have good day.'
And thus he took his leve, and wente his way.
But er that he hadde halfe his cours y-seyled,
280 Noot I nat why, ne what mischaunce it eyled,
But casuelly the shippes botme rente,
And ship and man under the water wente
In sighte of othere shippes it byside,
That with hem seyled at the same tyde.
And therfor, faire Pertelote so dere,
By swiche ensamples olde maistow lere,

morning. That night, however, one of the men dreamed just before dawn that a man was standing over his bed, who said, 'If you sail tomorrow, you will drown.' The man woke up, told his companion about the dream, and suggested that they wait one more day before setting sail.

266-289 "His companion, who was sleeping in the next bunk over, laughed at the man, and said, 'No dream is going to keep me from sailing tomorrow. I don't give a damn about your dreams because dreams are filled with nothing but nonsense. People are always dreaming about owls and apes and other crazy things, including things that never happened and never will happen. But it's no skin off my nose if you want to stay here and miss this golden opportunity to sail.' And so the next morning the unbelieving companion set out on the voyage by himself. But before he made it even halfway across the sea, somehow the ship's bottom split in two and sank in plain sight of all the other ships in the convoy, killing everyone on board. So you see, my beautiful Pertelote, no one can be too careful when it comes to dreams because many of them are to be feared.

That no man sholde been to recchelees
Of dremes, for I sey thee, doutelees,
That many a dreem ful sore is for to drede.

290   Lo, in the lyf of seint Kenelm, I rede,
That was Kenulphus sone, the noble king
Of Mercenrike, how Kenelm mette a thing;
A lyte er he was mordred, on a day,
His mordre in his avisioun he say.
His norice him expouned every del
His sweven, and bad him for to kepe him wel
For traisoun; but he nas but seven yeer old,
And therfore litel tale hath he told
Of any dreem, so holy was his herte.
300   By God, I hadde lever than my sherte
That ye had rad his legende, as have I.
Dame Pertelote, I sey yow trewely,
Macrobeus, that writ the avisioun
In Affrike of the worthy Cipioun,
Affermeth dremes, and seith that they been
Warning of thinges that men after seen.

And forther-more, I pray yow loketh wel
In the olde testament, of Daniel,
If he held dremes any vanitee.
310   Reed eek of Ioseph, and ther shul ye see
Wher dremes ben somtyme (I sey nat alle)
Warning of thinges that shul after falle.
Loke of Egipt the king, daun Pharao,
His bakere and his boteler also,
Wher they ne felte noon effect in dremes.
Who-so wol seken actes of sondry remes,
May rede of dremes many a wonder thing.

Lo Cresus, which that was of Lyde king,
Mette he nat that he sat upon a tree,
320   Which signified he sholde anhanged be?
Lo heer Andromacha, Ectores wyf,

NO FEAR

290-306 "Of course, there's the example of King Kenelm, the boy king of Mercia in old England, who dreamed of his own death just before he was murdered. His nurse explained the dream to him and told him to watch his back, but he didn't pay attention because he was only seven years old. I'd give anything for you to read that story, Lady Pertelote. And then there's the case of the old author Macrobeus who wrote about the dreams of the great Roman Scipio and argued that it's worth paying attention to dreams because they fortell the future.

307-317 "Furthermore, consider the story of Daniel in the Old Testament of the Bible, and ask yourself if the dreams in that story were mere nonsense. Read the story about Joseph, too, and ask the same question. Or look at the story of Pharoah in Egypt and his baker and his butler to see what they thought of the power of dreams. If you study the history of faraway kingdoms and lands, you'll find that dreams can be pretty amazing things. I'm not saying that all dreams foretell the future, but some certainly can.

318-336 "Oh, and don't forget the story about King Croesus of ancient Lydia in Turkey. Didn't he dream that he sat in a tree, which meant that he would be hanged? Then there's Andromache, the wife of Hector, the warrior of ancient Troy. The night before he died she saw in a

That day that Ector sholde lese his lyf,
She dremed on the same night biforn,
How that the lyf of Ector sholde be lorn,
If thilke day he wente in-to bataille;
She warned him, but it mighte nat availle;
He wente for to fighte nathelees,
But he was slayn anoon of Achilles.
But thilke tale is al to long to telle,
330   And eek it is ny day, I may nat dwelle.
Shortly I seye, as for conclusioun,
That I shal han of this avisioun
Adversitee; and I seye forther-more,
That I ne telle of laxatyves no store,
For they ben venimous, I woot it wel;
I hem defye, I love hem never a del.

Now let us speke of mirthe, and stinte al this;
Madame Pertelote, so have I blis,
Of o thing God hath sent me large grace;
340   For whan I see the beautee of your face,
Ye ben so scarlet-reed about your yën,
It maketh al my drede for to dyen;
For, also siker as *In principio*,
Mulier est hominis confusio;
Madame, the sentence of this Latin is—
Womman is mannes Ioye and al his blis.
For whan I fele a-night your softe syde,
Al-be-it that I may nat on you ryde,
For that our perche is maad so narwe, alas!
350   I am so ful of Ioye and of solas
That I defye bothe sweven and dreem.'

And with that word he fley doun fro the beem,
For it was day, and eek his hennes alle;
And with a chuk he gan hem for to calle,
For he had founde a corn, lay in the yerd.
Royal he was, he was namore aferd;
He fethered Pertelote twenty tyme,

dream how he would be killed in battle with the Greeks. She begged him not to fight, but he wouldn't listen to her, which is why he died that day by the sword of the Greek warrior Achilles. Anyway, that's a long story, and I should really get going since the sun is about to come up. Let me just say this, though: That dream I had last night doesn't mean I need a laxative, which I can't stand anyway. It means that something bad is going to happen to me.

337-351   "Now, let's stop talking about this and turn to happier things. God has really blessed me by giving you to me, Madame Pertelote. When I look at you—with those cute little ringlets of red around your eyes—all my fears just melt away. It really is true what they mean when they say *In principio, mulier est hominis confusion*, which

What it really means is: "In the beginning, woman brought the downfall of man."

... uh ... um, I guess means that 'Woman is man's joy and the source of all his happiness.' Yeah, that's it. Because when I feel your soft side at night, even though I can't mount you because our perch is so small, I'm still so happy that no nightmare or dream can bother me!"

352-366   And with that, he flew down from the rafters to begin the day, his hens following after them. He clucked for them to come to him when he found some corn in the yard, and all his wives would come running. He rustled his feathers twenty times for Pertelote and mounted her just as many times too before noon. He looked like a fierce lion as he paced too and fro around the yard on his tip-

And trad as ofte, er that it was pryme.
He loketh as it were a grim leoun;
360   And on his toos he rometh up and doun,
Him deyned not to sette his foot to grounde.
He chukketh, whan he hath a corn y-founde,
And to him rennen thanne his wyves alle.
Thus royal, as a prince is in his halle,
Leve I this Chauntecleer in his pasture;
And after wol I telle his aventure.

Whan that the month in which the world bigan,
That highte March, whan God first maked man,
Was complet, and passed were also,
370   Sin March bigan, thritty dayes and two,
Bifel that Chauntecleer, in al his pryde,
His seven wyves walking by his syde,
Caste up his eyen to the brighte sonne,
That in the signe of Taurus hadde y-ronne
Twenty degrees and oon, and somwhat more;
And knew by kynde, and by noon other lore,
That it was pryme, and crew with blisful stevene.

'The sonne,' he sayde, 'is clomben up on hevene
Fourty degrees and oon, and more, y-wis.
380   Madame Pertelote, my worldes blis,
Herkneth thise blisful briddes how they singe,
And see the fresshe floures how they springe;
Ful is myn herte of revel and solas.'
But sodeinly him fil a sorweful cas;
For ever the latter ende of Ioye is wo.
God woot that worldly Ioye is sone ago;
And if a rethor coude faire endyte,
He in a cronique saufly mighte it wryte,
As for a sovereyn notabilitee.
390   Now every wys man, lat him herkne me;
This storie is al-so trewe, I undertake,
As is the book of Launcelot de Lake,

toes, as it was beneath him to put his whole foot on the ground. He felt powerful and regal—as royal as a prince in his hall—and was no longer afraid.

367-377 The month of March—the same month when God had made the world and first made mankind—had passed, and the day was April 1. Proud Chanticleer, with his seven wives at his side, looked up at the bright sun, which was more than 21° through the sign of Taurus. His natural instinct alone told him that it was nine o'clock in the morning, and he crowed happily at the top of his lungs.

378-394 "The sun," he crowed, "has climbed across the sky more than 40°. Madame Pertelote, the light of my life, listen to the happy birds singing and the fresh new flowers sprouting from the ground. My heart is so happy!" But no sooner had he finished saying this than his happiness quickly vanished. God knows that happiness only lasts a moment. A poet should take note of this saying and write it in a poem sometime. Now, ladies and gentlemen, what I'm about to tell you is completely true, as true as that famous romance novel about Lancelot du Lac that women like to read so much. I swear it. Okay, back to the story.

That wommen holde in ful gret reverence.
Now wol I torne agayn to my sentence.

A col-fox, ful of sly iniquitee,
That in the grove hadde woned yeres three,
By heigh imaginacioun forn-cast,
The same night thurgh-out the hegges brast
Into the yerd, ther Chauntecleer the faire
400 Was wont, and eek his wyves, to repaire;
And in a bed of wortes stille he lay,
Til it was passed undern of the day,
Wayting his tyme on Chauntecleer to falle,
As gladly doon thise homicydes alle,
That in awayt liggen to mordre men.
O false mordrer, lurking in thy den!
O newe Scariot, newe Genilon!
False dissimilour, O Greek Sinon,
That broghtest Troye al outrely to sorwe!
410 O Chauntecleer, acursed be that morwe,
That thou into that yerd flough fro the bemes!
Thou were ful wel y-warned by thy dremes,
That thilke day was perilous to thee.
But what that God forwoot mot nedes be,
After the opinioun of certeyn clerkis.
Witnesse on him, that any perfit clerk is,
That in scole is gret altercacioun
In this matere, and greet disputisoun,
And hath ben of an hundred thousand men.
420 But I ne can not bulte it to the bren,
As can the holy doctour Augustyn,
Or Boece, or the bishop Bradwardyn,
Whether that Goddes worthy forwiting
Streyneth me nedely for to doon a thing,
(Nedely clepe I simple necessitee);
Or elles, if free choys be graunted me
To do that same thing, or do it noght,
Though God forwoot it, er that it was wroght;
Or if his witing streyneth nevere a del

395-429 It so happens that the night before, a sly and mischievious fox, who had been living in the nearby woods for the last three years, had entered the old woman's yard where Chanticleer and his wives lived. He'd slunk over to the bed of cabbages and had waited until mid-morning for the right time to pounce on Chanticleer, as all murderers wait to strike. Oh wicked, lurking murderer! You're just like the traitors Judas Iscariot, who betrayed Jesus, Ganelon of France, and Sinon of Greece, who caused the fall of Troy when he convinced the Trojans that the wooden Greek horse was a present. Oh Chanticleer, damn the day when you flew down from the rafters and into the yard! You should have payed attention to your dream and known that today would be a dangerous day for you. But, according to some philosophers, what God foresees is destined to happen and cannot be changed. Well, then again, any philosopher worth his salt would tell you that not everyone agrees that this is so. A hundred thousand men have tried to answer this question whether the future is already written or can be changed. I'm not really good at logic and picking apart the various arguments like St. Augustine can or like the philosopher Boethius or Bishop Bradwardine can. I'm not sure whether God's foretelling of an event means that it has to happen or whether I have free will and can choose to make it not happen.

430 But by necessitee condicionel.
    I wol not han to do of swich matere;
    My tale is of a cok, as ye may here,
    That took his counseil of his wyf, with sorwe,
    To walken in the yerd upon that morwe
    That he had met the dreem, that I yow tolde.
    Wommennes counseils been ful ofte colde;
    Wommannes counseil broghte us first to wo,
    And made Adam fro paradys to go,
    Ther-as he was ful mery, and wel at ese.
440 But for I noot, to whom it mighte displese,
    If I counseil of wommen wolde blame,
    Passe over, for I seyde it in my game.
    Rede auctours, wher they trete of swich matere,
    And what thay seyn of wommen ye may here.
    Thise been the cokkes wordes, and nat myne;
    I can noon harm of no womman divyne.

    Faire in the sond, to bathe hir merily,
    Lyth Pertelote, and alle hir sustres by,
    Agayn the sonne; and Chauntecleer so free
450 Song merier than the mermayde in the see;
    For Phisiologus seith sikerly,
    How that they singen wel and merily.
    And so bifel that, as he caste his yë,
    Among the wortes, on a boterflye,
    He was war of this fox that lay ful lowe.
    No-thing ne liste him thanne for to crowe,
    But cryde anon, 'cok, cok,' and up he sterte,
    As man that was affrayed in his herte.
    For naturelly a beest desyreth flee
460 Fro his contrarie, if he may it see,
    Though he never erst had seyn it with his yë.

    This Chauntecleer, whan he gan him espye,
    He wolde han fled, but that the fox anon
    Seyde, 'Gentil sire, allas! wher wol ye gon?
    Be ye affrayed of me that am your freend?

430-446 I don't really want to get into all that. My story is just about a rooster, who, as you already know, foolishly listened to his wife after having had that dream I told you about. Women's advice is more harmful than good. It caused Adam to get kicked out of Eden, where he'd been happy and doing just fine. Okay, okay. I'm only joking. I don't want to offend anybody by saying that women are full of foolishness. There are lots of books on that subject, and you can read them and make up your own mind. I'm just telling you what the rooster thought, not what I think. I don't think there's anything wrong with women.

447-461 Well, Pertelote was happily sunbathing in the sand, and Chanticleer was singing away, more happily than a mermaid (for the naturalist Physiologus tells us that mermaids sing very happily). And as he was singing, a butterfly caught his eye, which then made him notice the fox lying low in the bushes. Surprised, Chanticleer choked, sputtered out a "cok, cok," and instinctively started to run away.

462-510 Chanticleer was going to fly away, but the fox immediately said, "Hey wait, mister, where are you going? Don't be afraid. I'm a friend. Honestly, I'd be pretty evil if I intended to hurt you. I just wanted to listen to you sing because you have the voice of an angel. You

Now certes, I were worse than a feend,
If I to yow wolde harm or vileinye.
I am nat come your counseil for tespye;
But trewely, the cause of my cominge

470 Was only for to herkne how that ye singe.
For trewely ye have as mery a stevene
As eny aungel hath, that is in hevene;
Therwith ye han in musik more felinge
Than hadde Boece, or any that can singe.
My lord your fader (God his soule blesse!)
And eek your moder, of hir gentilesse,
Han in myn hous y-been, to my gret ese;
And certes, sire, ful fayn wolde I yow plese.
But for men speke of singing, I wol saye,

480 So mote I brouke wel myn eyen tweye,
Save yow, I herde never man so singe,
As dide your fader in the morweninge;
Certes, it was of herte, al that he song.
And for to make his voys the more strong,
He wolde so peyne him, that with bothe his yēn
He moste winke, so loude he wolde cryen,
And stonden on his tiptoon ther-with-al,
And strecche forth his nekke long and smal.
And eek he was of swich discrecioun,

490 That ther nas no man in no regioun
That him in song or wisdom mighte passe.
I have wel rad in daun Burnel the Asse,
Among his vers, how that ther was a cok,
For that a preestes sone yaf him a knok
Upon his leg, whyl he was yong and nyce,
He made him for to lese his benefyce.
But certeyn, ther nis no comparisoun
Bitwix the wisdom and discrecioun
Of youre fader, and of his subtiltee.

500 Now singeth, sire, for seinte charitee,
Let see, conne ye your fader countrefete?'
This Chauntecleer his winges gan to bete,
As man that coude his tresoun nat espye,

also have more feeling for music than any other singer. In fact, you sound just like your father, who was an excellent singer too. He would sing from the heart and so powerfully that he'd have to close his eyes and stand on his tiptoes and crane his slender neck to crow the notes. He was so proud of his ability to sing. I once read a story about how a boy broke a rooster's leg and how that rooster took his revenge years later when he decided not to wake the boy up on a very important day. That rooster was very clever, but he wasn't nearly as wise as your father. Yes, I know your mother and father— God bless him!—and have entertained them at my house before. I was hoping I could have you over sometime too. Now, would you please sing for me, sing like your father?" Chanticleer was so flattered that he began to beat his wings, not recognizing the treachery in the fox's voice.

So was he ravisshed with his flaterye.
Allas! ye lordes, many a fals flatour
Is in your courtes, and many a losengeour,
That plesen yow wel more, by my feith,
Than he that soothfastnesse unto yow seith.
Redeth Ecclesiaste of flaterye;
510　　Beth war, ye lordes, of hir trecherye.

This Chauntecleer stood hye upon his toos,
Strecching his nekke, and heeld his eyen cloos,
And gan to crowe loude for the nones;
And daun Russel the fox sterte up at ones,
And by the gargat hente Chauntecleer,
And on his bak toward the wode him beer,
For yet ne was ther no man that him sewed.
O destinee, that mayst nat been eschewed!
Allas, that Chauntecleer fleigh fro the bemes!
520　　Allas, his wyf ne roghte nat of dremes!
And on a Friday fil al this meschaunce.
O Venus, that art goddesse of plesaunce,
Sin that thy servant was this Chauntecleer,
And in thy service dide al his poweer,
More for delyt, than world to multiplye,
Why woldestow suffre him on thy day to dye?
O Gaufred, dere mayster soverayn,
That, whan thy worthy king Richard was slayn
With shot, compleynedest his deth so sore,
530　　Why ne hadde I now thy sentence and thy lore,
The Friday for to chide, as diden ye?
(For on a Friday soothly slayn was he.)
Than wolde I shewe yow how that I coude pleyne
For Chauntecleres drede, and for his peyne.

Certes, swich cry ne lamentacioun
Was never of ladies maad, whan Ilioun
Was wonne, and Pirrus with his streite swerd,
Whan he hadde hent king Priam by the berd,
And slayn him (as saith us *Eneydos*),

NO FEAR

Watch out, my lords! There are many flatterers in your courts who will try to deceive you. These people will make you feel much better than those who actually tell you the truth. Read what the Bible says about flattery, and then watch out for those trying to trick you.

511-534   Chanticleer closed his eyes, stood on his tiptoes, stretched out his neck, and began to crow at the top of his lungs. The fox, who was named Sir Russell, immediately jumped out of the bushes and grabbed Chanticleer by the throat, threw him on his back, and carried him off into the forest before anyone could follow fate. There's nothing we can do! It's too badown from the rafters this morning! And evedidn't pay attention to his dream! And this all happened on too, the day of the goddess Venus. Oh Venus, the goddess of sex and pleasure, how could you let Chanticleer die on your day? Chanticleer was humbly devoted to you and did everything in his power to have as much sex as he could, not to have children, but for sheer delight alone. Oh master poet Geoffrey of Vinsauf, if only I could find the words to damn Friday all to hell as vividly as you expressed your sorrow over King Richard I's death in your poetry. Then I'd be able to express my sorrow for Chanticleer!

535-554   The hens in the yard cried and grieved as they watched the fox snatch Chanticleer and carry him away. Never had there been such a ruckus, not even by the Trojan ladies when the Greek warrior Pyrrhus grabbed the Trojan king Priam by the beard and killed him with his sword, giving victory to the Greeks at Troy as the epic

540 As maden alle the hennes in the clos,
Whan they had seyn of Chauntecleer the sighte.
But sovereynly dame Pertelote shrighte,
Ful louder than dide Hasdrubales wyf,
Whan that hir housbond hadde lost his lyf,
And that the Romayns hadde brend Cartage;
She was so ful of torment and of rage,
That wilfully into the fyr she sterte,
And brende hir-selven with a stedfast herte.
O woful hennes, right so cryden ye,
550 As, whan that Nero brende the citee
Of Rome, cryden senatoures wyves,
losten alle hir lyves;
em slayn.
gayn:—

This sely widwe, and eek hir doghtres two,
Herden thise hennes crye and maken wo,
And out at dores sterten they anoon,
And syen the fox toward the grove goon,
And bar upon his bak the cok away;
560 And cryden, 'Out! harrow! and weylaway!
Ha, ha, the fox!' and after him they ran,
And eek with staves many another man;
Ran Colle our dogge, and Talbot, and Gerland,
And Malkin, with a distaf in hir hand;
Ran cow and calf, and eek the verray hogges
So were they fered for berking of the dogges
And shouting of the men and wimmen eke,
They ronne so, hem thoughte hir herte breke.
They yelleden as feendes doon in helle;
570 The dokes cryden as men wolde hem quelle;
The gees for fere flowen over the trees;
Out of the hyve cam the swarm of bees;
So hidous was the noyse, a! *benedicite*!
Certes, he Iakke Straw, and his meynee,
Ne made never shoutes half so shrille,
Whan that they wolden any Fleming kille,

poem *The Aeneid* describes. Lady Pertelote screamed the loudest—much louder than the wife of King Hasdrubal of Carthage when the Romans killed her husband and burned the city—and she'd been so upset that she committed suicide by burning herself alive. These hens cried like the Roman senators' wives cried when the emperor Nero killed their husbands and burned the city of Rome. But I digress—back to my story.

had that Canticlee
en worse that h
on a

555-582 Well, the old widow and her two daughters heard the commotion in the yard and ran outside to see what was the matter. They saw the fox running into the woods with Chanticleer on his back, and they cried out, "Oh my God! Help! Catch that fox!" as they chased after him. Some of the neighbors, including Talbot and Gerland, grabbed sticks and shovels and whatever they could find and joined in the chase as they screamed like banshees. Coll, the dog, ran after the fox too, and the cows and pigs were running around, scared from the shouting and the barking of the dogs. The ducks and geese were squawking and flying away and even the bees flew out of the hive, so terrible was the noise. God help us! Not even the peasant rebel Jack Straw and his lot were half as loud when they attacked Flemish merchants as this bunch was as they ran after the fox. They blew trumpets and hunting horns, and hearing them, you would've thought the sky itself was falling.

As thilke day was maad upon the fox.
Of bras thay broghten bemes, and of box,
Of horn, of boon, in whiche they blewe and pouped,
580   And therwithal thay shryked and they houped;
It semed as that heven sholde falle.
Now, gode men, I pray yow herkneth alle!

Lo, how fortune turneth sodeinly
The hope and pryde eek of hir enemy!
This cok, that lay upon the foxes bak,
In al his drede, unto the fox he spak,
And seyde, 'sire, if that I were as ye,
Yet sholde I seyn (as wis God helpe me),
Turneth agayn, ye proude cherles alle!
590   A verray pestilence upon yow falle!
Now am I come unto this wodes syde,
Maugree your heed, the cok shal heer abyde';
I wol him ete in feith, and that anon.'—
The fox answerde, 'in feith, it shal be don,'—
And as he spak that word, al sodeinly
This cok brak from his mouth deliverly,
And heighe upon a tree he fleigh anon.

And whan the fox saugh that he was y-gon,
'Allas!' quod he, 'O Chauntecleer, allas!
600   I have to yow,' quod he, 'y-doon trespas,
In-as-muche as I maked yow aferd,
Whan I yow hente, and broghte out of the yerd;
But, sire, I dide it in no wikke entente;
Com doun, and I shal telle yow what I mente.
I shal seye sooth to yow, God help me so.'
'Nay than,' quod he, 'I shrewe us bothe two,
And first I shrewe my-self, bothe blood and bones,
If thou bigyle me ofter than ones.
Thou shalt na-more, thurgh thy flaterye,
610   Do me to singe and winke with myn yë.
For he that winketh, whan he sholde see,
Al wilfully, God lat him never thee!'

NO FEAR

583-597 Ah, but Fortune changes course quickly, and she will sometimes unexpectedly help those she frowned upon just a moment ago! Despite the fear running through him, Chanticleer—who still lay on the fox's back—spoke up and said, "Mr. Fox, if I were you, I would turn around and say, 'Go away, dummies! Damn you all! You'll never get your rooster back because, now that I'm at the edge of the forest, I'm going to eat him right here and now.'" The fox answered, "Hey, yeah, that's a good idea!" But as soon as he spoke, the rooster pulled himself out of the fox's mouth and flew high up into a tree.

598-615 And when the fox realized that he'd lost the rooster, he said, "Oh Chanticleer, I'm so sorry! I must've scared you when I grabbed you and brought you out of the yard. But sir, I wasn't going to hurt you. Come on down and let me explain. I promise I'll tell you the truth, so help me God." "No way," Chanticleer replied. "Fool me once, shame on you—but fool me twice, shame on me! You're not going to trick me again and get me to close my eyes and sing with your flattery. God punishes those who look the other way instead of seeing!" "No," said the fox. "God punishes those who aren't careful and talk too much when they should hold their tongue."

'Nay,' quod the fox, 'but God yeve him meschaunce,
That is so undiscreet of governaunce,
That Iangleth whan he sholde holde his pees.'

Lo, swich it is for to be recchelees,
And necligent, and truste on flaterye.
But ye that holden this tale a folye,
As of a fox, or of a cok and hen,
Taketh the moralitee, good men.
For seint Paul seith, that al that writen is,
To our doctryne it is y-write, y-wis.
Taketh the fruyt, and lat the chaf be stille.

Now, gode God, if that it be thy wille,
As seith my lord, so make us alle good men;
And bringe us to his heighe blisse. Amen.

HERE IS ENDED THE NONNE PREESTES TALE.

NO FEAR

See? This is what happens when you're sloppy and not careful and listen to flatterers. This may have been a story about a fox and a rooster and a hen, but it's more a story of morality, my friends. As St. Paul says, we can learn something from the words others have written, so I hope you understand that this was a story about morality and not about barnyard animals.

Oh Lord, make us all good men if it be your will, and let us rejoice in you. Amen.

THAT'S THE END OF THE NUN'S PRIEST'S TALE.

Epilogue to the Nun's Priest's Tale

EPILOGUE TO THE NONNE PREESTES TALE.

'Sir Nonnes Preest,' our hoste seyde anoon,
'Y-blessed be thy breche, and every stoon!
This was a mery tale of Chauntecleer.
But, by my trouthe, if thou were seculer,
Thou woldest been a trede-foul a-right.
For, if thou have corage as thou hast might,
Thee were nede of hennes, as I wene,
Ya, mo than seven tymes seventene.
See, whiche braunes hath this gentil Preest,
10   So greet a nekke, and swich a large breest!
He loketh as a sperhauk with his yën;
Him nedeth nat his colour for to dyen
With brasil, ne with greyn of Portingale.
Now sire, faire falle yow for youre tale!'

And after that he, with ful mery chere,
Seide to another, as ye shullen here.

Epilogue to the Nun's Priest's Tale

1-14 And with that, our Host said, "Damn! What a great story, Mr. Nun's Priest! Bless your britches and your balls! And I'll bet that if you weren't a priest, you'd be a quite the cock among hens yourself! You could have all the women you wanted—more than a hundred of them, I bet. I mean, just look at the muscles on this priest! What a powerful neck and chest he has! And eyes as sharp as a hawk's! And what a great complexion. He doesn't need to use any of that fine Portuguese makeup or anything to hide any blemishes! Man, what a guy, and what a tale!

15-16 And after that, he happily spoke to another person in our group, as you'll soon hear.